THE RUSSO-TURKISH WAR, 1877

SPECIAL CAMPAIGN SERIES. No. 2.

THE RUSSO-TURKISH WAR
1877

A Strategical Sketch

BY

MAJOR F. MAURICE

THE SHERWOOD FORESTERS

WITH THREE MAPS

The Naval & Military Press Ltd

Published by

The Naval & Military Press Ltd
Unit 5 Riverside, Brambleside
Bellbrook Industrial Estate
Uckfield, East Sussex
TN22 1QQ England

Tel: +44 (0)1825 749494

www.naval-military-press.com
www.nmarchive.com

Cover illustration:
The Battle of Shipka Pass in August 1877

In reprinting in facsimile from the original, any imperfections are inevitably reproduced and the quality may fall short of modern type and cartographic standards.

Print and page size has been increased over the original publications to accommodate the oversized maps.

TO

GENERAL SIR THOMAS KELLY KENNY
G.C.B.

PREFACE

THIS small volume has no pretensions to be a history of the Russo-Turkish War of 1877–8. It deals merely with the strategy and major tactics of the decisive portion of the campaign in Europe. The majority of the English accounts of the campaign appeared shortly after the conclusion of the war, and were based upon the reports of newspaper correspondents, the narratives of eye-witnesses, and the despatches of the various Russian Generals. Since then, the Russian official history has been published · an excellent account of the operations of Osman Pasha's army has appeared from the pens of Mouzaffer Pasha and Talaat Bey; General Kuropatkin has written a detailed account of operations in which he took part, and a mass of other literature bearing on the campaign has seen the light in both France and Germany. The moment appears, therefore, to be opportune for the publication of an account in English. I hope I have shewn that the lessons of the war are not unimportant. The work will have fulfilled its purpose if it directs attention to a portion of Europe which is still of the greatest political interest.

For the benefit of those who may wish to make a fuller study of the campaign than I have been able to give, I have at the end of each chapter referred to those works which deal most completely with the incidents described. The list does not pretend to be exhaustive, but as many of the books on the campaign are difficult to obtain, I have confined myself to those which are in the library of the Royal United Service Institution.

The works referred to are:—*Geschichte des russisch-türkischen Krieges auf der Balkan-Halbinsel* 1877–8: Krahmer, Berlin, 1902, compiled by Krahmer from the Russian official account; referred to as Krahmer. *Kritische Ruckblicke auf den russisch-türkischen Kreig*, 1877–8, *Kuropatkin*, Berlin, 1885; translated from the Russian by Krahmer, referred to as Kuropatkin. *Défense de Plevna par Mouzaffer Pacha et Talaat Bey*, Paris, 1889; referred to as *Défense de Plevna*. *The War in Bulgaria*, by Lt.-General Valentine Baker Pasha, London, 1879; referred to as Valentine Baker. *La Guerre d'Orient, par un tacticien*, Paris, 1879; referred to as *La Guerre d'Orient*. *Turkey in Europe*, by Col. G. Baker, London, 1877; referred to as Baker. *The Defence of Plevna*, 1877, by Herbert, London, 1895; referred to as Herbert. *La Cavallerie Russe dans la guerre de 1877–8*, Paris, 1902. *The Russian Army and its Campaign in Turkey in 1877–8*, by F. V. Greene, U.S. Army, London, 1880; referred to as Greene. *The Russo-Turkish War, including an account of the Ottoman Power and the history of the Eastern Question*, by Captain Hozier; referred to as Hozier. *The Invasion of the Crimea*, Kinglake, vol. i., ii., London, 1877; referred to as Kinglake. *The Official Handbooks to the Russian and Turkish Armies*, published by the Intelligence Department. 1st Editions.

The large scale map of the theatre of war in Bulgaria is based upon the Austrian survey of 1881 of the Balkan States. This is the best map yet published. The spelling of the names has been brought into conformity with this map, with the exception of one or two names which appear also on Maps I and II. The varieties of spelling of the names in the various books and maps dealing with the campaign is very great, owing to the number of languages concerned. While I hope I have avoided any chance of confusion, I must ask my readers' indulgence if I have not attained complete uniformity.

COLCHESTER,   F. MAURICE.
    October, 1905.

CONTENTS

CHAPTER I

		PAGE
I	THE CAUSES OF THE WAR—	
	Sketch of the Eastern Question	3-5
	Immediate Causes of the War	6
	Troubles in the Balkan States	7
	The Declaration of War	8
II	THE RIVAL ARMIES—	
	The Russian Army	9
	Limitations to Strength of Russia	9
	Constitution of Russian Army	10
	Organization of a Russian Army Corps	11
	The Infantry	12
	The Cavalry	13
	The Artillery	14
	The Turkish Army	14
	Its Organization	15
	Condition of Army in '77	16
	The Infantry	17
	The Cavalry	18
	The Artillery	18

CHAPTER II

THE PLANS OF CAMPAIGN

I	THE RUSSIAN	23
	Preliminary Mobilization	23
	Bulgarian Contingent	24

CONTENTS

PLANS OF CAMPAIGN—*continued.*

	PAGE
Commander-in-Chief	25
The Russian Frontier	26
Position of Roumania	26
Roumanian Army	27
The Roads through Roumania	28
The Roumanian Railway	29
The Danube	30
Question of Advance through the Dobrudja	31
Reasons for choosing the Middle Danube Line	32
The Russian Plan of Campaign	32
Comments	33–5

II THE TURKISH—

The Commander-in-Chief	36
Distribution of Forces	37–8
Plan of Campaign	39
Comments	40

CHAPTER III

I THE RUSSIAN DEPLOYMENT—

Seizure of Barboshi Bridge	46
Occupation of left bank of Danube	47
Destruction of Turkish Monitors	48
Advance of Main Army	49
Participation of Roumania	50
Completion of Deployment	52
Comments	54

II THE PASSAGE OF THE DANUBE—

Position of Army on June 6	55
Passage at Brahilov	56
Zimmerman occupies the Dobrudja	58
Selection of point for Main Passage	59
Arrangements for Main Passage	60
The Passage at Simnitza	61
Comments	64

CHAPTER IV

THE RUSSIAN ADVANCE UP TO THE FIRST BATTLE OF PLEVNA—

	PAGE
Situation after the Passage of the Danube	69
Formation of Gourko's Advanced Guard	70
Formation of Western Army and Army of Rustchuk	71
Comments	72
Gourko's Advance	74
Occupation of Tirnova	75
Capture of Hainkioj Pass	76
Attack on Shipka Pass from the South	81
Capture of Shipka Pass	82
Comments	83
Operations of the Army of Rustchuk	85
Advance to the Jantra	86
Advance to the Kara Lom	88
Operations of the Western Army	89
Cavalry Reconnaissance to Plevna	89
Capture of Nikopol	91
Advance to Plevna	93
Operations of the Turkish Forces in the Quadrilateral	96
Osman's Advance to Plevna	97

CHAPTER V

THE FIRST AND SECOND BATTLES OF PLEVNA—

The First Battle of Plevna	105
Movements of the Russian Columns	106
Osman's Position at Plevna	107
Attack of the Northern Russian Column	109
Attack of the Southern Column	111
Comments	113
The Second Battle of Plevna	114
The Defensive Works at Plevna	115
Russian Dispositions for the Attack	118
Attack of Shakofskoi's Column	121
Attack of Veliaminov's Column	125
Comments	127

CHAPTER VI

THE TURKISH OFFENSIVE—

	PAGE
Gourko's Operations Beyond the Balkans	133
Suleyman's Move from Montenegro	134
Suleyman's Advance	137
Gourko's Retreat	138
Mehemet Ali	139
Situation of Russian and Turkish Armies on August 9	140
Comments	142
Russian Reinforcements	146
The Roumanian Army	147
Suleyman attacks Shipka Pass	148
Mehemet Ali's Offensive	152
Action at Ajazlar	153
Action at Karahasankioj	154
Action at Kaselievo	155
Situation of Western Army on August 22	159
Action at Pelisat	160

CHAPTER VII

THE CAPTURE OF LOVCHA BY THE RUSSIANS—

Formation of Skobelov's Detachment	167
Description of Lovcha	169
Turkish Position at Lovcha	171
Skobelov's Proposal for Attack	173
Force detailed for the Attack	175
Imeretinski's order for the Attack	176
Attack of the Right Column	179
Attack of the Left Column	180
Osman's March to Relieve Lovcha	182
Comments	184

CHAPTER VIII

THE THIRD BATTLE OF PLEVNA—

The Russian Reinforcements	191
Considerations as to their Disposal	192

	PAGE
THE THIRD BATTLE OF PLEVNA—*continued*.	
Distribution of the Western Army	199
Arrival of Reinforcements	200
Distribution of the Garrison of Plevna	203
Russian Plan of Attack	204
The preliminary Bombardment	206
Imeretinski's Operations south of Plevna	209
Orders for the General Attack	214
Movements of the Turkish Garrison	217
The Attack on the Southern Section	218
The Attack on the Centre Section	222
The Attack on the Northern Section	224
Turkish Counter-Attack in the Southern Section	228
The Russians withdraw	231
Comments	232

CHAPTER IX

EVENTS IN THE THEATRE OF WAR FROM THE THIRD BATTLE OF PLEVNA TO THE FALL OF MEHEMET ALI—

Mehemet Ali's Advance to the Banica Lom	237
Position of the Army of the Quadrilateral on September 16	239
Mehemet Ali's Difficulties	240
Attack on Verboca	241
Mehemet Ali's Recall	242
Second Attack on the Shipka Pass	242
Political Situation after Third Battle of Plevna	245
Position of Western Army on September 15	247
Appointment of Todleben	249
Arrival Convoy at Plevna	250
Osman Proposes to evacuate Plevna	253
Gourko's operations against Osman's Communications	257
Completion of the Investment	259

CHAPTER X

THE FALL OF PLEVNA—

Organization of a Covering Force	263
Distribution of the Investing Force	265
Osman's Preparations for a Sortie	267

THE FALL OF PLEVNA—*continued*.

	PAGE
Suleyman as Commander-in-Chief	270
Distribution of the Forces in the Quadrilateral	271
Suleyman's Advance	274
Action at Mecka	275
Suleyman's Advance on Elena	276
Comments	279
Gourko's Operations West of Plevna	280
Mehemet Ali at Arabkonak	282
Osman's Sortie from Plevna	283
Osman's Surrender	286
Strategical Lessons of Plevna	287
Kuropatkin's Tactical Deductions from Battles of Plevna	289
Final Phase of the Campaign	291

APPENDIX I

Order of battle of the Russian Army in Europe up to the second battle of Plevna. 296-7

APPENDIX II

Order of battle of the Turkish Army of the Quadrilateral, July 1st, 1877 298

APPENDIX III

Order of battle of Osman Pasha's Army, July 13th, 1877   299

APPENDIX IV

Order of battle of the Turkish Army of the Quadrilateral, August 20th, 1877 300

MAPS

I   MAP OF TURKEY IN EUROPE

II MAP OF COUNTRY BETWEEN THE DANUBE AND THE MARITZA

III MAP OF PLEVNA AND NEIGHBOURHOOD

Due to size and complexity these maps have not been reproduced in this edition.

CHAPTER I

(I) CAUSES OF THE WAR

Sketch of the Eastern Question—Immediate Causes of the War—Troubles in the Balkan States—The Declaration of War.

(II) THE RIVAL ARMIES

The Russian Army—Limitations to Strength of Russia—Constitution of Russian Army—Organization of a Russian Army Corps—The Infantry—The Cavalry—The Artillery—The Turkish Army—Its Organization—Condition of Army in '77—The Infantry—The Cavalry—The Artillery.

CHAPTER I

(I) Causes of the War

POLICY always influences strategy and the major operations of war. Some knowledge of the events leading up to the outbreak of hostilities is therefore indispensable to a proper understanding of the military history of a campaign. In the War of 1877–78 the policy of the Russian government had the most direct influence upon the scope of the operations. But in this case the political problem involved was the perennial Eastern Question. I do not, therefore, intend to do more than sketch the outline of a controversy which is still with us, and I will refer those who wish to fill in details, so far as they affected the campaign in the Balkans, to the authorities given at the end of this chapter.

" Men dwelling amidst the snows of Russia are driven by very nature to grow covetous when they hear of the happier lands, where all the year round there are roses and long sunny days. And since this people have a sea board and ports on the Euxine, they are forced by an everlasting policy to desire the command of the straits, which lead, through the heart of an empire, into the midst of that world of which men kindle thoughts when they speak of the Aegean, and of Greece, and the Ionian shores, and of Palestine and Egypt, and of Italy, and of France, and of Spain and the land of the Moors, and of the Atlantic beyond, and the path of ships on the ocean."[1]

Here we have the key to one side of the problem. On the other we have the constant anxiety of the nations of Western Europe, lest the approach of the Russian colossus to the Mediterranean should so alter the balance of power as to menace their rights and liberties. The maintenance of the integrity of the Ottoman Empire has always been a guiding principle of the policy of England and France, not from any love for the Turk, but from dread of Russia.

In the year 1904 a number of pamphlets have been published in Russia with the consent and assistance of the Russian government. They have been issued professedly with the object of explaining to the Moujik the general aims of Russian policy and the causes of the war with Japan. The following extract from one dealing with the history of the relations of Russia with Manchuria is significant:—

"Vladivostock was founded in 1860, and its bay was christened 'The Golden Horn.' The name serves as a reminder to Russia of another Golden Horn in the Nearer East which has been an object of keen longing for successive generations to the Russian people. There Russia has had to encounter dangerous and persistent opposition from other European nationalities. She has had, therefore, temporarily to turn her eyes elsewhere, and, bowing for awhile to the force of circumstances, to establish in a more distant

[1] *Kinglake*, vol. i., chapter 4.

country another 'Golden Horn.' Russians have long felt that only that nation which rules the sea and has a free outlet to the wide ocean can call itself powerful and can claim a world-wide importance, or can hope to develop fully its real strength."

Access to the Mediterranean has been for centuries the ultimate aim of Russian policy, and has led, directly or indirectly, to all the more recent conflicts between the Russian and Ottoman Empires. This policy has grown and developed, until Czars and statesmen have become its tools and not its authors. The professions of love of peace, so often in the mouths of Russian autocrats, have in themselves been generally honest enough; behind them, however, has been this policy of aggression, which has always meant war.

Ever since 1683, when John Sobieski stemmed the tide of Ottoman conquest, and the decline of the Turk in Europe began, Russia has, at intervals of from twenty to thirty years, been at war with the Ottoman Empire. She has regarded every victory merely as a step forward to the ultimate goal, every defeat as a check to be overcome by a fresh effort at the first opportunity.

The fact that the Russian church is intensely national, that the Turk rules or misrules many millions of Christians, and that that part of the earth held most sacred by Christians of all denominations is in Ottoman territory, has given Russian statesmen a ready pretext for interference in Turkish affairs, and has insured them the enthusiasm of the Russian people in the event of war.

The more immediate causes of the war of '77 may be traced from the Treaty of Paris of 1856, which concluded the Crimean war. By that treaty the position of Turkey in Europe was re-established. She was granted representation in the Concert of the Powers, and a buffer state was established between her and Russia. The latter was altogether excluded from access to the Danube, and was pledged not to put ships of war upon the Black Sea. Turkey in return gave pledges of reforms in the treatment of her Christian subjects.

True to her policy, Russia hardly allowed the signatures of her representatives to this treaty to dry, before she began to cast about for means to overcome the obstacles which had been placed in the path of her progress.

The fates were kind to her, as they usually are to those who know what they want, and concentrate all their efforts on its attainment. The Powers most interested in seeing that the stipulations of the Treaty of Paris were carried out were England, France and Austria. The two former, because the maintenance of the balance of power in the Mediterranean was essential to the prosperity of their commerce, and the security of their over-sea possessions. The latter, because Russian domination of the Danube threatened her existence as a nation. In 1866 Austria was humbled and defeated by the North German States under the leadership of Prussia. In 1870 France was crushed and the German Empire became the leading military power of the Continent. The interests of Germany in Eastern Europe were at that time comparatively unimportant. The chief aim of German diplomacy was to secure the friendly neutrality of the eastern neighbour in the event of the western neighbour attempting a *revanche*. An agreement was arrived at between Germany and Russia by which the latter undertook to throw no obstacle in the way of the consolidation of the German Empire, while the former agreed not to oppose Russian policy on the Eastern Question.

Russia had therefore only England to deal with. At that time the Manchester School was dominant in England, and the English army was in no condition to undertake single-handed an expedition against Russia. Seeing her opportunity the latter approached the Concert of the Powers under the guise of the champion of Christianity in Eastern Europe, and by a protocol, signed in London in March 1871, most of the limitations imposed upon her by the Treaty of Paris were abrogated. During the following years unrest, carefully fomented by Russian agents, showed itself in the Christian principalities of the Ottoman Empire.

In 1875 an insurrection broke out in Herzegovina. Montenegro and Servia took up arms. The movement spread eastwards into Bulgaria, and was repressed with great severity. Exaggerated stories of the events in the Balkans reached England, which was moved to horror of the Turk and all his ways, by the fiery speeches of Mr. Gladstone on the Bulgarian atrocities. Russia again saw her opportunity, and, in a second protocol, engineered by Russian diplomacy, the Powers were pledged to active interference in the Balkans on behalf of the Christian subjects of the Ottoman Empire, Russia well knowing that she alone of the Powers was in a position to take effective action upon the resolutions at which the conference had arrived.

Meanwhile Russian officers, and volunteers in Russian uniform, had been openly assisting Servia and Montenegro, and the Turks, who were making honest though tardy efforts to put their house in order, were roused to a state of exasperation which could only lead to war. Russia still protesting her desire for peace, mobilized her armies and moved to the frontier. A conference of the Powers, held at Constantinople with the object of finding a peaceful solution of the problem, ended early in '77 without result.

A second conference held, at Russian instigation, in London in March '77, and at which, contrary to the stipulation of the Treaty of Paris, Turkey was not represented, proposed that Turkey should disarm, in which event Russia was to do likewise.

The proposal contained, moreover, a reference to the Bulgarian atrocities in terms which could only be regarded by Turkey as an insult, and it was rejected by her *en bloc*.

On April 24 Russia declared war, and on the same day her armies crossed the frontier in three columns, the Russian Chancellor having a week before signed an agreement with Roumania, by which the Russian armies were to be allowed free movement through the latter's territory.[1]

(II) THE RIVAL ARMIES

The Russian

The size of Russia, and the millions who serve the Czar, so impress the imagination, that the limitations to the development of the fighting strength of the Slav Empire are often over-

[1] See Kinglake vol. i.; Hozier, vol. i.

looked. In 1877 the population of " All the Russias " totalled not much under 90,000,000 souls, of whom all males capable of bearing arms were liable to service. The Turkish army was recruited solely from the Mohammedan population, which at that time numbered not more than sixteen millions.

But the very size of her empire, which seems to make the power which can be exerted by Russia so irresistible, has, again and again, proved the chief obstacle in the way of military success. She herself in 1812 taught the world that a long line of communication may be made the surest weapon of defence against an invader. Since then she has had to put forth her utmost exertions to maintain a portion only of her total effective strength in arms upon or beyond her frontiers.

In 1877 circumstances combined to equalize the odds between the rival powers.

The Crimean war had left Russia in a state of financial exhaustion. To keep pace with modern progress, and to prepare for an effort to recover the ground lost in that struggle, it was necessary for her to develop her resources. New railways were needed, new fleets required to replace the vanished Black Sea Squadrons. The army required re-organizing and re-arming. For all this money was essential, and the purse strings were held by her late foes England and France.

Turkey, on the other hand, with the support of the Concert of the Powers in general, and of England in particular, inspired confidence on the exchanges of Europe, and she had no difficulty in raising all the loans she required. Much of this money went to build palaces on the Golden Horn, or found its way into the pockets of the greedy Pashas. But enough was left to provide the army with modern weapons, and the navy with some of the finest battleships then afloat. Thus it came about that the Turks entered upon the struggle better armed and equipped than the Russians, and with undisputed command of the sea. This, as will be seen, went far to counterbalance the apparent superiority of their enemy.

The re-organization of the Russian army on a modern basis was begun in 1863, but a fully developed system of universal service was not introduced till January, 1874. By the Imperial ukase then issued some 600,000 men became annually liable for service, and of these 150,000 were taken to form the annual contingent for the regular army. Service with the active army was for six years with the colours, nine in the reserve, and five in the Militia. All who were not taken for the active army served in the Militia for twenty years.

The officers of the Russian army were divided into two main classes :—

First, those officers who had completed the course of training in the military schools. They were for the most part men of good family and of good education, and were usually appointed to the Guard, the Rifles, or other selected corps. They rose rapidly through the lower ranks and monopolized appointments and commands throughout the army. Secondly, officers who had not been through the military schools who were men of lower class and indifferent education. They formed the majority of the regimental officers, they rarely rose even to the command of battalions; they were as a rule devoted to their men, but lived dull monotonous lives, and were without prospects or ambition. The staff was composed of officers who had been educated at the Staff College, which was recruited almost entirely from the first of the above classes. The Russian soldier was stolid and impassive, filled with devotion to the Czar, and responsive to good leading, but stupid and lacking in initiative, and generally intemperate.

The Army was organized in Army Corps. Each Corps consisted of two Infantry Divisions, composed of two brigades of two regiments of three battalions; each battalion had five companies. In the Guards, however, the regiments consisted of four battalions, each of four companies. To each Army Corps a Cavalry Division was attached, this consisted of two brigades, each of two regiments. One brigade of the Calvalry Division was composed of a regiment of Dragoons and a regiment of Lancers, the other of a regiment of Cossacks and a regiment of Hussars. The Dragoon, Lancer and Hussar regiments had each four squadrons, the Cossacks six sotnias[1]; so that each Army Corps had eighteen squadrons. Two Horse Artillery batteries, each with six 4-pounder guns, were attached to the Cavalry Division.

The fighting portion of the Russian Army Corps was completed by two brigades of artillery, one of three 9-pounder batteries, the other of three 4-pounder batteries; each battery having eight guns. The establishment of a Russian Corps consisted of about 3,000 sabres, 25,000 rifles and 108 guns; but no Corps during the campaign was ever at full strength. When hostilities began the infantry were being re-armed with a modern weapon. The Guard, Grenadier and

[1] The sotnia is a unit corresponding to a squadron.

Rifle regiments, and nine line divisions were armed with the Berdan rifle, a smallbore breech-loader sighted to 1,500 yards, which was abreast of the times; but the remaining twenty-seven line divisions were armed with the Krenk rifle, a converted breech-loader of the snider pattern, sighted only up to 600 yards. Of the troops employed in the European theatre of war only the Rifle brigades were armed with the Berdan rifle, up to the time of the arrival of reinforcements in August 1877.

The infantry tactics of the Russian Army were out of date in 1877. The strategical lessons of the Franco-German War had been carefully studied by the Russian General Staff, but its tactical lessons had been either misunderstood or altogether neglected. The traditions of Suvarov, whose favourite maxim was "The bullet is a hag, the bayonet is a queen," still had a strong hold upon the Russian infantry. They were trained to advance to the attack in column of companies, and to move to the assault while still at a distance from the position to be captured. The bayonet assault was looked upon as the one decisive feature in an infantry attack, no attempt was made to obtain superiority of fire over the enemy. In short the possibilities of the breech-loading rifle were not understood. There was no provision for a mobile battalion ammunition reserve which could follow the infantry in the attack. The supply of entrenching tools was inadequate, fifty spades, and seventy-five picks were allotted to a battalion. These were carried on the transport wagons, and were not, therefore, easily accessible in action.

In the cavalry, the Lancers and Hussars had the front rank armed with sword and lance, and the rear rank with sword and Berdan carbines. The Cossacks were armed with sword, lance and Berdan rifle. Some of the reserves which arrived during the course of the campaign were armed with the Krenk rifle. The Dragoons were armed with sword and Krenk rifle. The Guard Dragoons had received the Berdan rifle, and Dragoon regiments which were mobilized after the outbreak of hostilities received the Berdan rifle before starting for the theatre of war. The Dragoons were trained much on the lines of our mounted infantry. The Russian army at this time, alone of the armies of Europe, appreciated the importance of the fire of dismounted cavalry.

The Cossacks had an organization of their own, a compromise between their national customs and the requirements of a modern army. They formed a semi-regular force of natural horsemen, and had of recent years received some training with modern rifles. They were exempt from taxes and rendered military service in return, they provided their own horses and equipment, the Government supplying arms and ammunition; they were generally intelligent and accustomed to rely on their own resources; they were therefore good scouts, when under officers who knew how to use them, but were deficient in discipline and not trained to movements in formed bodies. They were organized in sotnias, or squadrons of 100 men. The Cossacks had acquired a great reputation in Europe, due chiefly to the terror with which they had inspired Napoleon's soldiers during the retreat from Moscow. But the work of pursuing an exhausted and dispirited army requires a very different standard of training from that necessary to fit cavalry to fulfil its rôle on a modern battlefield. The Cossacks in 1877 were at best irregular cavalry, and as such depended to a great extent for their efficiency upon their leaders. Under specially gifted officers who understood them they did good work, but as a body they failed to maintain their reputation.

The artillery in 1877 was probably the least efficient of the three arms. Both its training and its armament were antiquated. The Field Artillery were armed with four and nine-pounder bronze guns with a range according to the range tables of 2,560 and 3,200 yards respectively. The Horse Artillery were armed with a four-pounder gun. A few mountain batteries armed with a bronze three cwt. gun with a range of 1,500 yards, drawn by one horse, were also employed.

See Krahmer, chapters iv. and v.; *Handbook of the military forces of Russia*, 1st edition; Greeno, Part I.

The Turkish Army
The Turkish army was recruited solely from the Mohammedan population, Christian subjects of the Sultan were not allowed to bear arms, but paid a poll-tax in lieu of military service. It would perhaps be more accurate to say that they were compelled to take out annual licences to carry their heads, the receipt for the tax bearing the words "The bearer is entitled to keep his head for one year." Exemptions from service were frequent, and easily obtained by the upper classes. The burden of the service had therefore to be borne by not more than twelve million Mussulmans.

The army was divided into (i.) the Nizam, or active army, in which infantry served for four years and cavalry and artillery for five years; (ii.) the Ithiat, composed of men who had served their time in the

Nizam, who passed into this class to complete six years service ; (iii.) the Redif, composed of men who had passed through the Nizam and Ithiat, and of those who had escaped conscription ; service in the Redif was for eight years ; (iv.) the Mustaphiz composed of all men who had completed their time in the Redif, service in this class was for six years.

The Turkish army was organized into seven Army Corps, but these corps were purely territorial and administrative. Two corps were located in European Turkey, the remaining five in Asia Minor.

The army had no systematic organization for war, the real fighting unit being the battalion, which consisted of 800 men divided into eight companies ; the higher units were improvised as occasion required. The greatest confusion resulted from this. It was quite common for battalions of different corps to be serving in the same brigade. Thus it is often impossible to give any accurate account of the distribution of the Turkish forces during the war, and the numbers engaged can only be arrived at approximately.

Perhaps the most serious defect in the Turkish organization was the constitution of the Redif. This was divided into four classes, the first class consisting of men who had served in the Nizam, the third of men who had escaped conscription but who received a certain amount of military training. Men passed after four years service in the Redif from the first and third classes into the second and fourth respectively. The whole of the Redif was organized in battalions by classes. These battalions were formed and called out as complete units. The result of this system was that the Ithiat formed the only reserve to make good the losses in the battalions of the Nizam, and the battalions of the last two classes of the Redif had little military training. As a further consequence the Nizam battalions were, owing to their losses in the campaigns against the insurgent states, much below their establishment, the average strength at the beginning of the war was not above 500 men.

In spite of its constitutional defects of organization, the Turkish army was better prepared for war in the spring of 1877 than it had been for many years. The Ithiat and the 1st Division of the Redif had been called out to reinforce the Nizam, on the outbreak of the insurrection at Herzogovnia, in the winter of 1875. A large part of the 2nd Division of the Redif had been called out early in 1876 on the outbreak of war with Montenegro and Servia. The 3rd Division of the Redif had been called out in November, 1876, on the mobilization of the Russian forces in Bessarabia. Thus a far larger proportion of the Turkish army had, in April 1877, received some training for war than would have been the case if the Christian principalities under Turkish suzerainty had not risen.

Owing to the same causes the army was better clothed and equipped than at any previous period of its history. The Porte under pressure from the Powers made serious efforts to put its affairs in order, and a considerable proportion of the loans raised in Europe was expended upon the army. In 1877 seventy-five per cent. of the infantry were armed with the Peabody-Martini rifle sighted to 1,800 yards, as good a weapon of the kind as any then existing. This had an important influence on the course of the campaign, as the strength of the Turkish army lay in its infantry. The remaining twenty-five per cent of the Turkish infantry were armed with Snider rifles sighted to 1,300 yards. The infantry of the Egyptian contingent which consisted of twelve battalions were armed with Remington rifles.

The Turkish foot soldier only requires leading and training to make him one of the finest fighting men in the world ; he is sober, capable of enduring great privation, and a good marcher ; a fatalist by religion, he is without fear of death. While insufficiently trained to be able to manœuvre under fire and to attack, the Turkish infantry were by their natural qualities admirably suited for defensive tactics.

The infantry battalions were provided with an ammunition reserve, and with a full complement of entrenching tools, both carried on mules. They were trained to entrench themselves at once on occupying a position, whether it was to be held on the defensive in the first instance, or whether it had been captured from the enemy and was to be used as a stepping-stone for further advance. The supply of ammunition was one of the few effective organizations in the Turkish army, and the infantry were prodigal in its use. They frequently opened fire at a range of 2,000 yards when occupying field works, and were accustomed to keep up an uninterrupted fusilade, often without raising their heads over the parapet to aim. There was no organized commissariat. Rations were irregularly issued and in insufficient quantities; this led to the troops foraging for themselves, and caused much straggling. Practically each Turkish General had to make his own arrangements for supply and transport; this accounts to a great extent for the long halts, and the delays which so frequently occurred between the time of the receipt of orders to march, and the time the force actually moved off.

The cavalry were badly mounted and insufficiently trained to be able to manœuvre in formed bodies. The cavalry regiments were composed of six squadrons, each of 150 men. The Dragoon regiments were armed with Winchester repeating rifles and revolvers. In the Lancer regiments the flank squadrons were armed like the Dragoons, the remaining four squadrons having lances instead of rifles.

The artillery were armed with four and six-pounder steel, breech-loading Krupp guns. The batteries had each six guns, they were badly horsed, and the personnel had little or no technical instruction.

The junior officers of the army were recruited mostly from the ranks and were entirely without scientific training. The senior officers were generally appointed from the Mohammedan aristocracy and were dependent on favouritism and influence for their advancement. They looked upon their commands merely as sources of income, and every form of peculation was rife. The higher commanders had little knowledge of war, while the Staff was without practical training. Intriguing with the Court at Constantinople was constant, and a general who wished to retain his command had to keep a watchful eye on the Sultan and his advisers.

Still, however disastrous this interference from Constantinople proved during the campaign, it tended in some measure to increase the efficiency of the Turkish army in the spring of 1877. The pashas knew well that defeat meant certain disgrace and probable death. They therefore took care, during the campaigns with the insurgent states, to see that their men were at least passably equipped, and had received some training. The misappropriation of army funds and stores was for this reason less prevalent at the beginning of the war with Russia than it had been for many a year.

See Krahmer, chapter ii. ; *La Guerre D'Orient*, chapter i. (x); *Handbook of the Turkish Army*, 1st edition; *Défense de Plevna* (Introduction); Baker, chapters xiv., xv.

CHAPTER II

THE PLANS OF CAMPAIGN

I. THE RUSSIAN

Preliminary Mobilization—Bulgarian Contingent—Commander-in-Chief—The Russian Frontier—Position of Roumania—Roumanian Army—The Roads through Roumania—The Roumanian Railway—The Danube—Question of Advance through the Dobrudja—Reasons for choosing the Middle Danube Line—The Russian Plan of Campaign—Comments.

II. THE TURKISH

The Commander-in-Chief—Distribution of Forces—Plan of Campaign—Comments.

CHAPTER II

THE PLANS OF CAMPAIGN

I.
The Russian

IN order to give weight to her influence at the conference of the Powers assembled at Constantinople, and to be prepared for eventualities, Russia in November, 1876, mobilized her VIIth, VIIIth, IXth, Xth, XIth, and XIIth Corps.[1] The mobilization was the first undertaken by Russia since the introduction of universal service. The Russian General Staff had made an elaborate study of the mobilization of the Prussian army in 1866 and 1870, and the methods that had proved so successful in Germany were generally adopted. Russia had, however, an enemy to contend with which affected the whole of her administration whether Civil or Military. Corruption was a recognized institution amongst all classes. Poor officials who deserved well of the State were deliberately appointed even by the Czar himself to positions in which they could make money beyond their salaries. The junior officers and minor officials charged with the duty of calling up and enrolling reservists saw in the mobilization an opportunity of reaping a rich harvest. A way was found to enable reservists, who did not wish to serve and who could pay, to avoid the call to the Colours. Further, the new system of service inaugurated by the law of January 1874 had not become fully effective by

[1] For the order of battle of the Russian army, see Appendix I.

the Autumn of 1876, and the reserve was not at its full strength; as a consequence no single corps entered upon the campaign at its proper establishment. But with this exception the mobilization was smoothly carried out, and on the twenty-ninth day after the order calling the reserves to the Colours had been received, the six corps named above moved to their winter quarters. The VIIth and Xth Corps were destined for the defence of the coast and had their headquarters at Odessa[1] and Nikolaieff respectively. The VIIIth Corps was quartered about Tiraspol, the IXth at Balta, the XIth at Gouragalbina, the XIIth at Orgeieff. Headquarters were established at Kishenev. The last four corps formed the active army. In addition to the above a special corps of light troops was formed just before the declaration of war and placed under the command of Lieutenant-General Skobelov[2]; it was composed of the 4th Rifle Brigade, the Caucasian Cossack Division, the 23rd Don Cossack regiment of the 2nd division, and the 5th Engineer battalion. This corps was gradually drawn towards the frontier, and on April 23 was about Bestomak.

The IVth, XIIIth and XIVth Corps received the order to mobilize on December 10, and were intended to form part of the active army, but were not moved from their places of mobilization until May 8.

On April 29 it was decided to form the Bulgarian refugees, who had offered their services, into a special corps under Russian officers. The formation was com-

---
[1] See Map 1.
[2] Called Skobelov I, to distinguish him from Major-General Skobelov, who became famous later in the campaign.

pleted by the end of May, when it reached a total of about 6,000 men. Though these latter corps did not join the army till after the declaration of war, their formation had so far been decided on that it is reasonable to take them into consideration when discussing the original plan of campaign. The total Russian force available at the beginning of operations was thus about 200,000 men.

This army was placed under the command of the Grand Duke Nicholas, brother of the Czar, a man in the prime of life, who had done much towards the reorganization of the Russian army. His Chief of Staff was General Nepokoitschitzki, who enjoyed a great reputation in Russia, where he was known as "Our Moltke." He had indeed made a profound study of Moltke's methods, and both the system of mobilization and the strategic deployment of the Russian armies were planned on the German model.

In April it was known at the Russian Headquarters that the Turkish forces, between the Danube and the Balkans, were in two main divisions, some 60,000 men being reported about Widin, near the Servian frontier, while something over 100,000 were believed to be within the area bounded by the fortresses of Rustchuk Shumla, Varna and Silistria, known as the Quadrilateral. His intimate acquaintance with the character of the Osmanli, and the available information as to the condition of the Turkish armies, led the Russian Commander-in-Chief to believe that he might count on being able to assume the offensive and gain the initiative.

It is now time to examine the geographical and political conditions which influenced him in shaping his plan of campaign.

In 1877 the Russian Frontier, as established by the Treaty of Paris, started from a point on the Black Sea close to Tuzly, about thirty miles north of the northern mouth of the Danube, it ran thence due west for seventy miles to the Jalpuch river, which it met some ten miles west of Kubei. It then turned north, along the course of the Jalpuch, and ran from the source of that river to a point on the Pruth, thirty miles south of Jassy. Thence it followed the line of the Pruth to the Austrian frontier, twenty miles south-east of Czernovitz, the length of the frontier from Kubei to the latter place being about 200 miles. The whole of the territory west and south of this frontier line belonged in 1877 to the Principality of Roumania.

Roumania, though nominally under Turkish suzerainty, was virtually independent. The one anxiety of her government in the spring of '77 was to keep out of the impending struggle. Awed by the forces massing in Bessarabia, her statesmen decided to make a virtue of necessity, and concluded a convention with Russia, by which the latter was allowed free passage for her troops. Roumania further agreed to provide camping grounds, to furnish supplies on payment, and to allow the Russian armies the use of her railways, on the same terms as her own troops enjoyed.

It will be convenient here to say something of the Roumanian forces, which were destined later to play an important part in the struggle. On April 18 the Roumanian Government decided to mobilize their army, which was placed on a war footing for the first time under the existing constitution of the State. This measure was adopted to provide for contingencies in general, and more particularly to protect the frontier from Turkish reprisals, which were to be anticipated as a consequence of the very favourable terms accorded Russia. The little army was organized in two corps. Each corps consisted of two divisions, the division being composed of two Infantry Brigades and one Cavalry Brigade, with three batteries of eighteen guns. The nominal strength of each corps was 18,000 men, but the advance of the Russian army blocked the Jassy-Galatz line and prevented many of the reservists of the 2nd Corps from rejoining; it was therefore much under strength. At the end of May the total Roumanian force in the field was 32,000 infantry, 4,500 sabres and eighty-four guns. At that time the 1st Corps was posted along the Aluta and the 2nd between Ploesti and Bukharest.

The question of passage through Roumanian territory being satisfactorily settled, it remained for the Russian Commander-in-Chief to decide how he would deploy his forces preparatory to the passage of the first great obstacle he had to cross, the river Danube. It has been seen that the frontier between Russia and Roumania formed a rectangle. The shorter face of this rectangle led directly into the delta of the Danube, a country of marshes and lakes, liable during the spring months to sudden and deep floods, and therefore quite unsuited to military operations on a large scale. The greater part of the Russian army had therefore of necessity to cross the western face of the rectangle, and make a great left-wheel in order to deploy into the basin of the Danube. The whole movement had to be pivoted on the left flank, which was within striking distance of the enemy. Had the Turks been an enterprising foe the movement would have been most hazardous. But the well-known lethargy of the Turkish Generals made the risk one which might legitimately be taken. Still there remained a risk. The Turks were known to have a strong flotilla on the Danube. Their fleet was in undisputed command of the Black Sea, and the central or Sulina channel of the Danube was navigable by ships of war. The first care, therefore, of the Russian Commander-in-Chief was to provide for the security of the pivot upon which the deployment depended.

The Russian Headquarter Staff had next to consider how this left-wheel could be carried out. The roads leading from Russian Bessarabia across the Pruth, (a river navigable to barges) and into Roumania, were:—

1. The road from Kishenev to Jassy, and thence by Roman, Bakau, Fokchany to Bukharest.

2. That from Kishenev to Jassy, thence by Berlat and Tekutch to Fokchany.

3. The road from Jassy along the valley of the Pruth to Galatz.

4. A road from Bendery to Leova, and thence by the Pruth Valley road to Galatz.

5. A road from Bendery by Kubei, Bolgrad, and Reni to Galatz.

6. A road from Akkerman by Tatar Bunar to Ismail, and thence to Reni and Galatz.

It will be noticed that these roads may be divided

into two classes, those which converge at Fokchany and those which converge at Galatz. Through these two points the whole Russian army had to pass. The strategic deployment, therefore, was a very delicate operation and required most careful timing and calculation. The roads were generally good, but, during the wet weather in May and June, those running along the Pruth and Sereth were often flooded, and would be much cut up by heavy transport columns. The Russians were, however, able to reckon on some assistance from the waterway of the Pruth. A line of railway ran from Odessa to Kishenev, crossed the Pruth at Umgeni and passed through Jassy, Tekutch, Brahilov, Ploesti, and ran thence to Bukharest, and the Danube at Giurgevo. Circumstances, however, limited the possibilities of this line of railway. The gauge changed at the frontier station Umgeni, and the Roumanian rolling stock was quite insufficient for the requirements of a large army. The line was single, and was so badly laid that only short trains could be run, and not more than eight of these in one direction in one day. The line was, therefore, almost valueless to Russia for the movement of troops, and was chiefly used for the transport of supplies and material.

In deciding upon the direction of the advance beyond the line Fokchany-Galatz, the Russian Commander-in-Chief had to determine where he would make his main attempt to cross the Danube. From the Servian frontier the Danube flows in a general easterly direction for some 300 miles. After passing Rassova it turns north for eighty miles to Galatz, whence it again flows eastwards into the Black Sea. At Widin the river during the dry season is about 800 yards wide, and below that town it gradually widens till at Galatz the banks are more than a mile apart, and when in flood the river in its lower reaches is as much as four miles wide. The southern or Bulgarian bank, except at one or two points, commands the northern or Roumanian bank, the latter is marshy, except at the ordinary points of passage, and during the spring months is often flooded. The trade routes cross the river between the following towns, in each case the name first given is that of a Roumanian town:— Kalafat-Widin, Piketi-Rahova, Turnu-Nikopoli, Simnitza-Sistova, Giurgevo-Rustchuk, Oltenitza-Turtukai, Kalarashi-Silistria, Gurajalomitza-Hirsova, Brahilov-Matchin, Ismail-Tultcha. Of these points Widin, Rahova, Nikopoli, Sistova, Rustchuk, Turtukai, Silistria, Hirsova, Matchin and Tultcha were fortified, Widin, Rustchuk and Silistria were strong places in good repair, the fortifications at the remaining places being either improvised works or old forts in bad condition.

The ultimate objective of Russia was Constantinople. The most direct routes from Bessarabia to the Turkish capital were those running through Brahilov and Ismail by Varna. These roads ran through the territory between the Danube, where it flows northwards, and the Black Sea. This area is called the Dobrudja. Through it the Russian army had advanced in 1828, when the Russian generals Witgenstein and Diebich had in a brilliant campaign brought Turkey to her knees. But the conditions in 1828 were very different to those in 1877; then Russia was in undisputed command of the Black Sea, in 1877 this advantage rested with Turkey. Diebich as he moved South was able to shift his base from port to port on the west coast of the Black Sea. The Dobrudja is a barren and unhealthy country, full of swamps and marshes and with few and indifferent roads. Diebich's army did not exceed 50,000 men, and the experiences of his campaign proved conclusively that it would be quite impossible to maintain an army of 200,000 men, without the assistance given by the command of the sea, in that desolate region. The southern portion of the Dobrudja consists of the Quadrilateral. To advance through this area it would be necessary to mask by considerable detachments the four fortresses, whence comes the name ; and again the problem of supplying these detachments for a length of time presented great difficulties. Further, the command of the sea would allow Turkey to land her troops at Varna, on the flank of such an advance. The Danube below Rustchuk was, for these reasons, considered unsuitable for the main passage of the Russian army.

Westward of Nikopoli all roads leading from the Danube converged upon Sofia. An advance by them was dismissed as necessitating a wide detour to reach Constantinople, and entailing a line of communication through Roumania exposed to attack by an army operating from the Quadrilateral. There remained, therefore, the portion of the Danube between Nikopoli and Rustchuk. Good roads led thence through Lovcha and Tirnova, by the most practicable of the Balkan passes, direct upon Adrianople and Constantinople. The rivers Lom and Jantra would form a screen protecting the communications from the Quadrilateral, while the Vid would serve the same purpose against a Turkish force based on Widin. Also by avoiding the Dobrudja and moving through Roumania the railway, the roads, and the resources of that fertile land would become available. This line of advance led direct into Bulgaria, where the Christian population would give material assistance. On these considerations the Russian plan of campaign was based. It was decided to make the Odessa-Kishenev-Jassy railway the main line of communication, Kishenev the advanced base in Russia, and to move a force from Galatz and Brahilov into the Dobrudja, to screen the deployment of the main army between Giurgevo and Nikopoli. The latter was to cross the Danube between those two places, and, after detaching forces to the lines of the Lom and the Vid to observe the Turkish armies, known to be in the Quadrilateral and about Widin, to push a strong mobile column by Tirnova through the Balkans on Adrianople. It was confidently expected that the rapid and bold advance of this latter force would frighten the Sultan into surrender.

Nepokoitschitzki's studies of the 1870 campaign and of Von Moltke's strategy had led him to a false conclusion. Had he been content to carry his plan of campaign up to the passage of the Danube, and arranged his strategic deployment so that on crossing that river he would have been in superior force to either of the detachments, into which the Turks had weakly divided their forces; had he set himself the task of crushing the enemy's armies, before proceeding to threaten their capital, he might have passed as an apt disciple of the great Prussian. Moltke did not carry his original plan of campaign beyond the first collision with the French.

His strategic deployment was so arranged that his armies should meet the enemy in superior force; his dispositions made the chances of success upon the battlefield in his favour. But though Paris was his ultimate objective, just as Constantinople was that of Nepokoitschitzki, the first task he kept before him was the defeat of the enemy's main armies in the field. This is the aim of sound strategy, not the occupation of capitals, and of so-called strategic points, which are of no value except in so far as they assist in the defeat and destruction of the enemy upon the battlefield.

The whole art of war does not, of course, consist in seeking out and attacking the enemy wherever he may be. Generalship aims at being stronger than the enemy at the decisive point, at meeting him when he is at a disadvantage. Threatening an enemy's communications, his capital or his base may be and often is an effective means of attaining these results, but while he has armies still in the field they are effective only so far as they lead to the defeat of those armies. It is a far cry from the Danube to Constantinople. Nepokoitschitzki's plan of campaign depended upon the moral effect of a rapid advance on the Turkish capital. But however rapid such an advance might be there would be time for either of the main Turkish armies to intervene; in other words, the success of the plan depended upon movements of the enemy which could not be foreseen. It is useless to threaten an enemy if the latter can counter the blow before the threat becomes effective. Thus while it is sound strategy to menace some point such as an important railway or road junction, a mountain pass or river crossing, which is vital to the enemy, provided the latter must either abandon the point in danger or manœuvre to cover it and thus accept battle on ground not of his choosing, this operation is of no value if the enemy can first threaten a point which is equally vital to his assailant. In such a case the initiative, which it is the object of every commander to gain, passes from the latter to the former. Indeed an army which has once been committed to such a blow in the air is, when the enemy makes his counter stroke, in a far worse position than an army which is not involved in some extensive strategic enterprise. For in all probability attention will be fixed upon such a movement, the enemy's manœuvre will come as a surprise, and hasty and ill-considered preparations be made to meet it. Time and space are therefore all-important factors in a strategic problem.

The Russian plan of campaign was based upon an under estimate of what the enemy could do, a by no means uncommon fault, which invariably brings its own punishment. For their campaign in Europe the Russians had prepared a force of 200,000 men; some 60,000 were destined for that in the Caucasus. With the latter I am only concerned in so far as it affected the campaign in Europe. It was intended that the army of the Caucasus should invade Asia Minor, and sweeping the shores of the Black Sea, advance on Scutari. This operation was planned in the same optimistic spirit which devised the dash through the Balkans on Constantinople. Their desire to be strong in both theatres of war led the Russians to be strong in neither. 20,000 men would with the assistance of local levies have sufficed to defend the passes of the Caucasus against Turkish aggression. The Russians were soon to feel the want of the 40,000 men who might have been employed in the main theatre of war in Europe.

In May, 1877, no less than seven corps had not been mobilized. Nepokoitschitzki should have learned from Moltke that it is impossible to be too strong at the decisive point. He was proposing to contain two armies of the enemy, which together would not be much inferior to the force he could put in the field south of the Danube, and with the small body he would then have available to make a rash forward movement into the heart of Turkey. He forgot that the command of the sea would allow Turkey to bring troops from her Western European provinces, from Africa, or from Asia Minor, and rail them to or beyond Adrianople quicker than he could move his men through the defiles of the Balkans. No doubt he was influenced by Diebich's dash through the Balkans to Burghas in 1829, which wrung from the terrified Sultan the Peace of Adrianople; but that movement was the consequence of substantial victories previously gained. To follow up success boldly is a very different operation to rashly pressing forward with an undefeated enemy in rear. Russia was to learn the lessons we have been so often taught, that there is no greater mistake than to despise your enemy, and that the objective of sound strategy is the defeat of the enemy's army.

II. The Turkish Plan of Campaign. The wars with Servia and Montenegro and the troubles in Bosnia, Herzegovina, Macedonia and Bulgaria led to the Turkish army in Europe being widely dispersed in the spring of 1877. In the month of March Turkey had forces in

Bosnia, in Herzegovina, about Novibazar, on the southern frontier of Servia, about Widin on its eastern frontier, in Albania, about Sofia in Southern Bulgaria and in the Quadrilateral and Dobrudja in Eastern Bulgaria. Thus her troops were scattered from the Adriatic to the Black Sea. When it became apparent that war with Russia was inevitable, an attempt was made to establish a *modus vivendi* with the disaffected States, and to concentrate a part at least of the forces available for the European theatre of war within the Quadrilateral.

Abdul Kerim Pasha was appointed by the Sultan to the Chief Command in Europe. He was seventy-one years of age, and was a Pasha of the old school. He thought slowly, spoke little, never put foot to the ground, or except under the direst necessity put his horse out of a walk. He had acquired a certain reputation as a student of the art of war in Turkey, owing to the fact that he had studied in Vienna. He had commanded the Turkish army which operated against Servia, but conducted the greater part of that campaign from a house in Sofia. His right-hand man and the real director of operations was the commander of the Shumla corps, Ahmed Eyoub Pasha, a man who was a born fighter, but was without any scientific military training.

Abdul Kerim's first effort was to concentrate. Unfortunately this laudable attempt was carried out in a perfunctory manner, and was much interfered with by the civil governors of towns and provinces, who, frightened by being left without troops in the midst of a disaffected Christian population, appealed to the Sultan against Abdul Kerim's orders, which directed the various units to assemble in the

THE PLANS OF CAMPAIGN

Quadrilateral. The marches and counter-marches, due to Abdul Kerim's vacillation, and the intriguing with the Palace at Constantinople, make it difficult to follow the movements of the Turkish forces prior to the declaration of war; but at that time the approximate distribution of the Turkish army in Europe was as follows:—

At Widin along the western frontier of Servia, and on the Danube from the Servian frontier to Rahova, under Osman Pasha :—

> 50 battalions.
> 10 squadrons.
> 15 batteries.
>   Total, 30,000 men.

Along the Upper Danube, between Rahova, Nikopoli and Sistova :—

> 15 battalions.
> 4 squadrons.
> 5 batteries.
>   Total, 10,000 men.

In Rustchuk and along the Danube to Sistova, under Kaisserli Ahmed Pasha :—

> 20 battalions.
> 5 squadrons.
> 2 batteries (exclusive of fortress artillery).
>   Total, 12,000 men.

In Silistria, under Salami Pasha :—

> 12 battalions.
> 3 squadrons.
> 3 batteries.
>   Total, 9,000 men.

In Shumla, and Eski Dzuma, under Ahmed Eyoub Pasha :—

>65 battalions.
>30 squadrons
>>(including irregular cavalry).
>
>15 batteries.
>>Total, 55,000 men.

In the Dobrudja and along the lower Danube under Ali Pasha :—

>20 battalions.
>4 squadrons.
>6 batteries.
>>Total, 18,000 men.

In Varna, under Reschid Pasha :—

>12 battalions.
>2 squadrons.
>2 batteries.
>>Total, 9,000 men.

In addition to the above, 45 battalions, 12 squadrons and 8 batteries, total 25,000 men, were divided as the reserve to these forces between Sofia, Tirnova, Adrianople and Constantinople. Abdul Kerim thus had under his orders a force of about 170,000 men. There were 15,000 men at this time in Bosnia under Veli Pasha, 50,000 in Herzegovina and Montenegro under Suleyman Pasha, 20,000 in Albania under Ali Saib Pasha, 10,000 at Novibazar under Mehmet Ali Pasha. The Turks had besides some 45,000 men available under arms scattered in small bodies throughout European Turkey and in Crete.

It will be seen that Abdul Kerim's concentration was of the vaguest. The Quadrilateral is an area of about seventy miles by sixty, and even into this space he had only brought a portion of his force. His plan of campaign was to adopt a purely passive defence. He had learnt in Vienna that a river was an obstacle which had never yet stopped the advance of an army, and with Oriental fatalism he decided to make no effort to cope with the inevitable, and to give up any attempt to defend the line of the Danube. He proposed to entice the Russians into the Quadrilateral, and to swoop down upon them, while they were engaged in either masking or besieging the four famous fortresses.

Such a plan of campaign is more than puerile. Even the youngest spider does not expect to catch flies without spinning a web. Abdul Kerim might have foreseen that the reasons which led him to wish that the Russians should enter the Quadrilateral, would keep them out of it. Except as one more example to prove that a passive defence is no defence there is nothing to be learned from Abdul Kerim's strategy. But it is worth while considering what he might have done.

The disturbed state of the Christian provinces of European Turkey, and the dissemination of the Turkish forces, which resulted from this, precluded any idea of an offensive campaign. At the same time Adbul Kerim was in no way obliged to sit still, and allow the enemy to choose his point of attack. Indeed few generals could have had greater inducements, or better opportunities, to adopt a policy of active defence. Everything was to be gained by delaying the Russian advance. Either England or Austria, or both, would probably intervene if the campaign were protracted and indecisive. It was well known that Roumania had from necessity, and not from love, concluded the convention with Russia.

An early check to the Russian advance would probably awe the revolting Christian provinces into some semblance of order. Were the enemy allowed to gain early successes the insurgents would be encouraged to renewed efforts.

In all her many struggles against Russia, Turkey had never had such opportunities as she possessed in the spring of 1877 for delaying the Russian advance across the Danube. Turkey's best means of defence was her fleet, which Abdul Kerim had left altogether out of his calculations. It has been seen that the mere existence of the Turkish Black Sea squadron compelled Russia to allot two Army Corps to the defence of her coasts. But the Turkish fleets not only caused the enemy to make detachments, they greatly increased the Turkish powers of concentration. The reserve forces of the Ottoman Empire were even more widely scattered than was her active army, at the time of the Russian declaration of war. Turkey could draw upon Egypt, Tripoli, Crete, the islands of the Aegean, and Asia Minor, and land her troops at whichever port the course of events made the most suitable. The power to transfer force to any desired point would, in the hands of a more instructed commander than Abdul Kerim, have been the surest weapon of defence against Russian invasion. It was not upon the sea alone that the Turkish flag flew without challenge. Turkey had, in April 1877, seven armoured and eighteen unarmoured ships of war upon the Danube, and a fleet of twenty armoured vessels off the Sulina mouth, and to these at that time Russia could not oppose a single ship. We have seen the difficulties which Russia had to overcome in order to deploy her forces in Walachia, how her corps had to execute a difficult wheel, pivoted upon her left flank, and how all the roads, by which her left columns could move, converged on Galatz. Had Abdul Kerim used the weapon which was placed in his hands, and in conjunction with the fleet secured Reni, Galatz and Brahilov, he would not only have checked the Russian advance, but would have turned it in the direction he wished, a direction which the enemy had condemned as unsuitable. It is quite certain that no Russian forces would have ventured south of the line Fokchany-Galatz, as long as a Turkish force was established in the neighbourhood of the latter place. By taking the initiative in this way Abdul Kerim could have influenced the direction of the Russian advance, not by sitting under the shadow of the fortresses of the Quadrilateral and wishing the enemy to follow him there.

See Greene, part ii. (Introduction); Krahmer, chapter xi.; *La Guerre D'Orient* (Introduction).

CHAPTER III

(I) THE RUSSIAN DEPLOYMENT

Seizure of Barboshi Bridge—Occupation of Left Bank of Danube—Destruction of Turkish Monitors—Advance of Main Army—Participation of Roumania—Completion of Deployment—Comments.

(II) THE PASSAGE OF THE DANUBE

Position of Army on June 6—Passage of Brahilov—Zimmerman Occupies the Dobrudja—Selection of Point for Main Passage—Arrangements for Main Passage—The Passage at Simnitza—Comments.

CHAPTER III

(I) The Russian Deployment

THE plan, devised by the Russian Staff for the deployment of their army in Walachia, depended upon the security of their left flank. To protect this it was necessary that the first step of the invasion should be the occupation of Reni, Galatz and Brahilov, which commanded the only firm and secure landing places in that region of swamps and marshes where the Danube takes its final bend eastwards. A short distance south of Galatz the river Sereth flows into the Danube; at its mouth it is 180 yards wide, and during the wet months of April and May it is a swift-flowing and deep river. During the 140 miles of its course which crossed the line of the Russian advance, there were only three bridges, at Roman, at a point between Tekutch and Fokchany, and at Barboshi near Galatz. The Tekutch bridge was narrow and in bad repair, that at Barboshi was a modern, iron, rail and road bridge, some 300 yards long. There had been heavy rains during the month of April, and the floods of the Sereth and the Danube had filled the marshes near Barboshi, and made the construction of a military bridge well-nigh impossible. It will be remembered that all the southern roads, available for the Russian deployment, converged on Galatz; they passed thence over the

Barboshi bridge. To secure this bridge was then a matter of great moment to the Russians. A Turkish flotilla was known to be in the Sulina channel of the Danube, and Turkish troops were in the Dobrudja; it was necessary, therefore, to act swiftly and secretly. The Russian agreement with Roumania was to be ratified by the parliament of that country on April 29. The Russian Commander-in-Chief reckoned that this fact would be known in Turkey, and that a declaration of war would not be expected prior to that event. The Russian troops were quietly moved up to the frontier. The formal declaration of war was made on April 24, and from the earliest hours of that day they poured into Roumania.

The task of securing the Barboshi bridge was allotted in the first instance to a specially formed column composed of the three Don Cossack regiments attached to the XIth Corps (29th, 31st and 40th Don Cossacks), two battalions of the 41st regiment, two Field and two Cossack batteries. These were placed under the command of Colonel Biskoupski, the Chief Staff Officer of the XIth Corps. It assembled during the night of April 23-24 on the frontier between Kubei and Bolgrad, and crossed at 3 a.m. on the 24th. The cavalry moved by Hadzi Abduly and Reni, on Galatz, which was reached at 6 p.m. that day. The distance from Kubei to Galatz is about fifty miles; they were delayed for close on five hours at the Pruth by having to cross the flooded river in boats, but reached the Barboshi bridge a little before 7 p.m. The remainder of the detachment starting at the same time as the cavalry reached Reni between 5 and 6 p.m. Here the column was unexpectedly delayed, two Turkish gunboats were discovered to be at the mouth of the Pruth, and the ferry over that river had been damaged. The gunboats steamed off shortly afterwards down the Danube, and the column began to cross at 10 p.m. By 9 a.m. on the 25th one battalion of the 41st regiment and the two Cossack batteries had crossed, and with these Biskoupski advanced on Galatz and reached the bridge about midday. The remaining battalion and the field batteries were delayed in crossing the Pruth by a storm, and did not reach Galatz until 8 p.m. The leading battalion had marched the fifty miles in thirty-four hours in spite of the long delay at the Pruth. Biskoupski had requisitioned carts to carry the packs of the infantry who were thereby enabled to make a noteworthy march.

The Roman entrenchments, on the plateau commanding the bridge, required little improvement to make them suitable for modern artillery, and when, on the 25th, the Turkish monitors, charged with the destruction of the Barboshi bridge, arrived off the mouth of the Sereth, they were repulsed by the Russian guns already in position.

During the morning of the 26th detachments of the XIth Corps occupied Ismail and Kilia, after marches little less remarkable than that of Biskoupski. Thus, before the Turks were well aware that hostilities had begun, the Russians had secured all the points of passage over the Danube, at and below Brahilov, and behind the screen thus formed could move their columns through Roumania in safety.

During the 26th and 27th the greater part of the

11th Infantry Division and the 2nd Brigade of the 32nd Infantry Division reached Galatz. During the 28th and 29th the first Brigade of that Division, the 7th Engineer Battalion, the Black Sea Naval Brigade and the heavy artillery arrived at Galatz. They had been moved down from Jassy by train, but had been delayed on the way by the deficiency of rolling stock and the bad condition of the permanent way of the Roumanian railway.

The Russian Naval Brigade at once set to work to neutralize the Turkish flotilla. The mouth of the Sereth was mined, and the Barboshi bridge was thereby secured against attack by the Turkish gunboats. By April 30 a line of mines was established across the Danube at Reni and Brahilov. The main Turkish fleet, which was off the Sulina mouth, was thus cut off from the flotillas of the Danube. Batteries were established at Brahilov, Galatz and Reni. The Turkish river monitors were unable to cope with the Russian batteries because the latter were established on commanding ground, which allowed them to direct a plunging fire upon anything in the river, and the former were not provided with any deck protection, and could not obtain the elevation necessary to enable them to reply to the field guns. The Turkish Eastern Danube flotilla was, early in May, driven to take refuge in an arm of the river at Matchin. An attempt on the part of the Turks to break out on May 11 was frustrated by the batteries at Brahilov, and the *Louft-i-Djelil*, the principal vessel of the squadron, was blown up. On May 25 her sister ship, the *Havzi Rahman*, was destroyed by a daring attack by Russian steam pinnaces, fitted with spar torpedoes. The loss of these two fine vessels caused the greatest discouragement in the Turkish navy. No serious attempt to obtain command of the Danube was made after this date. The Turkish river flotilla had proved of little advantage to the Turks. The Turkish navy was commanded by Hobart Pasha, an Englishman who had entered the Turkish Service. He was a dashing and enterprising sailor who had made his name as a blockade-runner during the American Civil War, and who possessed the Sultan's confidence. Yet the fact of his being a foreigner was sufficient to ensure him the hostility of the Turkish Pashas. All his plans were frustrated by intrigue. His subordinate commanders were disloyal and did not carry out his orders, while Abdul Kerim, with whom he should have been working in the closest co-operation, actually requested that he should on no account be allowed to enter the Danube. The sea-going squadron, therefore, could not act in conjunction with the river flotillas, which in turn were independent of each other, while there was no combined action between the naval and land forces. The energetic action of a few Russian sailors on light pinnaces railed to the Danube sufficed to counteract the naval strength of Turkey in the river.

While these events were taking place on the Danube the Russian army of invasion was moving through Roumania. It had crossed the frontier on April 24 at Umgeni, Bestamak and Kubei, and advanced in three main columns, covered by the cavalry. On the right the 8th and 12th Cavalry Divisions and the 21st, 26th and 37th regiments of Cossacks moved from

Umgeni by Jassy, Roman, Bakau to Fokchany. In the centre the infantry and artillery of the XIIth Corps moved by Umgeni, Jassy, Berlat to Fokchany. The left column crossed the Pruth at Leova and moved by Faltsi to Galatz and Brahilov. This column consisted of the specially formed body placed under the command of Skobelov I, composed of the Caucasian Cossack Cavalry Division, the 23rd Don Cossack Regiment, the 4th Rifle Brigade and the 5th Battalion of Engineers. Skobelov's command was destined to occupy successively all possible points of passage on the Danube above Brahilov, and to screen the deployment of the Russian army. It was followed by the 11th Cavalry Division and the infantry and artillery of the VIIIth Corps. The movements of the XIth Corps, which with the exception of the 11th Cavalry Division formed what was called the detachment of the Lower Danube, have already been described. The IXth Corps was to be moved by rail, with the exception of the 34th Don Cossack regiment, which followed the march of the left column. The 36th Division of the VIIth Corps, which with the Xth Corps had charge of the defence of the Black Sea coasts, was moved up from Akerman and relieved the troops of the XIth Corps at Kilia, Ismail and Reni.

By May 8 the VIIIth, XIth, and part of the VIIth Corps were concentrated about Reni, Galatz and Brahilov, while the XIIth Corps was about Tekutch. The cavalry, with Skobelov's Light Division in support, had occupied all points of passage over the Danube, as far south as Gora-Yalomitza. From the Yalomitza to the Aluta the Danube was watched by the Roumanian troops, who handed over their posts to the Russians as they advanced, and took ground further to the west. Thus early in the day the Russians had established a preponderating force at the angle of the Danube near Galatz, and had secured the left flank of their advance into Walachia.

The Turks meanwhile contented themselves with an aimless bombardment of the defenceless Roumanian towns on the northern bank of the river, the only result of which was to drive the Roumanians more than ever into the arms of Russia. The latter had at first received the Russians coldly, and had regarded the movement of the Slav armies through their territory as a necessary evil. But the useless and savage attacks of the Turks upon the Roumanian towns which lie along the Danube aroused a feeling of irritation in the country, which strengthened the hands of the Russo-phil party. The officers of the army, which had for the first time been placed on a war footing, were eager to gain distinction on the field of battle, and Prince Charles of Roumania, who was something of a stranger in his country, was anxious to establish himself in the affections of his people by appearing as a victor at the head of the forces of the Principality.

Popular feeling in Roumania began, therefore, to favour active co-operation with Russia. On May 11 relations with the Porte were finally broken, and on the 15th Roumania proclaimed her independence. A few days later a second agreement was concluded with Russia, by which the latter recognized Roumania as an independent kingdom; and undertook to make Turkey cede to Roumania the Turkish

Dobrudja, as far south as the Kustenji-Tchernavoda line of railway, and to provide Roumania with 200,000 rifles. In return Roumania agreed to cede to Russia that portion of Roumanian Bessarabia which lies between Reni and the Black Sea, to declare war on Turkey and to maintain an army of 70,000 men. Difficulties arose as to the terms on which the Roumanian army was to serve, and these were not finally settled till a later date. The Russian Staff was inclined to regard the pretensions of their allies to be considered soldiers with some amusement, and to look on any active assistance from the Roumanian army as unnecessary and undesirable. At the end of May the Roumanians were allotted the task of watching the Danube, west of the Aluta, and were denied any active rôle.

Even as early as May 8 it had become apparent to the Russian Head Quarter Staff that they had under-estimated the force required for the campaign. None of the Army Corps with the active army was at full strength, and the garrisons of the towns on the Lower Danube, which were necessary to the security of the Russian left flank, had eaten up a considerable portion of the active army. On May 8, therefore, the order was given for the three Reserve Corps, the IVth, XIIIth, and XIVth, to join the active army.

The deployment of the active army as originally constituted was completed by May 24, by which date 150,000 Russian troops had entered Roumania. One Division and the Cavalry of the IXth Corps were at Slatina. The remaining division of the IXth Corps, the VIIIth and XIIth Corps were at Bukharest. Half the XIth Corps was at Budesti. The remaining half of the XIth Corps, half of the VIIth and some units of the XIIIth were about Brahilov, Galatz and Reni, guarding the left flank. The greater part of the cavalry, and Skobelov's Light Division, watched the passages of the Danube, from the Aluta, where they connected with the Roumanian army, eastwards, and formed a screen effectually concealing the deployment from Turkish observation.

The Russian Staff had every reason to congratulate themselves on the way in which this deployment had been carried out. The movement had been one of exceptional difficulty, as they had at their disposal but two main lines of march and a single line of rail. The latter proved of even less assistance than had been anticipated. The Roumanian rolling stock was so deficient, that not more than five trains a day could at first be forwarded, and these were all required for the torpedo boats, pinnaces, and heavy artillery which were needed to deal with the Turkish flotilla. Further the spring of 1877 was an abnormally wet one. Shortly after the declaration of war both the Pruth and the Sereth were in flood. The bridge at Skuleni was three times carried away, while the Pruth at Leova, where it is usually forty-five yards wide, overflowed its banks to a distance of three miles. The roads along the valleys became well-nigh impassable, and a special provision of bridging material which had been made proved quite inadequate. But all difficulties were overcome, an army of 150,000 men had been deployed in thirty days, the greater part of it having marched 300 miles.

The Russian Staff had thoroughly realized the danger to their left flank, and had understood that the surest way to obviate the danger was to effect a surprise. Their plans were carefully and secretly elaborated before war was declared. The construction of batteries at Galatz and Brahilov was begun with the assistance of Roumanian labour as early as April 17. Careful provision was made for securing the important Barboshi bridge and for neutralizing the Turkish monitors.

It is interesting to note that Turkey appealed to Europe against the violation by Russia of international law, in that the latter had begun active operations before declaring war. In 1904 Japan has acted in the same manner, and on the same principles, as Russia in 1877 : this time it is Russia that has appealed to Europe. In 1877 the success of the improvised Russian torpedo boats against the Turkish monitors was hailed as introducing a new era in maritime warfare, and as dooming the armoured battleship to extinction. The battleship has survived for close on thirty years, and, after having once more been doomed by the success of the Japanese torpedo boats at Port Arthur, has in the battle of the Tsushima Straits given a final answer to its critics.

The general methods of the Russian deployment were no less excellent than its details. The cavalry and light troops were pushed forward to screen the movement, which was well calculated to mislead the enemy as to the real line of advance. The massing of troops about Galatz and Brahilov led Abdul Kerim to anticipate that the main Russian advance would be through the Dobrudja. Thus a necessary measure for the protection of the deployment was made a part of the general offensive scheme. No information that Abdul Kerim was able to obtain by the end of May led him to conclude that the main Russian advance would cross the middle Danube. An army which has adopted a passive defence has this essential weakness that, having to conform to the enemy's movements, it is dependent upon information which a skilful enemy can with little difficulty make misleading.

(II) THE PASSAGE OF THE DANUBE

The Russian Commander-in-Chief had intended to attempt the passage of the Danube on June 6. But the railway had not been able to bring up the necessary bridging material, and heavy rains had delayed the march of every column. On that date the IXth Corps, less the 5th Division, had moved southward towards the Danube to Turnu Magurelli. The XIIth Corps had reached Fratesti. Half the XIth had moved down to Oltenitza. The VIIIth Corps and the 5th Division of the IXth Corps were at Bukharest. The XIIIth Corps had arrived complete at Ploesti. The other half of the XIth Corps maintained touch with the left flank column, which then consisted of half the XIVth Corps at Galatz, and half the VIIth eastward of that place. The remainder of the XIVth Corps was on the march to Galatz, which it reached by June 13. The Cavalry and Skobelov's Light Division carefully watched the Danube from Oltenitza to the Aluta, west of which lay the two Roumanian corps. The advance troops of the IVth Corps had reached Bukharest, but the greater part had not yet crossed the Roumanian frontier.

General Zimmerman was placed in command of the force which was destined to guard the left flank. This was composed of the XIVth Corps, and a division of Cossacks, about 25,000 men and 108 guns. The division of the VIIth Corps, which garrisoned the points of passage east of Galatz, was also under his command.

The Grand Duke Nicholas intended that Zimmerman should cross into the Dobrudja, before the passage of the river by the main army was attempted. Great quantities of timber were floated down the Sereth, and collected at Brahilov, and on June 12 the construction of a bridge between Brahilov and Getchet was begun. The mines laid in the river secured the work from interruption by the Turkish gunboats, and the flooded state of the right bank prevented Turkish patrols from moving along the river, so that they did not discover what was going on. These same floods, however, hindered the construction of the bridge. The Danube was fifteen feet above its normal level, and the river at the point selected for the passage was 2,500 yards wide. Zimmerman reported that he could not cross until the waters abated. He received in reply a peremptory order from Head Quarters, that the river must be passed on June 22. It was found impossible to complete the bridge by that date, but a large number of boats and rafts had been collected at Galatz, and a proportion of men trained in rowing. Zimmerman determined to secure the Budschak Hills, which commanded the marshes on the Turkish bank, opposite Galatz. The passage was begun at 3 a.m. on the 22nd by two parties, each consisting of five companies from regiments of the 1st Brigade of the 18th Division. The landing was hotly opposed by a Turkish detachment on the Budschak Hills, but on the arrival of Russian rein-

The Russian Crossing at Brahilov.

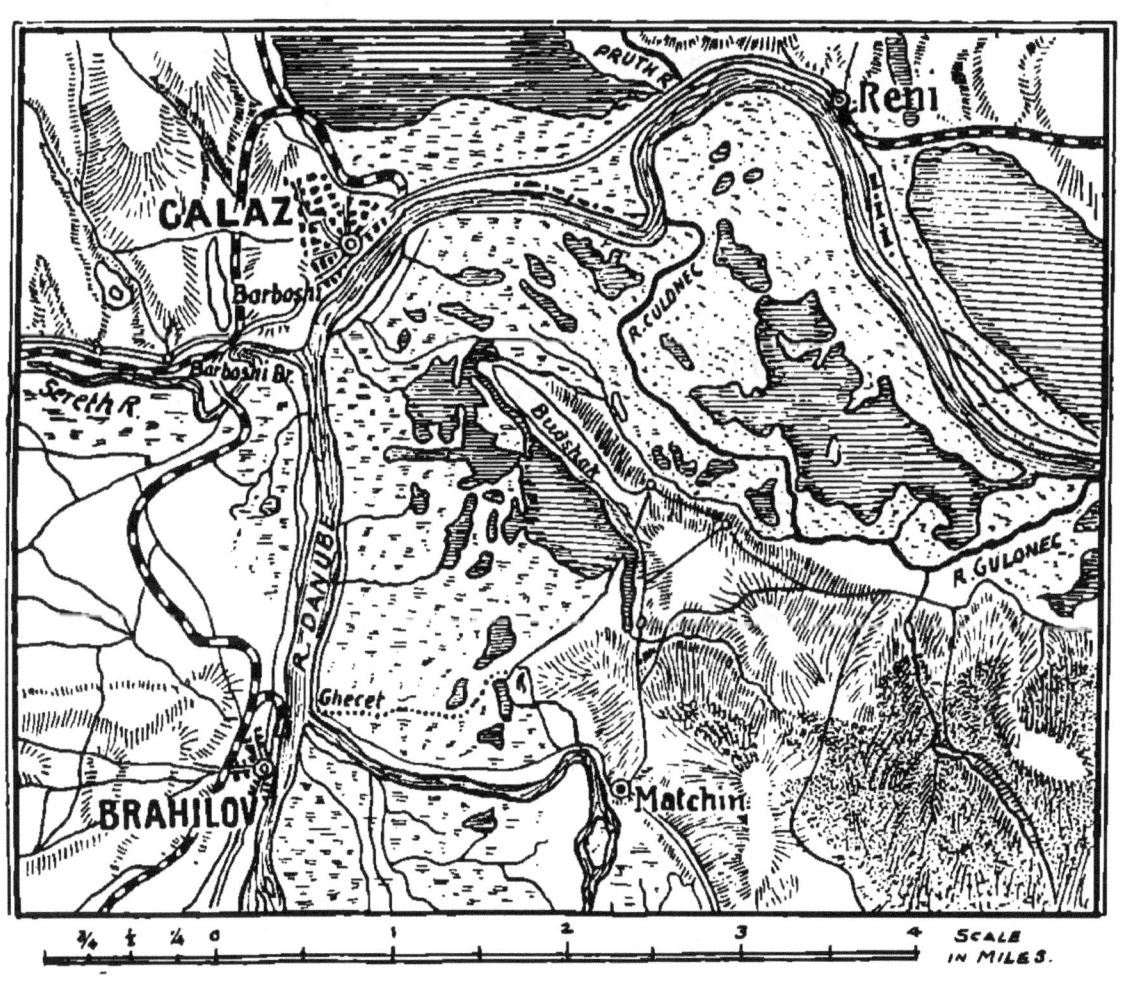

forcements at eleven o'clock the Turks withdrew to Matchin, and the next day abandoned that place too, and allowed Zimmerman to complete his crossing without further opposition. During the next few days Iskatchi, Tultcha and Hirsova were occupied by the Russians without striking a blow. By the end of June the Turks had abandoned the Dobrudja as far south as the Tchernavoda-Kustenji line of railway. The XIVth Corps advanced slowly and reached that line by July 19. Zimmerman established himself here, and took no further active part in the campaign, beyond containing a force of some 15,000 Turks under Ali Pasha,[1] apparently considering that he had fulfilled his part by securing the Lower Danube against the enterprises of the Turkish forces in the Quadrilateral.

Hobart Pasha's fleet was still a cause of anxiety at Russian Head Quarters. In the second week of July, therefore, when the whole of the XIVth Corps had entered the Dobrudja, the 36th Division of the VIIth Corps was moved back to Akkerman to watch the Black Sea littoral, and its place in the Danube Delta was taken by the 61st Infantry Regiment, the 4th Don Cossacks, and a battery, all from the IVth Corps.

Meanwhile the preparations for the crossing of the main army were pushed forward. The reasons which led the Commander-in-Chief to make his crossing between Rustchuk and Nikopoli, have already been explained. The selection of the actual point of crossing depended upon the nature of the country on either bank, and the state of the river. It was essential to the success of the undertaking that the point selected should

[1] These numbers include the garrisons of Silistria and Turtukai.

be kept secret to the last possible moment. It was therefore necessary to find a place, out of reach of Turkish observation, in which the immense mass of bridging material needed could be collected, and from which it could be rapidly transported to the chosen point. The river Aluta fulfilled these conditions. Timber could be accumulated on its banks in any quantity and floated down to the Danube. The point of passage had therefore to be near, and below, the mouth of the Aluta. The nature of the banks of the Danube, between Nikopoli and the radius of the strong Turkish fortress of Rustchuk, limited further choice to three points. Two of these, Flamunda[1] and a point just south of Turnu-Magurelli, were close together, both being in the neighbourhood of Nikopoli. At this place the Turks were known to have a number of heavy batteries and two monitors. The third point was between Simnitza and Sistova. This had obvious advantages. A good road led up to Simnitza, and from Sistova ran the road to Tirnova and the Shipka Pass, by which it was intended to make the main advance. There were two islands at this point in the river, one of which formed a backwater in which bridging material could be collected, the other would materially shorten the length of bridge necessary. The Turkish forces, which could oppose the passage, were, with the exception of small garrisons at Nikopoli and Sistova, within the Quadrilateral. The strong defensive line of the Jantra at Biela, which town commanded the main roads leading from the Quadrilateral to Sistova, was within an easy day's march of the latter place. The chances of a

[1] *See* Map II.

force which crossed at Simnitza anticipating a Turkish movement from the Quadrilateral on the Jantra were clearly much greater than those of a force crossing near Nikopoli. The only disadvantage of Simnitza was that the northern bank at that point was very low, and was liable to floods, which might seriously interfere with the bridging operations. On these grounds the Grand Duke Nicholas decided that the crossing should be made at Simnitza, if the state of the river permitted it, if not, at Flamunda.

On June 20 ten steam pinnaces were brought by rail to Giurgevo, and launched above Rustchuk, where they placed a line of mines across the river. A few days later a similar line was laid just above the mouth of the Aluta. The movement of the Russian army to the banks of the Danube began on June 19. The XIth Corps was ordered to relieve Skobelov's Light Division, and to hold the Danube from Kalarashi[1] to the river Vede. The 9th Division of the VIIIth Corps, the 4th Rifle Brigade, and the artillery of the VIIIth Corps, moved to Piatra[2]; the 14th Division of the VIIIth Corps and four pontoon battalions to Siaka; and the XIIth Corps and the Bulgarian contingent to Salsia; the IXth Corps with the exception of its cavalry division, which moved to Slatina, to Segarcia. The 1st Brigade of the Caucasian Cossack Division marched to Simnitza, the 2nd Brigade and the XIIIth Corps were ordered to Alexandria to form the general reserve.

It had originally been intended that the crossing should be attempted on June 24, but the troops had not reached the positions indicated by that time,

[1] *See* Map I. [2] *See* Map II.

and the pontoon park had not arrived. It was therefore decided to postpone the passage till the night of the 26th-27th. The most elaborate precautions were taken to keep the Russian plans secret. The VIIIth Corps was to be the first to cross, and its commander alone was informed that Simnitza was to be the point of passage. The grouping of the army pointed to a passage at Flamunda, and confidential instructions were issued to the Commanders of the IXth and XIIth Corps to prepare to cross the river at that point. The Czar himself aided in the deception. He publicly announced his intention of coming to the Danube to see his army cross into Bulgaria. He established his Headquarters at Turnu Magurelli, which is near Flamunda, and spent the days immediately preceding the crossing in scanning the south bank near that point through a telescope.

On the 25th the final orders for the passage were issued. The VIIIth Corps and the 4th Rifle Brigade were ordered to Simnitza, and directed to cross the river during the night of the 26th-27th in boats. The XIIIth Corps was directed from Alexandria to Piatra. The IXth Corps was to make a feint of crossing at Flamunda. The XIIth Corps was to take ground to its right towards Piatra. Siege batteries, which had been erected opposite Rustchuk and Nikopoli bombarded those places throughout the 25th, 26th and 27th. On the evening of the 26th the troops destined to make the first crossing were quietly collected at Simnitza, five batteries of Field Artillery were established on the north bank, 104 pontoons and more than 100 boats were brought up in carts, launched in a small creek near Simnitza, and floated down to the point of passage.

The 14th Division under General Dragomirov were the first troops to attempt the passage. Dragomirov formed his division into six detachments, each consisting of twelve companies of infantry, and sixty Cossacks. A battery of eight mountain guns was attached to each of the first two detachments, and four field guns to the other four. Each detachment consisted of about 2,500 men. The troops were ordered in no circumstances to fire a shot until the south bank was reached.

The Turks had a company of Mustaphis close to the mouth of the Tekir Brook, the point selected for landing, and had altogether about 4,000 men about Sistova. The first Russian detachment embarked at 1 a.m. The actual time taken by the detachments in crossing varied from about $\frac{3}{4}$ hour to $1\frac{1}{2}$ hours. As the boats of the first detachment gained the southern shore they were fired on by the Turkish outposts. They succeeded, however, in gaining the cliffs and driving back the Turkish skirmishers. The latter were quickly reinforced from the direction of Sistova, and the position of the Russians was for a time critical. Five of the Russian boats were sunk by the fire of a Turkish battery from Sistova, which took up a position on the left bank of the Terek, two mountain guns being lost, but the Russian guns on the north bank gradually obtained the mastery, and the continual arrival of reinforcements enabled the Russians to establish themselves. By eight o'clock on the 27th Dragomirov had driven the Turks off the cliffs which commanded the landing-place. By 9 a.m. a steamer from Turnu Magurelli arrived on the scene, and in two journeys was able to bring a complete regiment across the river. This reinforcement made the success of the crossing certain. The whole of the 14th Division was established on the south bank by 10.30 a.m.

The Turks had to oppose the passage Ismid Pasha's brigade of four battalions and a field battery, the whole under Ahmed Namdy Pasha. One battalion was in Sistova, the remainder were camped at a point about two miles to the east of that town and one and a half miles from the river. Ahmed Namdy Pasha on the first alarm sent forward two battalions, which were gradually forced back as the Russian boats landed more and more men. The moment that it became clear that the Russians were making a serious attempt to force the passage of the river, it was Ahmed Namdy Pasha's duty to throw in every man he had available, to oppose the Russians on the river bank, and to delay them by every means in his power, pending the arrival of reinforcements from Rustchuk, distant only thirty-five miles. By sending up his reinforcements piecemeal, he allowed the Russians to obtain a foothold on the right bank, and the success of the crossing was thereby assured. In fact, though he had been more than a month at Sistova he was taken completely by surprise. A commander acting on the defensive must be prepared with a plan of action to meet every possible movement of his enemy. The attacker being able to choose time and place has two deadly weapons at his service, surprise and the initiative, to counteract them the defender must be ready to act on the instant. To begin making plans when the blow has fallen is to go half way to meet defeat.

The steady advance of Dragomirov's division cut the Turks in two, part of their force retiring on Rustchuk, while the remainder fell back on Sistova and joined the battalion left in garrison. The 4th Rifle Brigade, which followed the 14th Division across the river, and one of Dragomirov's brigades were directed against Sistova, the remaining Brigade followed up the Turks retiring on Rustchuk, and covered the attack on the former place. After a short sharp resistance the Turks evacuated Sistova about 2 p.m. and fell back on Biela. By 9 p.m. the whole of the VIIIth Corps with the exception of its cavalry division was across the Danube. The work of ferrying over troops was continued steadily through the night of the 27th-28th; by the morning of the 28th the 25th Division of the XIIIth Corps was across, the remaining division crossing later the same day. The bridging material which had been collected in the Aluta was put together at Slatina and floated past the guns of Nikopoli during the night of the 27th-28th and the two following nights. The construction of the bridge was begun on the 28th, on which day the Emperor crossed. On the 29th work was interrupted by the appearance of a Turkish monitor, which, however, disappeared without firing a shot. On the 30th a storm further delayed the work, but by the morning of July 2 the bridge was complete. The cavalry of the VIIIth Corps, followed by Skobelov's division and the Bulgarian contingent, now crossed over. The XIIth Corps began crossing on the 3rd, and was followed by the 1st Division of the XIIIth Corps.

The IXth Corps began the passage on the 7th, then came the cavalry of the XIIIth Corps, and after them the XIth Corps, less the 2nd Brigade of the 32nd Division, the 2nd Brigade of the 11th Cavalry

THE PASSAGE OF THE DANUBE 65

Division and the 31st Don Cossacks, which were left to hold Olteniza[1] and Giurgevo, and to prevent the Turkish garrisons of Silistria and Rustchuk raiding the Russian communications in Roumania. The IVth Corps, with the exception of the detachment (61st Regiment and 4th Don Cossacks) left under Zimmerman's orders to hold the Danube Delta, had by this time concentrated at Bukharest; but it was not established on the right bank of the Danube until the end of July.

The passage of the river cost the Russians only 800 killed and wounded, the Turks admitted a loss of 700. The passage of such an obstacle as the Danube had been made with astonishing ease. The Russians deserved the success they had won. Their plans were well thought out, every precaution had been taken to mislead and deceive the enemy. When ready to strike they had struck with energy and decision. The Turks on the other hand waited for the blow to fall, and suffered the inevitable penalty of a purely passive defence.

To scatter troops along a line, whether it be a river, a mountain chain, or a geographical frontier, is to be weak at all points. The Turks could only hope to defend the river line successfully by constant and energetic patrolling on the enemy's bank and by holding reserves on their own bank ready to concentrate rapidly when required.

The total want of co-operation between the Turkish army and navy is a point which we English soldiers would do well to consider. Their overwhelming force of iron monitors gave the Turks a weapon, which, if it had been used in conjunction with their army, either

[1] *See* Map I,

for reconnaissance or still better for active offence, might have indefinitely postponed the Russian passage of the river. Mutual jealousy between the services, and want of understanding by each of the needs and capabilities of the other led to inaction and defeat. The Turkish river flotillas, being independent of each other, adopted no concerted plan of action. The military commanders failed to keep the naval officers informed of their plans and movements and of such information about the enemy as they possessed. The moral effect of the Russian successes at Galatz appears to have paralysed the Turkish gunboats, which were quite unable to cope with the Russian field guns when these were posted on commanding positions, as they were unable to obtain the necessary elevation, and were not supported by their own field artillery.

>Krahmer, chapter xvi.
>*Guerre D'Orient*, part i. chap. iv.

CHAPTER IV

THE RUSSIAN ADVANCE UP TO THE FIRST BATTLE OF PLEVNA

SITUATION AFTER THE PASSAGE OF THE DANUBE—FORMATION OF GOURKO'S ADVANCED GUARD—FORMATION OF WESTERN ARMY AND ARMY OF RUSTCHUK—COMMENTS—GOURKO'S ADVANCE—OCCUPATION OF TIRNOVA—CAPTURE OF HAINKIOJ PASS—ATTACK ON SHIPKA PASS FROM THE SOUTH—CAPTURE OF SHIPKA PASS—COMMENTS—OPERATIONS OF THE ARMY OF RUSTCHUK — ADVANCE TO THE JANTRA—ADVANCE TO THE KARA LOM — OPERATIONS OF THE WESTERN ARMY—CAVALRY RECONNAISSANCE TO PLEVNA—CAPTURE OF NIKOPOLI—ADVANCE TO PLEVNA—OPERATIONS OF THE TURKISH FORCES IN THE QUADRILATERAL—OSMAN'S ADVANCE TO PLEVNA.

CHAPTER IV

THE RUSSIAN ADVANCE UP TO THE FIRST BATTLE OF PLEVNA

THE situation with which the Grand Duke Nicholas had to deal, after the passage of the Danube had been sucessfully accomplished, presented many difficulties. The information at his disposal was to the effect that 50,000 Turks were garrisoning the fortresses of Widin, Nikopoli, Rustchuk, Turtukai, Silistria and Varna; Osman Pasha was reported to have a field force of 40,000 men and 100 guns about Widin; the main Turkish army in the neighbourhood of Shumla was estimated at 60,000 men and 230 guns; about 15,000 men and 40 guns were opposing Zimmermann in the Dobrudja; in addition it was known from Turkish papers that Mehmet Ali was preparing to leave Albania, and Suleyman Pasha, Montenegro, which would bring a reinforcement of 50,000 men into the field. As regards his own forces, though the advance through Roumania and the passage of the Danube had been affected with little loss, no unit was up to its establishment. The wet weather and the marshes on the banks of the Danube had produced a lengthy sick list. The mobilization arrangements were new, and had not been tested, and, as has been explained, they had failed to bring the reserves to the colours to the extent which had been anticipated. The protection of the line of communications and the security of the coast against the enterprises of the superior Turkish fleet necessitated many detachments from the main army. It was, therefore, to be expected that the Grand Duke Nicholas would make some modification in his original plan of campaign. But the blind confidence in themselves and the unreasoning contempt for their adversaries, which have always been characteristic of the Russians at the beginning of their wars, over-ruled all counsels of prudence.

On June 30 Lieut.-General Skobelov's command was broken up, and in its place a special advanced guard corps was formed, consisting of the Bulgarian contingent (six battalions), the 4th Rifle Brigade, two sotnias of Plasstuns (Cossack infantry), fourteen mountain guns, a Brigade of Dragoons (8th and 9th Dragoons and one battery), a mixed Brigade of Hussars and Cossacks (9th Hussars, 30th Don Cossacks and a battery), a Brigade of Don Cossacks (21st and 22nd and a battery), half a squadron of Guard Cavalry, one sotnia of Ural Cossacks and a mounted detachment of Engineers; in all $10\frac{1}{2}$ battalions, $31\frac{1}{2}$ squadrons, 18 Horse Artillery, and 14 mountain guns.[1] These were placed under the command of Lieut-General Gourko, who commanded a division of guard cavalry and was brought specially from St. Petersburg. He had orders to advance as rapidly as possible on Tirnova and

[1] This detachment was thus made up from Skobelov's division, one cavalry regiment from the VIIIth Corps, two from the IXth Corps, and some details.

Selvi, and on receipt of a definite order from Headquarters to push on and seize one or more of the Balkan Passes. He was to bring about a rising of the Christian population south of the Balkans, and disperse any Turkish detachments he might find in the Valley of the Tundja.

The IXth Army Corps[1] under General Krudener, called the Western Army, was ordered to seize Nikopoli, to advance thence to the line of the Vid and secure the Russian left flank. The XIIth and XIIIth Corps, called the Army of Rustchuk, under the command of the Czarevitch, were ordered to Biela and instructed to occupy the line of the Jantra, to contain the Turkish forces in the Quadrilateral, and if all went well to reduce the fortress of Rustchuk. The VIIIth Corps was directed to push forward on Tirnova and support Gourko's force, while the XIth and IVth Corps, less the detachments guarding the communications, were to form a general reserve in the neighbourhood of Simnitza. Zimmermann, with the XIVth Corps and the detachment of the 16th Division of the IVth Corps, was directed to secure the line of communications against any enterprises from the Quadrilateral, and to keep the Turks in that area as much occupied as might be.

From this it will be seen that the Grand Duke Nicholas had not considered it necessary to alter the plan of campaign drawn up by the General Staff before the declaration of war.

[1] The two Cossack regiments of Skobelov's division which had not joined Gourko were formed into the Caucasian Cossack brigade and attached to this Corps to replace the 9th Hussars and 9th Dragoons.

This plan of campaign aimed at bringing the war to an early conclusion by a rapid advance through the Balkans into Roumelia. Clearly then the point at which the campaign was to be won was to be looked for somewhere on the line of advance of the force which was to make this dash. Yet the dispositions he proposed to make would only allow the Grand Duke Nicholas to concentrate at this decisive point, which was of his own choosing, Gourko's advanced guard detachment, the VIIIth Corps, and possibly if all went well part of the XIth and IVth Corps, that is to say at the very most 60,000 men. This is a striking example of the results of the policy of making detachments. At this period Russia had mobilized not less than 320,000 men for the prosecution of the war, yet less than one-fifth of this total could be made available for the movement which was to bring the Sultan to his knees. 60,000 men were committed to the campaign in the Caucasus, two corps were required for the protection of the Black Sea coast, and a considerable detachment from another for the garrisons of the towns in the Delta of the Danube. Another corps was considered necessary to contain the Turkish troops in the Dobrudja, and to secure the communications as far south as Tchernavoda. But even this proved to be insufficient to assure the Russian communications. Silistria, Turtukai and Rustchuk were known to be occupied by large Turkish garrisons, and the danger of their making a raid across the Danube had to be provided against. For this purpose a brigade of the XIth Corps and a brigade of the 11th Cavalry Division were left to hold Kalarashi, Oltenitza, and Giurgevo. Similarly until Nikopoli was captured a garrison had to be found for Turnu Magurelli, and to cover the all-important bridge at Simnitza. For these duties the remainder of the 16th infantry division of the IVth Corps was allotted, all in fact of that corps which had at this time arrived on the central Danube. The general reserve nominally composed of the XIth and IVth Corps was therefore in reality not available for any of the purposes for which a general reserve is required. Further the Grand Duke Nicholas had decided to make two more detachments, and these the most important of all, the XIIth and XIIIth Corps were directed to contain the Turks in the Quadrilateral, while the IXth Corps was needed to prevent Osman Pasha and the Turks in Western Bulgaria from interfering with the Russian right flank. And so four-fifths of the mobilized strength of Russia was dissipated on what were, according to the Grand Duke Nicholas's plan of campaign, minor operations.

Recently the Russian War Office has, in reply to its critics, announced that during the first thirteen months of the war with Japan it has delivered at Harbin 13,087 officers, 761,471 rank and file, 146,408 horses and 1,521 guns. It is known that about 61,000 men and 60 guns were either in Manchuria at the outbreak of hostilities, or reached the theatre of war by road. Therefore the Russians had south of Harbin during the first thirteen months of the war a total of 823,000 men and 1,580 guns. It is often asked what has become of this stupendous army. In Manchuria the Russians have, partly owing to want of preparation, and partly owing to the necessity of holding important fortresses and towns, and of protecting a long line of communication, been committed to a policy of detachments not very unlike that adopted by them in 1877. When we see how it came about that the Grand Duke Nicholas, before a single important engagement had been fought, could only put one-fifth of his mobilized force into the field, for what he intended to be the decisive operation of the war, it may help us to understand what has become of Kuropatkin's 800,000.

The Grand Duke's main army was engaged in three distinct operations. The first was Gourko's raid through the Balkans; the second the Czarevitch's advance to the Jantra; the third Krudener's advance to the Vid. In order to avoid confusion it is necessary to deal with each separately, but it must be remembered that they were simultaneous operations.

I. Gourko's advance into the Balkans The greater part of the cavalry of Gourko's detachment crossed the Danube on July 3, and the whole column concentrated the next day in the neighbourhood of Kozlovec,[1] whither the 4th Rifle Brigade had moved after the capture of Sistova. Gourko's infantry bivouacked on the night of the 4th at Akcair, the cavalry at Habeli, Karaisan and Ovca Mogila. No opposition was encountered, and information was obtained that Tirnova was occupied by five battalions of Turkish infantry with guns and cavalry.

The process of getting the Russian army across the bridges at Sistova proved a slow one, and in accordance with instructions from Headquarters, that the advance was not to be pushed forward too zealously until more troops had reached the south bank, the column remained halted on the 5th, the day being spent in bringing up

[1] See Map II.

the transport, and in gaining touch with the cavalry of the Western Army, which was watching the Sistova-Plevna road, and with that of the army of Rustchuk, which on this day occupied Biela. The next day but a short march was made, and on the night of the 6th the infantry reached Batak, and the cavalry the line of the Rusita. Confirmation was received of the report that Tirnova was occupied, and it was further discovered that the enemy were entrenching there and expecting reinforcements from the direction of Osman Bazar.

Gourko decided to leave his infantry where it was, and to make a reconnaissance with the whole of his mounted troops. The Dragoon Brigade was ordered to move from its bivouac at Murad-Bey by Mihalca and Kajabunar on Tirnova. The Don Cossack Brigade was directed to send strong patrols from Novinikup Stari, to demonstrate against Tirnova from the north and east, and to be prepared to support the Dragoons with the remainder of the Brigade. The 9th Hussars with four guns moved from Suhindol where they were bivouacked, and followed the Dragoons, for whom they formed the reserve. The 30th Don Cossack regiment with two guns remained at Suhindol to cover the right flank from the direction of Lovcha and to keep touch with the Caucasian Cossack Brigade which belonged to Krudener's Western column and was at Bulgureni.

Tirnova lies in a basin surrounded by the foot-hills of the Balkans, the approaches to it run between low hills covered with dense scrub. It is of great importance as a road centre, the routes from the Danube converging to cross the Jantra by a stone bridge, and again branching out to the Balkan passes. The Turks offered no opposition to Gourko's advance to Kajabunar, and a party of about 400 of their cavalry was surprised near that place, while watching the main road, which Gourko had purposely avoided, and fell back on Tirnova. Gourko keeping his reserves in hand on the high ground overlooking the town, dismounted his Dragoons, pushed them forward, and supported them with all his guns. The Turkish garrison consisted of a regiment of cavalry, five battalions and a battery, but it had not expected attack from the west, and had neglected to take proper military precautions. The boldness with which the dismounted Russian cavalry were handled, and the wide front covered by them in their advance, made the Turkish Commander believe that he was in the presence of a superior force, and he evacuated the town after a perfunctory resistance. This important strategic point was captured with the loss of only two men and eight horses wounded.

On the 8th Gourko brought up his Infantry, and used his cavalry on that and the day following in an extended reconnaissance of the Balkan passes. He discovered that all the passes were watched by the Turks with the exception of a difficult defile, some fifteen miles east of the main Shipka Pass, called the Hainkioj Pass (which had apparently been neglected because it was considered impracticable) and that on the 9th a force of five battalions with mountain artillery had reinforced the Mustaphis' garrison of the Shipka Pass and had begun constructing works commanding the road from Tirnova. On this information Gourko based his plan of campaign. This was to seize the Hainkioj Pass with his main body, while a detachment left at Tirnova should demonstrate against the Shipka Pass. He then proposed to move by Kazanlik and to attack the Shipka Pass from the south. This plan was submitted to Headquarters, and on the evening of the 11th Gourko received the Grand Duke's authority to carry it out, with the intimation that he would be supported by a Brigade of the VIIIth Corps, which would arrive at Tirnova by midday on the 12th, and that one regiment of this Brigade and one battery would be sent to Gabrova on the 14th to demonstrate against the Shipka Pass from the north. The field troop of Engineers, escorted by the sotnia of Ural Cossacks, started on the morning of the 10th to make a detailed reconnaissance of the Hainkioj Pass and to do what was possible to improve the track. On the same day strong patrols were sent towards the Elena, Travna and Shipka Passes to attract the attention of the Turks to those points. On the 11th Gourko received from General Rauch, who was conducting the reconnaissance of the Hainkioj Pass, a sketch with a detailed report of the route to be followed. On this he based his orders.

The detachment was to move by Prisova-Plakovski-Kolibi-Popovci-Ruscovci to Hainkioj. All supply, ammunition, and transport vehicles and animals, except the battery ammunition wagons and the pack animals, were to remain in Tirnova; five days' biscuit was to be carried for the men, and three days' hay for the horses; the infantry and cavalry were ordered to carry as much additional ammunition as possible in their pockets. Ten infantry and ten cavalrymen were allotted to each gun and ammunition wagon to assist in getting them over difficult ground. No fires were to be lighted after crossing the summit, and every precaution was to be taken against noise. Lastly, General Rauch was directed to collect all available supplies in the villages on the road.

The 9th Hussars and one battalion of the Bulgarian contingent was left at Tirnova as escort to the baggage and supply column. The 30th Don Cossacks, with two guns, also remained to furnish the cavalry for the Brigade of the VIIIth Corps, and to take part in the attack against the Shipka Pass from the north. The remainder of the detachment assembled at Prisova on the morning of July 12 and marched at 10.30 a.m. in the following order :—the 4th Rifle Brigade and the two sotnias of Plasstuns, then the two mountain batteries, followed by the Dragoon Brigade, five battalions of Bulgarians, and lastly the Cossack Brigade. The column bivouacked on the night of the 12th–13th at Kolibi.

On July 12 there were eight Turkish battalions in the Shipka Pass, three companies of Nizams watched the southern end of the Hainkioj Pass, five companies were at Tvardica where the Elena Pass enters the Tundja Valley, two battalions at Kazanlik, four at Kazan, three at Slivno and two at Jeni Zagra. Raouf Pasha, the Turkish Minister of Marine, had been sent forward by the Sultan, who was alarmed at the ease with which the Russians had forced the passage of the Danube, to organize the defence of the Balkans. He had at his disposal twenty-one battalions, twelve squadrons and $2\frac{1}{2}$ batteries, divided among the detachments named above. His Headquarters were at Slivno.

Gourko resumed his march at 6 a.m. on the 13th, and now the real difficulties of the venture began. The small detachment of Engineers were incessantly at work, but in spite of their utmost efforts the guns had to be dragged by hand for the greater part of that day.

At midday he halted at Ruskovci to give his men a meal. During this halt he wrote to Headquarters asking that a Brigade of the VIIIth Corps should be sent to hold the Hainkioj Pass, and to secure his line of retreat. He stated that if this were done he hoped to push on to Magliz on the 16th and attack Kazanlik and the southern end of the Shipka pass on the 17th. He asked that a demonstration should be made from the North against the Pass on the 16th and 17th, and proposed to advance on Philippopolis after the passes had been occupied. To this the Russian Headquarters replied that it was impossible at present to send a whole brigade to Hainkioj, as this would dangerously weaken the garrison of Tirnova, but that the 36th Infantry regiment and the 30th Don Cossacks would advance on the 16th against the Shipka Pass and attack on the 17th. Gourko was directed to content himself for the present with securing the passes, and until receipt of further orders he was to limit his operations after this had been done to sending patrols towards Philippopolis and Hermanli.

By the evening of the 13th four sotnias of Cossacks and all the infantry and mountain guns had crossed the summit, and they bivouacked that night on the southern slopes of the Balkans. At 10.15 next morning the first Russians debouched from the defile into the beautiful valley of the Tundja, and completely surprised a detachment of three companies of Nizams, who fled after a short resistance in the direction of Slivno pursued by the four sotnias of Cossacks, the only cavalry who at that time had reached the southern end of the pass. The distance from Tirnova to Hainkioj is forty miles, and the difficulties of the mountain track, which had hitherto only been used by the Bulgarian goatherds, were very great. From the col to the mouth of the pass in the Tundja Valley there is a drop of 3,000 feet in five miles ; it was necessary to dismount the greater part of the cavalry and to employ them in lowering the mountain guns over the rocks and through a dense scrub. Gourko spent the 14th in collecting his tired column in the valley, and in pushing out patrols in all directions to gain touch with the enemy. His advanced cavalry occupied Esekci on the road to Kazanlik, and Kuzosma on that to Tvardica. The situation which Gourko had to face was sufficiently serious. Tvardica was reported occupied by four battalions ; he was informed that from 5 to 6,000 Turks were about Kazanlik and the southern end of the Shipka Pass. Slivno, thirty miles to the east, was in direct communication with Shumla, the Headquarters of the Turkish army in the Quadrilateral, while only fifteen miles to the south lay Jeni Zagra, to which point Turkish troops could be railed from Adrianople and the south. Gourko decided that his greatest chance of success lay in prompt action. Part of the cavalry of his main body, the Horse Artillery battery, and the rear-guard did not, however, reach him till late on the 15th ; that day was spent in sending strong cavalry patrols to Tvardica, Jeni Zagra, Eski Zagra and Kazanlik. The first of these, which consisted of two sotnias of Cossacks, subsequently reinforced by a regiment of Dragoons and four guns, succeeded in driving the Turks out of Tvardica by skilful use of dismounted fire. Two more squadrons sent towards Jeni Zagra cut the telegraph line, but came upon four battalions of infantry and a battery and were repulsed.

On the night of the 15th-16th the 9th Hussars and 6th Bulgarian battalion came in from Tirnova. At 6 a.m. on the 16th Gourko advanced on Kazanlik, leaving four battalions of the Bulgarian contingent, two mountain batteries, and the 26th Don Cossacks to guard the Hainkioj Pass. This detachment was instructed to follow on the evening of the 17th, by which time Gourko expected that the Shipka Pass would be in his hands, and that he would be able to communicate through it with Russian Headquarters.

The cavalry was soon engaged with small bodies of the enemy and made slow progress. By 7 p.m. the column had only reached Magliz. It was then necessary to give up any hope of reaching Kazanlik that night. At dawn on the 17th the advance was resumed in three columns, and after a short fight the cavalry succeeded in enveloping the town, and as usual advanced to the attack dismounted. The Turks fearful of being cut off made but a poor resistance and abandoned the place, leaving 400 prisoners and three guns in the hands of the Russians. Pushing on in pursuit, the latter at 3 p.m. secured the village of Shipka and a Turkish camp with a quantity of supplies. But Gourko, finding that his men were exhausted, decided that it would be useless to think of attacking the Turks in the Shipka Pass that evening.

It will be remembered that the 17th was the day indicated by Gourko for a simultaneous attack on the pass from north and south. The force to make the attack from the north consisted of the

36th Orel regiment from the 9th Division of the VIIIth Corps, two sotnias of Cossacks, and four guns, about 2,000 men in all, under General Derojinski. This little column occupied Gabrova without opposition on the 15th. Derojinski received instructions from Headquarters to advance on the 16th towards the northern end of the Shipka Pass, but not to commit himself to a decisive attack until he heard that Gourko had occupied Kazanlik and was moving against the pass from the south.

On the 16th the detachment, with the exception of two companies left at Gabrova, occupied the northern end of the pass after a slight skirmish. During the night of the 16th–17th Prince Sviatopolk Mirski, the commander of the 9th Division, arrived and took command of the column. Though he was without news of Gourko he ordered an attack on the morning of the 17th. We have seen how Gourko was prevented from keeping his part of the agreement, and Prince Mirski's isolated attack upon a superior enemy in position had no chance of success. He was repulsed with a loss of two officers and seventy-seven men killed, four officers and 128 men wounded. On the evening of the 18th a belated message arrived from Gourko stating that he would not be able to attack on the 17th, and ordering a combined effort on the morning of the 18th. Meanwhile on the morning of the 18th Gourko summoned the Turkish commander in the pass to surrender, but receiving no answer advanced to the attack. Being in his turn unsupported from the other end of the pass he was repulsed with a loss of more than 300 men. Early on the 19th Gourko prepared to renew the combat, but was met by a Turkish flag of truce sent to enquire on what terms he would accept capitulation. Terms were drawn up, but when after some delay nothing further was heard from the Turks, Gourko sent forward his skirmishers ; about 2 p.m. as the latter were approaching the summit of the pass they met the advanced troops of the Gabrova detachment. The Turks had, under cover of the negotiations, evacuated all their positions. Prince Mirski had heard on the afternoon of the 18th that reinforcements were on their way to him from Tirnova. He had, therefore, sent forward the whole of the 36th regiment, and it was nine companies under Major-General Skobelov the younger, who had arrived with these reinforcements, which met Gourko's advanced troops on the summit of the pass. Three mountain and five Krupp guns and a quantity of stores were abandoned by the enemy, who, finding that the two Russian columns were at length acting in unison, had left all their impedimenta and retired by mountain tracks.

The Turkish garrison in the Shipka Pass which had opposed these attacks consisted of seven battalions and nine guns, 4,000 men in all, under Kouloussi Pasha. The latter had moved into the pass from Kazanlik on the 13th, and had at once proceeded to prepare defensive positions against an attack from the direction of Gabrova. Five successive positions facing north had been placed in a state of defence, but no attack from the direction of Kazanlik appears to have been anticipated. On the 19th the Turkish column under cover of the negotiations retired by side tracks on Philippopolis.

Gourko's capture of Tirnova and the Balkan Passes

will always be a striking example of what can be done by mobile troops boldly handled. How far the orders which sent him on his raid were judicious will be discussed later, when the conduct of the war by the Russian Headquarters is reviewed. But Gourko's execution of those orders shows that dash and judgment which are characteristic of great cavalry leaders. The lessons of this achievement are particularly important to us, now that our cavalry is armed with an infantry rifle and carefully trained to shoot and to fight on foot.

Gourko depended for his success chiefly on moral effect, to which the capture of Tirnova may be said to have been entirely due. With his Cossacks, Dragoons, and guns he was, by working over a wide front, able to impose upon his enemy the belief that he had with him a strong force of all three arms. He knew well that, as the result of a rapid advance, his numbers would be increased tenfold by rumour, and he was careful to take advantage of this fact. He was, however, never led by his success to change boldness for rashness. He used the time required by the infantry to overtake him at Tirnova, to explore a wide circle of country, and all the passes of the Balkans that he could reach; and again, while waiting for the rear of his column to toil slowly through the Hainkioj Pass, he pushed his reconnoitring patrols far into the Tundja Valley.

His failure to co-operate with the Gabrova column is another example, added to the many in military history, of the futility of framing for days ahead plans which are dependent for their execution on what the enemy may do, and of the difficulty of ensuring united action between two forces which are not in direct communication. The cases in which our columns in South Africa failed to co-operate at the critical moment are fresh in the memories of most of us. Napoleon's dictum that a double line of operations is unsound is still true. Telegraphy has, however, made it possible to keep forces which are separated still under the control of one man; and they are then working on a single line of operations in the sense in which Napoleon understood the phrase. It is probable that in the near future wireless telegraphy will still further extend the bounds within which different bodies of men may be controlled by one commander. But except where there is some sure means of exchanging information, and receiving and issuing orders, between forces which are working apart, failure to co-operate will still be the rule and not the exception.

La Cavallerie Russe dans la guerre de 1877-8. Krahmer, chapters xviii, xix. *Guerre D'Orient*, Part II, chap. i. and v.

II.
The Operations of the Army of Rustchuk

It will be remembered that the XIIth and XIIIth Corps under the Czarevitch were ordered to advance to the line of the Jantra, mask the Turkish army in the Quadrilateral, cover the Russian left flank, and if possible to seize Rustchuk. This force received the name of the army of Rustchuk. After crossing the Danube the XIIth Corps had moved to Pavlo, and on July 5 its cavalry division advanced on Biela, and secured that town, and its important bridge over the Jantra after a trifling skirmish. The neglect of the Turks to hold Biela can only be explained by the general apathy which marked their operations at this period. At

Biela was the one bridge over the Jantra between Tirnova and the Danube, and the roads running west from the Quadrilateral to Central Bulgaria and the Middle Danube united at this point. The river Jantra offered a strong defensive position; at Biela it is 150 yards wide, and of an average depth of six feet; the banks are steep and difficult, and the only points of passage between it and Tirnova are a few fords impracticable for guns or wheeled vehicles. Biela was therefore of the utmost importance to the Russians, whether to enable them to defend the line of the Jantra (since to defend a river successfully it is essential to have free access to the enemy's banks), or to allow them to carry on offensive operations within the Quadrilateral.

On July 6, part of the infantry of the 33rd Division arrived and occupied Biela, and on that and the following days the cavalry of the 12th Corps was engaged in constant skirmishes on the right bank of the Jantra, their right being gradually extended by the cavalry of the VIIIth Corps, which, with the exception of the 8th Dragoons with Gourko, was attached to the XIIIth Corps, as the 13th Cavalry Division had not yet crossed the Danube. On July 9, the infantry of the XIIth Corps, which had assembled at Biela, received orders to advance on Rustchuk, its cavalry being directed to move to the line of the Lom, while that of the XIIIth Corps was to move on the Kara Lom. The infantry of the XIIIth Corps were ordered to Kaseljevo to cover the operations of the XIIth Corps against Rustchuk.

Meantime the course of events had convinced the Grand Duke Nicholas of the correctness of his original plan of campaign. Gourko's successes, and the ease with which Tirnova had been captured, confirmed him in the belief that a rapid advance with his main force through the Balkans would be the surest means of bringing the war to a successful conclusion. He sent orders to the Czarevitch on July 9 to observe Rustchuk and the Turkish army in the Quadrilateral, and to be prepared to detach a large part of his army to join the main advance. Accordingly the Czarevitch checked his advance, and on July 11 his army occupied the following positions: the infantry of the XIIth Corps held the Jantra from Biela to Krivina with one brigade in reserve at Biberlik, and one regiment pushed forward as advanced guard to Obretenik. Of the infantry of the XIIIth corps, one brigade was in Biela, another along the Jantra south of that place, the remaining division being in reserve at Pavlo. The cavalry of the 12th Division held the line Mecka-Trestenik-Stroko-Abalva. Three regiments of the 8th Cavalry Division held the line Ablava-Osikova-Cairkioj.

From July 12 to 17 the Czarevitch's cavalry was occupied in carrying out reconnaissances towards Rustchuk, Rasgrad and Osman Bazar, and became engaged in a number of skirmishes with Turkish cavalry and infantry in the neighbourhood of those places.

The news of the capture of Nikopoli by the IXth[1] Corps on July 16, and Gourko's occupation of the Hainkioj Pass, caused the Grand Duke Nicholas again to modify his orders.

This time he appeared to consider that the shortest road to victory would be to crush the Turkish army in the Quadrilateral, and the easy success at Nikopoli

[1] *See* part iii. of this chapter.

seems to have overcome any doubts as to the expediency of operating within the radius of the great Turkish fortresses. The Czarevitch again received orders to push forward to the Lom and Kara Lom, and to be prepared to besiege Rustchuk.

The XIth Corps, with the exception of the 2nd Brigade of the 32nd Division—and the 2nd Brigade of the 11th Cavalry Division, which had been left with the 31st Don Regiment, and two batteries, to hold Giurgevo and Oltenitza,[1] and prevent any raids against the line of communications,—had now crossed the river Danube. It was ordered to Rahovica,[2] about ten miles north-east of Tirnova, to support the right flank of the Rustchuk army, while the IVth Corps was directed on Biela to form the reserve. The cavalry of the XIIIth Corps also came into line and was ordered to cover the front of the XIth Corps. In accordance with these orders the XIIth Corps was once more pushed on Rustchuk. On July 18 the left wing of the army of Rustchuk reached Pirgos, the centre was on the Kara Lom, and the right at Kaselievo, while the cavalry reached the line of the Rustchuk-Rasgrad railway and the river Solenik.

On July 24, just as the Czarevitch was in a position to begin active siege operations against Rustchuk, he received orders from the Grand Duke Nicholas that these must be for the present abandoned, and that he must resume his rôle of observation until Plevna was captured. It is now time to follow the operations of the western army, and to see what had brought the little town of Plevna into such prominence.

Krahmer, chapter xx.   *Guerre D'Orient*, part ii. chapter vii.

[1] *See* Map I.   [2] *See* Map II.

III.
Operations of the Western Army

The IXth Army Corps under General Krudener had been directed to seize Nikopoli, advance to the line of the Vid, protect the right flank of the Russian advance, and neutralize Osman Pasha's force, which was believed to be in the neighbourhood of Widin.

On July 9 the Western Army was distributed as follows :—

The Caucasian Cossack Brigade, which had up till now formed part of Skobelov I's advanced guard force, but from this date came under the orders of the Commander of the IXth Corps, was at Bulgareni, the 19th regiment and two batteries were at Stizari, the 20th regiment, two batteries, the 9th Lancers and 9th Don Cossacks were at Pety Kladenica, the remainder of the Division was at Orese. The 31st Infantry Division was still at Simnitza and had not begun to cross the river.

On July 7 Col. Tutolmin, who commanded the Caucasian Cossack Brigade, reported that he had received information from Bulgarians that a company of Nizams had occupied Plevna ; this was confirmed the next day by patrols from the 30th Don Cossacks, which had been sent by Gourko to gain touch with Tutolmin, and had actually entered Plevna. Tutolmin asked Krudener to support him as soon as possible with an infantry battalion to enable him to seize Plevna. Krudener replied that this would not be practicable until Nikopoli was taken. He allowed the 5th Infantry Division and his cavalry to remain halted during the 9th and occupied himself in getting the remainder of his corps across the Danube. The opportunity was thus lost. At 5 a.m. on the 10th Krudener was informed by Cossacks that Plevna had been entered the previous evening by a force of cavalry, infantry and artillery, which had come from Nikopoli. This report seems to have made Krudener believe that the Turks were engaged in a general retirement. On the 11th the Cossacks reported that Plevna was held by at least four battalions with six guns and that the Turks were entrenching themselves. That evening Krudener collected the whole of his corps on the right bank of the Danube.

The troops met by the Caucasian Cossack Brigade were three battalions of infantry and four guns under Atouf Pasha who had been detached from the garrison of Nikopoli. When the patrols of the 30th Don Cossacks entered Plevna it was occupied only by some invalid soldiers from the garrison of Nikopoli under charge of a few details. On the Russians entering the town these latter retired to Rahova, and on July 8 the commandant of Nikopoli received information of these events from Rahova. He promptly despatched Atouf Pasha to occupy Plevna in order to keep open his communications with Osman Pasha, and with the Turkish forces in Roumelia and Sofia, by way of Lovcha and Orkhanie.[1] Atouf Pasha arrived at Plevna on the 9th, a few hours before the first patrols of the Caucasian Cossack Brigade approached the town.

On July 12 Krudener moved on Nikopoli, and the batteries of Turnu began a bombardment of that town. Nikopoli was garrisoned by a Turkish force of between 8,000 and 9,000 men, some 5,000 being Redifs, who were badly found in clothing and equipment. The fortifications had been designed to meet an attack from the

[1] *See* **Map I.**

Roumanian bank of the Danube; the Turks had supplemented these by earthworks to the south and east of the town, but they were not complete at this time.

On the 13th the Caucasian Cossack Brigade, with the exception of three sotnias, was moved to Bresljanica,[1] being relieved at Bulgareni by the 19th regiment and a battery. To this regiment the remaining three sotnias of the Cossacks were attached. The 124th regiment with three batteries was left at Simnitza to guard the bridge until it was relieved of that duty by the IVth Corps. Krudener proposed to attack Nikopoli with all his force except the detachments at Bulgareni and Simnitza.

During the night of the 14th–15th Krudener established a battery of forty guns within about 2,000 yards of the Turkish trenches to the south of the town. The attack was made at 4 a.m. on the 15th in two main columns. The left column, under Lt.-General Schilder-Schuldner, with whom were the Caucasian Cossack Brigade and the 9th Lancers, was directed to secure the bridges over the Osma, to prevent any interruption from the direction of Plevna, and to advance against Nikopoli from the west; the main column under General Krudener moved forward from the south and south-east, its right covered by three sotnias of Cossacks. After sharp fighting the advanced line of Turkish trenches was captured, and by nightfall the Russians formed a semicircle round the town with their flanks on the Danube. At daybreak on the 16th the Turkish Commander, Hasan Hairi Pasha, finding that the Russians had gained a commanding position upon the high ground to the south of the

[1] *See* Map II

town, and that there was no prospect of breaking through their lines, decided to surrender. The Russians secured some 7,000 prisoners, about 100 guns, two gunboats and a quantity of stores. They had lost thirty-one officers and 1,310 men killed and wounded.

The capture of Nikopoli was of great importance to the Russians as it removed any immediate danger of an attack on the Simnitza Bridge, and provided them with a strong bridge-head for a more permanent bridge, which would certainly be required in the event of a protracted campaign. The heavy Russian losses were due to the fact that the infantry did not give the artillery sufficient time to prepare the way for their advance, and that in several cases battalions moved to the assault without making any effort to subdue the enemy's fire. The comparative ease with which Nikopoli was captured appears to have inspired the Russian Staff with contempt for Turkish fortifications. They overlooked the fact that, though Nikopoli was classed as a fortress, the attack was delivered against improvised works, ill provided with ammunition and stores.

On the 16th Krudener busied himself in collecting his scattered troops, and refilling his supply and ammunition columns, his artillery ammunition being almost exhausted. He had also to arrange for the disposal of his numerous prisoners, and to provide for the government of Nikopoli.

On the evening of the 17th his troops were disposed as follows :—three regiments and the artillery of the 31st Division were in Nikopoli, the fourth was still at Sistova ; the Caucasian Cossack Brigade, the 20th regiment of the 5th Division and three batteries were at Muselimselo ; the 17th regiment with three batteries was at Gradesti ; the 18th regiment with three batteries was at Samlijevo ; the 19th regiment had two battalions, with two sotnias and a battery at Trestenikturski, the remaining battalion of the regiment was at Bulgareni ; the 9th Lancers and 9th Don Cossacks were at Sejkova. It will be remembered that the remaining two regiments of the 9th Cavalry Division were with Gourko.

The Russian Headquarters now began to be anxious that Plevna should be occupied as early as possible, and during the 17th sent Krudener three telegrams to hasten his movement on that place ; finally in the early hours of the 18th a direct order reached him that he was to send forward the Caucasian Cossacks at once and support them with what infantry he could. Krudener thereupon ordered Lt.-General Schilder-Schuldner, the commander of the 5th Division, to occupy Plevna with the 17th, 18th, 19th regiments, the 9th Lancers, the Caucasian Cossack Brigade and thirty-two guns. The 9th Don Cossack Regiment was ordered to watch the lower Vid and cover Schilder-Schuldner's right flank.

Plevna bears the same relation to the Vid that Biela does to the Jantra. In itself it is a town of little importance, but as the point on which the main roads leading from Sofia and Western Bulgaria to the Middle Danube and the Quadrilateral converge, it was of the greatest value to the Russians, who intended to use the line of the Vid to screen the right of their advance to the Balkans. Schilder-Schuldner moved in two columns, the first, with which he was himself, marching from Nikopoli by Bresljanica, the second from Bulgareni by Sgalevica. The columns bivouacked on the night of the 18th–19th about twenty miles apart, on the two roads leading from Rustchuk and Nikopoli to Plevna. During the 19th the Cossack cavalry covering the advance engaged a superior force of Turks in the neighbourhood of Plevna and had to fall back, but failed to discover that Osman Pasha had himself arrived at that place, which the Turks had now occupied with twenty-five battalions, ten batteries and a cavalry regiment.

Krudener's operations up to this point were marked by want of foresight. His dispositions lead to the conclusion that he had not taken Osman Pasha into his calculations and that his thoughts in the first instance were centred on Nikopoli. Now it is a sound principle to give your enemy credit for doing what will be most advantageous to himself and most inconvenient to you. Clearly Krudener should have taken steps to cover his advance on Nikopoli against possible interruption from the direction of Widin, where Osman Pasha was known to have a field force superior to any Krudener could oppose to him. The Caucasian Cavalry Brigade which had gained touch with Atouf Pasha's battalions was withdrawn to take part in the operations against Nikopoli. Had this cavalry been employed in work round Plevna and in learning what was going on in the direction of Widin, it is probable that Krudener would have discovered that the occupation of the line of the Lower Vid and of Plevna as its key were of greater importance to the Russian plan of campaign than the immediate capture of Nikopoli. To withdraw cavalry which has once gained contact can rarely be justified. Still less justifiable is Hassan Hairi's surrender of Nikopoli. Had he held out but four days Osman Pasha's arrival must have obliged Krudener to give up his attack on the place and devote himself to the protection of the Simnitza bridge. Surrender is never excusable except under the direst necessity. The commander of a fortress or post is, in most cases, cut off from communication with his friends when attacked. He, therefore, is in no position to judge what will be the effect of his surrender. At any moment the enemy may be compelled to retire from some cause of which he is ignorant. Considerations of humanity should not affect him, for he cannot know that the situation may not require the sacrifice of his last man. In the last resort he will have detained as long as possible a force of the enemy, which when he is disposed of is free to operate elsewhere.

Krahmer, chapter xxi. *Guerre D'Orient*, part ii, chap. i (iv.)

IV. The Operations of the Turkish Forces up to July 19

At the time of the passage of the Danube at Simnitza by the Russians, Abdul Kerim's field army[1] in the Quadrilateral was disposed as follows—Fuad Pasha's cavalry division and the infantry divisions of Nedjib and Assaf Pasha were at Shumla,[2] the whole formed as a corps under the command of Ahmed Eyoub Pasha. A mobile brigade consisting of 8 battalions, 5 squadrons and 2 batteries had been made up from the garrison of Rustchuk, and was under Mustafa Zefi Pasha at that place. A second corps under Salik Pasha was in process of organization at Eski-Dzuma, and detachments from it held Osman Bazar and Tirnova. A division

[1] *See* Appendix II.   [2] *See* Map I.

made up from the Egyptian contingent was at Varna, but was not yet ready to take the field. The Turkish Commander-in-Chief had, therefore, about 30,000 mobile troops under his hand, and some 45,000 were garrisoning the various towns and fortesses in the Quadrilateral.

The ease with which the Russians had made good the passage of the Danube aroused the greatest anxiety in Constantinople, and on July 3 Abdul Kerim at Shumla received a peremptory order from the Sultan to advance and check the further progress of the invaders. Accordingly on the 4th Fuad Pasha's Cavalry Division, consisting of a Brigade of Circassian Cavalry, a Brigade of Regular Cavalry and Assaf Pasha's Infantry Division, under Ahmed Eyoub Pasha, were ordered to move on Rustchuk by Rasgrad. This force was to be joined at Rustchuk by Mustafa Zefi Pasha's Brigade, when the whole was to move on the Jantra. Nedjib Pasha's Infantry Division was left at Shumla and the Egyptian contingent at Varna, while Salik held Osman Bazar and Tirnova.

It is difficult to fathom Abdul Kerim's intention from these orders. He had certain information that the Russian crossing was at Sistova. Whether his object was to cover Rustchuk or to act on the flank of a Russian march to the Balkan Passes, an advance with his whole army to the line of the Jantra and the occupation of Biela was clearly his best course. From Shumla to Biela is a distance of about fifty miles. Had he directed the whole of his strong division of cavalry on Biela on receipt of the Sultan's orders he would have anticipated the Russians at Biela, and could have safely concentrated four divisions of infantry behind the Jantra. The only explanation possible appears to be that he was opposed to any active operations outside the Quadrilateral, and was determined to keep his force within that area till the last possible moment.

Moving leisurely by the main Shumla-Rustchuk road, Ahmed Eyoub effected a junction with Mustafa Zefi Pasha's Brigade, outside Rustchuk, on July 9, the cavalry moving on the Jantra by the Rustchuk-Biela road. The latter engaged the Russian cavalry advancing on Rustchuk, but before the action had become in any way serious orders for a general retirement were received from Abdul Kerim. Mustafa Zefi Pasha retired with his Brigade into Rustchuk, Ahmed Eyoub moving back on Rasgrad by the way he came, his retirement being harassed as we have seen by the cavalry of the XIIth and XIIIth Russian Corps.

The news of Gourko's advance on Tirnova paralyzed Abdul Kerim, and caused the immediate recall to the fortresses of the Quadrilateral of the troops he had let go with such an effort. The result of this irresolution and of Gourko's appearance south of the Balkans was an order from Constantinople recalling Abdul Kerim. On July 19 Mehmet Ali Pasha arrived at Shumla and took over the supreme command of the Turkish armies.

Osman Pasha, in the west, had before the outbreak of war organized his command in three divisions, the 1st under Adil Pasha, the 2nd under Izzet Pasha, the 3rd under Hasan Hairi Pasha. Osman was in the prime of life, and a soldier by nature and education. A man of active habits, he was in bad odour with Abdul Kerim and the Pashas of the old school, who considered bodily

H

activity of any kind as contrary to Moslem tradition, and derogatory to the dignity of a Pasha.

Osman took the greatest pains to equip and train his three divisions as a mobile field force, and having got them into some sort of order he laid proposals for using them before Abdul Kerim. He fully understood that the only effective means of defending the Danube was an offensive campaign in Roumania. He therefore proposed to cross the river near Kalifat, and act against the Russian right flank. Abdul Kerim vetoed this proposal and ordered him to remain in observation of the Servians who were known to be negotiating with both the Russians and Roumanians. This anxiety of Abdul Kerim to provide for every possible contingency is typical of his military policy, such as it was, and was a common weakness of the Turkish generals in this war. A check to the Russian advance would have been the surest means of keeping Servia quiet.

Shortly after the outbreak of war Abdul Kerim, in accordance with his policy of dissemination, withdrew twenty battalions from Osman Pasha's field force to watch the Middle Danube. Hassan Hairi Pasha was ordered to occupy Nikopoli with twelve of these battalions and four batteries. In spite of being thus weakened Osman again applied for leave to assume the offensive as soon as he heard that the Russians were crossing the Danube at Sistova. This request was also refused, but on July 8 Abdul Kerim received direct instructions from the Sultan that Osman Pasha was to advance. The latter's intention was to occupy the Teteven Balkans south of the Trojan Pass, while making good a line of retreat through Orkhanie on Sofia. He hoped to secure Plevna and Lovcha and to draw in the garrisons of Nikopoli and Rahova. If opportunity offered he proposed to advance on Tirnova and join hands with the army of the Quadrilateral. Abdul Kerim consented to this plan of operations, but only on the condition that at least half Osman's army was left to garrison Widin, to hold and watch the Servian frontier. Thus Osman Pasha could only move east with nineteen battalions, one cavalry regiment, nine batteries and a company of Engineers.

Osman's battalions had been weakened by the campaign in Servia, and in accordance with the Turkish Military policy, which formed all the reserves for the first line into fresh battalions, they had not been reinforced. Their average strength was therefore at this time about 500. The total force with which Osman was able to take the field did not much exceed 11,000 men.

He received his orders to advance on July 10. The 11th and 12th were spent in making arrangements for the various garrisons to be left behind, which were placed under the command of Izzet Pasha. The Field Force was organized in two divisions, under Adil Pasha and Hassan Sabri Pasha.[1] It started from Widin on the 13th and reached Arcener that day, a distance of twelve miles. During the march it was fired on by Roumanian batteries on the left bank of the Danube.

On the 14th Prince Charles of Roumania reported to Russian Head Quarters that Osman was on the march from Widin. At this period the Russians had a very poor opinion of the Roumanian forces, and earlier reports

[1] *See* Appendix III.

which had been received from the latter had proved inaccurate. Prince Charles's information was therefore disregarded and no attempt was made to investigate its truth. At four o'clock on the afternoon of the 14th Osman reached Drenovatz on the Lom. Here he was informed by a telegram from the Sultan that the Russians had attacked Jeni Zagra and Kazanlik, and directed to hasten his march. The advance was resumed after a short halt, and Vishidrina, forty-five miles from Widin, was reached by midday on the 15th. During the halt there Osman received an order by telegram from Abdul Kerim to occupy Plevna as soon as possible with the object of assisting the garrison of Nikopoli. In consequence he sent forward three battalions under Emin Pasha at midnight to reinforce Atouf Pasha at Plevna. On the 16th the main body reached Altemir on the Skit River. A distance of sixty-eight miles had been covered in four days; the roads were in very bad condition, and at many points it had been necessary for the infantry to man-handle the guns over bad ground. The only water to be had was from the rivers and streams which were many miles apart. The troops were exhausted and Osman decided to halt at Altemir till the afternoon of the 17th. Starting again at 3.30 p.m. on that day, the column reached Kneza where it bivouacked. Here it was joined by three battalions from Rahova. At dawn on the 18th the force arrived on the river Isker. The bridge had been allowed to fall into ruin, and there was considerable delay in getting the column across the river. Osman heard here of the fall of Nikopoli. Mahala was reached about midday, and after a four hours' halt he continued his march to Metropolja,[1] where he arrived at 6 p.m. There he found one of Atouf Pasha's outposts. He considered that it would be dangerous to march with tired troops by night in proximity to the enemy, and therefore collected his column and halted until dawn. He arrived in Plevna early on the 19th. In the 6½ days he had marched 110 miles through difficult country, and his troops had suffered much from heat and want of water. This march must therefore take rank among the finest achievements of Osman Pasha and his men.

Krahmer, chapter **xxi**. *Guerre d'Orient*, part ii., chapter iv. *Défense de Plevna*, chapter i.

[1] *See* **Map II.**

CHAPTER V

THE FIRST AND SECOND BATTLES OF PLEVNA

The First Battle of Plevna—Movements of the Russian Columns—Osman's Position at Plevna—Attack of The Northern Russian Column—Attack of the Southern Column—Comments—The Second Battle of Plevna—The Defensive Works at Plevna—Russian Dispositions for the Attack—Attack of Shakofskoi's Column—Attack of Veliaminov's Column—Comments.

CHAPTER V

THE FIRST AND SECOND BATTLES OF PLEVNA

THE news of Osman's departure from Widin had, as has been pointed out, reached Russian Head Quarters at Tirnova on July 14, but by a strange omission it was not communicated to General Krudener. The anxiety of the Grand Duke Nicholas to anticipate Osman on the line of the Vid is, however, evident from the frequent instructions sent to the Commander of the IXth Corps during the 17th and 18th, urging him to secure Plevna. Krudener had apparently overlooked the possibility of an offensive movement by Osman, and was much occupied by arranging for the administration of Nikopoli, the safe custody of his prisoners, and replenishing his supply and ammunition columns; the latter particularly presented difficulties as there had been some delay in getting ammunition across the Danube.

On the 17th he ordered a general movement south and south-west from Nikopoli, but it was not until midday on the 18th that he directed an immediate advance on Plevna, and then only in consequence of peremptory orders from Head Quarters. General Schilder-Schuldner received instructions at 2.30 p.m. on the 18th to march at once with his Division (the 5th), the 9th regiment of Don Cossacks and the Caucasian Cossack Brigade, and to secure Plevna the next day. Schilder-Schuldner's troops were already in bivouac when the order reached them, they were very scattered and the roads were bad; very little progress was therefore made on the afternoon and evening of the 18th. The positions occupied on the night of the 18th–19th were as follows :—

The 1st Brigade 5th Division, and four batteries, with whom was Schilder-Schuldner, were at Sejkova, they did not, however, all reach that place until 2 a.m. on the 19th; the 9th Don Cossack regiment was at Kreta; the Caucasian Cossack Brigade was at Trancevica; two Battalions of the 19th regiment (2nd Brigade 5th Division), and two sotnias detached from the Caucasian Cossack Brigade and a battery were on the Plevna-Biela road just north of Poradim; the remaining battalion of the 19th regiment was at Bulgareni; the 20th regiment (2nd Brigade 5th Division) was at Muselimselo on the Osma about five miles south-west of Nikopoli. Schilder-Schuldner's force was thus in two divisions, one on the Plevna-Nikopoli road, the other on the Plevna-Biela road. He had, on the afternoon of the 18th, issued orders for both columns to march direct on Plevna, but the troops on the Biela road did not get their orders till very late, and did not act upon them till the 19th.

Osman Pasha immediately on arrival at Plevna pushed detachments down the Nikopoli and Biela roads, and on the afternoon of the 19th Schilder-Schuldner's northern column became engaged with some Turkish cavalry and a battery north of Bukova. As he had not received any communication throughout the day from his other column, and as it was getting late, Schilder-Schuldner, who reached Calisovat with his column in the forenoon of the 19th, decided to postpone his attack till the next day, and after bombarding the Turkish position on the Janik Bair[1] for some hours he went into bivouac near Verbitza. The 19th regiment, after a slight engagement, went into bivouac at Sgalevica; the Caucasian Cossack Brigade, which had spent the greater part of the morning in endeavouring to gain touch with the troops on its flanks, reached the same place at 4 p.m.

The position occupied by Osman Pasha had much in its favour. The town of Plevna is situated in a hollow between the Grivitsa and Toultchenitza streams, which unite just north-west of the town, and flow into the Vid at Opanetz. North of the town a range of hills called the Janik Bair runs parallel to the Grivitsa; the southern slopes fall abruptly into that stream, but on the north side the ground drops gently into the Bukova and affords little cover to an attack. On the east the circle of heights runs just west of the village of Grivitsa, then south-west to the Toultchenitza brook; here the chain of hills is broken by numerous brooks which flow into the two main streams, and is commanded by a parallel ridge which runs south from the village of Grivitsa and east of Radischevo. From the Toultchenitza brook the hills immediately encircling Plevna start from a point just north of the village of Brestovetz, and run north-east past Krischin to the bridge where the Sofia road crosses the Vid.

The Vid at Plevna is sixty yards wide and is fordable

[1] See Map III.

at many places, except in the rainy seasons. On the left bank of the river west of Plevna is an open undulating plain. The hills are, generally speaking, treeless and devoid of cover of any kind, except occasional patches of scrub and low bush, but to the south of the town, on the left bank of the Toultchenitza about Krischin there are a number of vineyards and orchards.

Atouf Pasha had taken steps to put Plevna in a state of defence immediately on his arrival, and Osman Pasha had in the short time at his disposal extended this work, but on July 20 only a few field-works commanding the Biela road and the neighbourhood of Grivitsa and some light trenches near Opanetz had been constructed, and some of the buildings of the village of Bukova had been loopholed.

It has been explained that the strategic importance of Plevna lay in its being the point of junction of roads running east, west, north and south through Bulgaria. This fact contributed greatly to the tactical strength of the position. No fewer than six roads, the main roads to Widin, Sofia, Lovcha, Pelisat, Rustchuk and Nikopoli, radiate from Plevna, and these allow ready communication to all parts of the circle of hills which has been described above. Plevna itself thus formed a position from which reinforcements could be rapidly sent to any threatened point on the line of defence, and as these roads run for the most part along the valleys of the many streams which flow into the Vid, a defending force holding a position round Plevna is provided with a perfect system of covered communications.

Osman Pasha had made a personal reconnaissance of the enemy's position on the afternoon of the 19th. He had made up his mind that the Russian main force was to the north of Plevna, and that the force east of Grivitsa was only intended to make a demonstration. It must be remembered that the Caucasian Cossack Brigade did not, owing to its wanderings, become engaged on the 19th.

Osman had at his disposal, including Atouf Pasha's detachment, 25 battalions, 10 batteries and 6 squadrons.

These he disposed as follows—

The cavalry, with 2 battalions and 2 batteries, occupied the high ground about Opanetz, 1 company being detached to hold Dolna Netropolje, and 2 companies to cover the bridge over the Vid. 8 battalions and $3\frac{1}{2}$ batteries held the ridge of the Janik Bair; 3 battalions and a battery occupied the hill just west of the village of Grivitsa, 4 battalions connected the latter with the Janik Bair, occupying a line through points 7 and 8. 1 battalion and half a battery held the hill at point 18, just south of Plevna, which commanded the valley of the Toultchenitza. 5 battalions and 3 batteries formed the general reserve and were posted at point 9, where Osman established his head quarters. The remaining 2 battalions covered the front between the Grivitsa and Toultchenitza brooks, on the line between points 13 and 16.

At 4 a.m. on the 20th Schilder-Schuldner deployed the whole of the northern column (six battalions and four batteries) for the attack on the ridge south-west of Verbitza, keeping only one battalion in reserve. Without waiting to reconnoitre the enemy's position, or to gain touch with his other column, he directed his artillery to open fire at 4.30 a.m., and three-quarters of an hour later, before the guns had had time to prepare the way effectually, ordered the infantry to advance.

The five battalions which formed the first line advanced rapidly across the ravine, through which flows the Bukova brook, which separated them from the enemy, their right covered by the 9th regiment of the Don Cossacks. The Russian infantry moved forward with fixed bayonets, drove in the Turkish outposts, and rushed the enemy's first positions on the spurs of the Janik Bair, which commanded the ravine, almost without firing. The Turkish skirmishers fell back before the violence of their onset on to the main crest of the Janik Bair, and here an obstinate engagement took place, the Russians making good their hold on the spur No. 3 south-east of Bukova and defying the efforts of the Turks to drive them out. They were, however, unable to advance further up the open slopes leading to the crest of the ridge.

The Turkish position at this time extended from the village of Bukova, which was held as an advanced post on the left flank, along the spur No. 4 to the crest of the Janik Bair, while the Russian advanced troops held the ground from point No. 3 along the line of the 200 contour to about the point where it meets the brook which flows from point 7 into the Bukova stream. Osman Pasha now sent three battalions to reinforce the left of his position on the Janik Bair. About the time these battalions had reached point 4, two battalions of the 18th Regiment of Russian infantry, which were working down the Bukova stream, became involved in the gardens and inclosures of Bukova village and were surprised by fire from the houses and garden walls. The Turks now delivered a counter attack from point No. 4, drove the Russians from the outskirts of Bukova, and attacked and defeated their reserves, who were cramped in the narrow gorge and were thrown into confusion by the fugitives from Bukova. The Russians maintained their hold on point No. 3 for some time longer, but their retreat was threatened by the success of the Turkish counter attack and they were compelled to retire. The losses at this point were very heavy, General Knorring, the Brigadier of the 1st Brigade, was hit, as was the Commander of the 17th regiment. General Pokhitonov, who commanded the artillery of the Vth Corps, collected the remnants of the 17th and 18th regiments, and succeeded in withdrawing them at seven o'clock to the heights on the right bank of the Bukova brook; here he held his ground until 11.30 a.m.

Meanwhile Colonel Kleinhaus with the 19th regiment and one battery attacked the Turkish positions just north-west of the village of Grivitsa. Here too the infantry, after a short bombardment, advanced on the Turks with bayonets fixed. The latter held and had partially entrenched three lines of defence, the first near point C, the second near point 7, and the third near point 6; they also held the line between points 13 and 16. Kleinhaus succeeded in working round the right flank and in establishing himself on the ridge near point D. A panic ensued amongst the Turks holding the advanced positions, and they fled in confusion, carrying with them a battalion which had been sent to reinforce point 7. The troops holding point 6, however, stood fast, and the Russians came under a heavy artillery fire from Osman's reserve batteries posted near point 9. The Russians suffered heavily on the open slopes about point D, Colonel Kleinhaus and three of the Majors of the regiment fell. Once more Osman by a timely despatch of reinforcements (1½ battalions) enabled the Turks to deliver a counter attack, and the Russians were driven slowly back. Major Baraschev, who was now in command of the regiment, finding that the enemy was being strongly reinforced, and that in consequence of the heavy losses which the 19th regiment had sustained it would be hopeless to attempt to carry the strong Turkish positions on the east side of the town, decided to withdraw at 9 a.m.

While the 19th regiment were engaged in their attack the Cossack Brigade had moved round to Radischevo. Colonel Tutolmin, its commander, finding that the ground was unsuited for cavalry, contented himself with bringing his battery into action on the spur at point G. His guns were, however, outranged by the superior Krupp guns of the Turks, and had no influence on the course of events. At 9 a.m. he saw that the 19th regiment was falling back, and he spent the remainder of the day in covering their retreat on Bulgareni.

Schilder-Schuldner heard of the repulse of the 19th regiment at 9.30 a.m. About the same time he was informed by the 9th regiment of Cossacks that Turkish cavalry, supported by infantry and artillery, were working round his right flank. He therefore ordered a retirement, which was begun at 11.30 a.m. The 20th regiment and two batteries which came up at this time from Muselimselo [1] enabled the hardly tried 17th and 18th regiments to get away without further loss. Schilder-Schuldner withdrew with the 1st Brigade, the 20th regiment of the 2nd Brigade, and the 9th

[1] *See* Map II.

Cossacks to Bresljanica. The 19th regiment and the Caucasian Cossack Brigade fell back to Bulgareni. The Turks made no attempt to pursue.

The Russians lost seventy-four officers and 2,771 men killed and wounded. It is difficult to ascertain the Turkish losses, which are said to have amounted to about 2,000.

The failure of Schilder-Schuldner's attack on Plevna was due in the first instance to faulty reconnaissance, and the ignorance of the enemy's movements which follows therefrom. The Russians had actually had cavalry in Plevna on July 8, yet on the night of the 18th and 19th there was no Russian cavalry within twelve miles of that place. The responsibility for this rests of course with Russian Head Quarters and with Krudener, but there was little in Schilder-Schuldner's conduct of the attack which is in accordance with the recognized principles of tactics. It can never be anything but foolhardy to order two columns which are widely separated, and are not in communication, to make a convergent attack upon a position which is known to be occupied by an enemy of whom there is no recent or exact information.

In neither column was the cavalry employed to reconnoitre the enemy's position with a view to the attack, nor does Schilder-Schuldner appear to have made any personal reconnaissance. Had this been done it was hardly possible that the Russians should have failed to discover the fact of Osman Pasha's arrival.

Practically the whole available Russian force was deployed in the first instance. Schilder-Schuldner kept only one battalion, or about a twelfth of his strength, in reserve and even this was early thrown into the fight. Had the Turks been able to make any real pursuit nothing could have saved the Russians from a complete disaster, but Osman's men were worn out by their marches and want of sleep.

The Russian infantry flung themselves upon the Turkish positions without waiting for any artillery preparation, and without themselves preparing the way for their advance with infantry fire.

Finally the almost complete inaction of the Caucasian Cossack Brigade should be noted as another instance of the evils following the want of connection between the Russian columns, which prevented Schilder-Schuldner from exercising any proper control on the battlefield.

Briefly, the mistakes committed by the Russians were due to careless reconnaissance and contempt for the enemy. Their faults were so very similar to our own in the early days of the South African war, before we learnt to treat the Boers with proper respect, that they deserve to be carefully considered by English soldiers.

The Second Battle of Plevna The failure of July 20 did not create much alarm at Russian Head Quarters, where the effect produced by Gourko's successes in the Balkans was still fresh. Schilder-Schuldner's failure was regarded as a temporary check, and Krudener was ordered to drive back Osman at once, a division from the IVth and two brigades from the XIth Corps being placed at his disposal for the purpose. Krudener having himself examined the Turkish positions about Plevna, reported that Osman was receiving reinforcements, and was entrenching, and that he did not consider himself strong enough in the circumstances to venture the attack. The Grand Duke Nicholas was, however, still optimistic. He apparently considered that the reports of Osman Pasha's strength had been exaggerated, and that the fact of his having made no pursuit on the 20th was a proof of his weakness. Krudener therefore received explicit orders to attack as soon as possible.

Osman Pasha had evidently been impressed by the vigour of Schilder-Schuldner's infantry attack. His first request to Mehmet Ali, the new Turkish Commander-in-Chief, was for reinforcements, and for authority to effect a junction with Raouf Pasha, who commanded the Turkish army of the Balkans. The latter request Mehmet Ali refused; he ordered Osman to hold on to Plevna and to entrench himself. At the same time he placed at his disposal all the Turkish troops in Western Bulgaria, at Sofia[1] and Novi Bazar. Osman at once brought up a brigade from Widin, and eight battalions from Sofia. Thus after providing six battalions and a battery to hold Lovcha, he had at his disposal thirty-three battalions, five squadrons and fifty-eight guns, about 22,000 men, for the defence of Plevna. These he organized into two divisions and a General Reserve. Each division consisted of twelve battalions, two squadrons and twelve guns. The General Reserve was composed of nine battalions, one squadron, and thirty-four guns. The 1st Division under Adil Pasha was in charge of the northern section, on the right bank of the Grivitsa[2] stream from Opanetz to the village of Grivitsa. The eastern and southern sections were allotted to the 2nd Division under Hassan Pasha. One brigade (six battalions and a battery) under Rifaat Pasha was

[1] *See* Map I.   [2] *See* Map III.

despatched on July 25 to hold Lovcha,[1] in order to secure the passage of the Osma at that point, and to prevent any Russian enterprises against Osman's communications with Sofia. Systematic defensive works were begun. By the 30th two redoubts at Opanetz[2] and an open work south of the village, commanding the main bridge over the Vid, had been constructed. The line of defence ran thence along the Janik Bair, on which epaulements had been constructed at points 4, 5 and 6. These were connected by shelter trenches, and an open advanced work had been thrown up at point 3.

Two redoubts at points 7 and 8, which subsequently became known to the Russians as Grivitsa No. 1 and Grivitsa No. 2, had also been finished. The works on this section were connected and extended by infantry shelter trenches; their garrison absorbed seven battalions, leaving five for the reserve of the section.

The second section of the defence ran south-west from the village of Grivitsa, about 2,000 yards north of Radischevo. The works in existence on the 30th were some shelter trenches on the spur at point 14, and at points 9, 10 and 11 gun epaulements connected by shelter trenches. Trenches were also erected at points 17 and K, commanding the valley of the Toultchenitza, and a gun epaulement flanked by trenches at point 19. These works were garrisoned by five battalions. Some trenches were thrown up to guard the bridge over the Vid, and were garrisoned by one battalion. No. 2 Section was therefore held by six battalions in the works, six forming the section reserve.

I do not propose in describing the Turkish works

[1] *See* Map I.   [2] *See* Map III.

at Plevna, to go into details of trace and profile. These were adapted to the arms in use in 1877 and are not (with some exceptions) applicable in these days of powerful artillery and long-range rifle fire. Curiously enough one of the exceptions is the infantry shelter-trenches used by the Turks. These were generally of the type which we to-day call "Boer trenches," that is to say they were deep, and narrow, with perpendicular sides. The stiff clay soil of the country round Plevna, which would stand at any slope, lends itself as well to this style of trench as does the soil of South Africa. The general principles on which the Turkish works were constructed are, however, worthy of note, as they are as applicable to warfare in this year of grace as they were in 1877.

The greatest care was taken in the siting of all redoubts and shelter trenches. Uniformity was not attempted, in each case the nature of the ground was the ruling factor. Protection from enfilade fire was everywhere provided, and whenever the ground admitted, arrangements were made for two or even three tiers of infantry fire. The reserves and supports were provided with overhead cover and approaches to the fire trenches. Overhead cover was also subsequently provided for troops in the firing line, and since it was impossible to make enough cover for these inside the works the gunners alone were provided with bombproof cover there, and that for the infantry firing line was made some distance in rear of the trenches and connected with them by means of covered ways. Rifle pits and short trenches for sharpshooters were constructed in advance of the main line of works. Lastly, every care was taken to improve and extend the already excellent system of communications inside the defences.

It must be understood that the system of defence as described above was gradually developed, and was not complete during the early battles round Plevna. Indeed the spade was used with unceasing energy until the surrender.

Krudener had at his disposal, in addition to Schilder-Schuldner's troops, which had been repulsed on the 20th, three regiments of the 31st Division, the 9th regiment of Lancers, and eight batteries. Of the other troops of the IXth Corps, the 124th regiment of the 31st Division was still in charge of the bridge-head at Sistova, and the 9th Hussars and 9th Dragoons were with Gourko. On the 29th Krudener was joined by the 30th Division of the IVth Corps, the 1st Brigade of the 32nd Division Infantry (XIth Corps), and the 1st Brigade of the 11th Cavalry Division; and on the same day he received orders to advance and drive the Turks out of Plevna. He decided to leave the 19th regiment, which had been so severely handled on the 20th, to garrison Nikopoli. This made his available force thirty-six battalions, thirty squadrons, and twenty-two batteries (170 guns), about 35,000 men in all. Lt.-General Prince Shakofskoi (who commanded the XIth Corps) had received orders from Head Quarters on the 22nd when he was at Dzuljunica, N.E. of Tirnova, to reinforce Krudener at once with one Infantry and one Cavalry Brigade. He reached Karaagac-bolgarski, about fifteen miles east of Plevna, on the 27th. Here he got into touch with the Caucasian Cossack Brigade, and learnt from them that Lovcha had been occupied the previous day by the Turks. On the 28th he directed General Skobelov II, who had joined him on the march from Tirnova, to advance on Lovcha with the Cossack Brigade and to endeavour to occupy that place. Skobelov reported that the Turks there had taken up a good defensive position, and were busily engaged in strengthening it, and that at least one Infantry division would be required in addition to the Cossack Cavalry Brigade if Lovcha was to be secured. Shakofskoi thereupon ordered Skobelov to keep a watch on Lovcha, and after reconnoitring the Turkish position at Plevna arranged for a meeting with Krudener.

The two men were of very different character. Krudener had the reputation of being a good soldier, but a man who was inclined to take life easily. Shakofskoi was a man who believed that nobody but an aristocrat could be a good general; he was very quick-tempered and impetuous, and was in no sense a scientific soldier.

The positions occupied on the evening of the 29th were as follows:—Lockarev's Cavalry Brigade of the 9th Cavalry Division was at Bresljanica. The 31st Infantry Division was at Kojulovce. The 5th Infantry Division was at Trestenik-Turski. The 30th Division was at Karaagac-bolgarski. The 1st Brigade of the 32nd Infantry Division and the 1st Brigade of the 11th Cavalry Division were at Poradim. The Caucasian Cossack Brigade was at Bogot. The whole force thus occupied a semi-circle, with its centre at Plevna, on a radius of about twelve miles.

The two Generals agreed to organize their troops as follows—

Fifth Infantry Division (nine battalions and five batteries), under Schilder-Schuldner.

Thirty-first Division (nine battalions and five batteries), under General Veliaminov.

One Brigade of the 30th Division, one Brigade of the 32nd Division, and two squadrons of the 11th Lancers (twelve battalions, six batteries, two squadrons), under Prince Shakofskoi.

A Cavalry Brigade composed of the 9th Lancers, 9th Don Cossacks and two squadrons of the 11th Dragoons (twelve squadrons and one battery), under General Lockarev.

The Caucasian Cossack Brigade (twelve squadrons and one battery) was under the command of General Skobelov II.

The 2nd Brigade of the 30th Division, with four batteries, two squadrons of the 11th Lancers, and two squadrons of the 11th Dragoons (six battalions, four squadrons, and four batteries) formed the general reserve under General Krudener.

It was decided that the attack should take place on the 30th. Lockarev was to cover the right flank, with his right on the Vid, which he was to cross, in the event of the infantry attack being successful, to cut the enemy's line of retreat on Sofia. Veliaminov, with Schilder-Schuldner in support, was to attack the enemy's positions north of the Grivitsa brook, moving from Kojulovce. Shakofskoi was to advance from Poradim by Radischevo and attack the southern front of the enemy's position. Skobelov was to cover Shakofskoi's left and rear, and in particular to watch for any movement in the direction of Lovcha. Shakofskoi was so impressed by the importance of having this service effectually carried out, that he reinforced Skobelov with a battalion of the 125th regiment and four guns. Krudener with the general reserve was to be on the Plevna-Biela road near Poradim.

It will be seen from these proposals that it was intended to attack the Turks with two separate columns, one moving from the north-east, the other from the south-east, and that the general reserve, a long way in rear, formed the only connecting link between the two attacks. It is generally believed that these dispositions were due to Shakofskoi, who had a profound contempt for the Turks, and considered that the failure of the 22nd was caused by Schilder-Schuldner's incapacity and want of determination. He had a great belief in himself and wished to have as free a hand as possible. Shakofskoi was socially Krudener's superior, and almost his equal in military rank. His insistence on the above plan, which had this much justification, that he had by personal reconnaissance discovered the importance of the heights about Radischevo, overpersuaded Krudener, who consented to it against his better judgment. On the morning of July 30 the Turkish positions were enveloped in a thick fog, under cover of which Veliaminov advanced to within 2,000 yards of the Grivitsa No. 1 redoubt (point 8), when he deployed about 7 a.m. and waited for the fog to clear. At 8.15 the Turkish Commander of the Grivitsa No. 1 redoubt discovered the presence of a Russian force in his front, and sent back for reinforcements. At nine o'clock the fog began to lift and an artillery duel began. At 10 a.m. Schilder-Schuldner arrived with the 5th Division and took up a position in support of Veliaminov. The artillery duel lasted until

3 p.m., at which hour Veliaminov received orders from Krudener to advance to the attack.

Meanwhile Shakofskoi advanced in two columns, one from Sgalevica, the other from Pelisat, and succeeded in occupying Radischevo at 9 a.m. Here he too became engaged in an artillery duel with the Turkish guns at points 14 and 10. On the extreme Russian right General Lockarev deployed in front of the Turkish works about Opanetz, but being unable to make any progress, he remained in observation. On the extreme Russian left Skobelov under cover of the fog succeeded in reaching Krischin, and taking the Turks completely by surprise, gained possession of the heights above that place. Advancing with two squadrons and four guns, he managed to work his way through the vineyards down the spur L to within 1,000 yards of the outskirts of Plevna. He discovered the Turkish reserves massed on the east side of the town and some Turkish cavalry west of the town on the Sofia road.

About 8.30 a.m. Skobelov hearing Veliaminov's guns, brought his battery into action near point 23. The Turks immediately brought a battery against him, and advanced to attack him in superior numbers. This compelled Skobelov to fall back on Krischin. He had, however, noticed that from the heights immediately east of Krischin, which subsequently became famous as the " Green Hills," Shakofskoi's left could be enfiladed. Junous Bey, who commanded in this section, also realized the importance of these hills and sent a battalion forward to occupy ridge J. Skobelov found near Brestovetz the greater part of Tutolmin's Brigade, which had been directed to watch the Plevna-Lovcha road. He decided to make an effort to secure a position on the Green Hills. After throwing out patrols to his flanks to secure his communication with Shakofskoi and to give him warning of any attempt against his line of retreat, Skobelov directed Tutolmin to remain in observation on the Lovcha road, with three sotnias and two guns, and with the remainder of his force, nine sotnias, one battalion, and four guns, he advanced about 12.30 p.m., and after a severe engagement succeeded about 3 p.m. in driving the Turks from the ridge J of the Green Hills and in maintaining himself there during the remainder of the day, covering Shakofskoi's left, being opposed by Junous Bey with four battalions. At 2.30 Shakofskoi at Radischevo decided that his artillery had sufficiently prepared the way for the attack, and ordered an advance. The 125th and 126th regiment were directed against the Turkish works at points 11 and 14 respectively. The three battalions of the 126th regiment moved forward without firing, and succeeded in reaching the valley of the Suluklia stream without much loss; they assembled in some dead ground close under the trenches at point 14, which they enveloped and captured after a short struggle. Two battalions immediately advanced to assist the 125th in its attack on the works at point 11. Tahir Pasha who commanded here was obliged to evacuate the advanced redoubt, near point 15, which was indeed little more than a shelter trench, his left being exposed by the loss of the spur at point 14. He fell back on Hassan Sabri's reserve. These successes gained by the Russians on the south-east front coincided with Skobelov's capture of hill J. In order to relieve the pressure on this part of his position Osman called upon Adil Pasha to send a part of the reserves of the northern section to reinforce Hassan Sabri.

The Turks took up a strong position on the line from point 34 to point 10, and checked every effort of the Russians to make headway against them. The 126th regiment established itself on the ridge between points 15 and 13, but was unable to advance beyond it, the 125th regiment extending across the valley of the Suluklia towards point 17. It was now about 5 p.m. and Shakofskoi, having learnt that Krudener was sending a regiment to support his attack, ordered the 118th regiment to reinforce his right. Still the Russians were unable to check the deadly fire poured from the Turkish front. Seeing that the 119th regiment, which had been sent him from the general reserve, was approaching, he ordered the 117th regiment, supported by a battery on the spur east of point 16, against the works at point 11. This movement was at once met by the Turkish reinforcements from the northern section, and the 119th regiment had on its arrival to be employed at once against a Turkish counter-attack which issued from point 10, against the right of Shakofskoi's attack.

Shakofskoi's men were throughout exposed to the direct fire of the batteries with the Turkish general reserve, and to enfilade fire from batteries on the Janik Bair. He had left the greater part of his own artillery behind, on the high ground south-east of Radischevo, and his infantry without artillery support were unable to establish superiority of fire over the Turks at any point. Soon after 6 p.m. the last of Shakofskoi's reserves had been thrown into the fight and his attack came to a standstill. Two companies of the 125th regiment did indeed succeed in creeping down the valley of the Toultchenitza and in getting behind the Turkish trenches just north of point 17, but they were overwhelmed by fire from both banks of the ravine and almost annihilated.

Krudener, on hearing of Shakofskoi's advance, had at 2.40 p.m. directed Veliaminov to move to the attack. From a reconnaissance made during the artillery duel he came to the conclusion that the Grivitsa No. 1 redoubt (point 8) was the key to this part of the position. It was therefore given as the objective of Veliaminov's attack. The latter directed the 121st, 123rd and 122nd regiments (in that order from north to south), against the redoubt, the 17th and 18th regiments were held in reserve in rear of his right, while the 20th regiment was directed to move down the Grivitsa valley and gain touch with Shakofskoi. The leading battalions advanced, in accordance with the usual Russian tactics, in column and without firing until within close range of the Turkish positions. They then came under a well-sustained and deadly fire, and were made to deploy. Owing to the skilful use to which the Turks had put the ground the Russians were almost everywhere exposed to cross and enfilade fire. The whole of the nine battalions directed against this part of the position were deprived of any power of movement by the intensity of the Turkish fire, and suffered enormously, the 121st regiment alone losing twenty-nine officers and 1,006 men. The 20th regiment was early diverted from its first objective to assist in the attack. It suffered the same fate, and on the right the 18th and 17th regiments, with the exception of a single battalion of the latter, were themselves drawn into the deadly tangle in their efforts to support their comrades. Thus no fewer than seventeen Russian battalions paid the penalty for attempting to advance within close range, before gaining superiority of fire over the enemy, and were massed on the open slopes, west and north-west of Grivitsa village, unable to do more than make an ineffective reply to the deadly fire which was being poured upon them.

At 4 p.m. Krudener had sent off the 119th regiment and a battery to reinforce Shakofskoi. He therefore had one infantry regiment, the 120th, in reserve. About 6 p.m. Adil Pasha finding that Veliaminov had apparently no more men to bring into line, and that the fire of the Russians opposed to him was slackening, began a counter-attack from the crest of the Janik Bair, which forced back Veliaminov's right. Krudener gradually used up two battalions of the 120th in efforts to check this movement, but these troops were unable to do more than delay the inevitable, and Krudener directed the remaining battalion of the 120th and a squadron of Lancers to take up a position to cover a general retirement, and ordered Veliaminov to draw off under cover of darkness. Assisted by the 124th regiment, which arrived during the night from Sistova, Veliaminov succeeded in making good his retreat.

On the left Shakofskoi was forced back by a counter-attack, and was only saved from destruction by darkness and the weariness of the Turkish troops. Krudener's attack had ended in a complete failure, and resulted in a loss of 168 officers and 7,167 men, about 23 per cent. of his whole force. The

Turks reported their losses 1,200 killed and wounded.

In this battle Krudener had tried to avoid some of the mistakes which had led to failure on the 20th. He and Shakofskoi had both personally reconnoitred the Turkish positions, and the whole of the forenoon of the 30th had been devoted to the artillery preparation for the infantry attack. But in neither case had the Russian general gone far enough. Personal reconnaissance by a commander is a very necessary antecedent to an attack, but it is not in itself sufficient. A commander must find out not only what positions an enemy holds but how he holds them, where he is weak, and where he is strong. This can only be done by a screen of skirmishers feeling the enemy's position along the whole front. The enemy can then be held where he is found to be strong and attacked at his weak point. " On s'engage partout et on voit " was Napoleon's favourite description of his method of beginning an attack on an enemy in position. Krudener had neglected any such preliminaries to battle. He flung his force in two columns against those parts of the Turkish position which his reconnaissance had led him to believe should be at first secured, without knowing in what strength they were held.

He did not display any greater skill in his use of artillery. Long range bombardment is not a sufficient preparation for an infantry attack. To be used effectually artillery must be employed in closest co-operation with infantry, infantry skirmishers must advance and hold the enemy in his positions during the preliminary bombardment, or the latter will retire under cover and appear fresh and unshaken, when the artillery have ceased fire, to meet the infantry attack. Further the artillery must advance and co-operate with the infantry in that attack. This appears to have been entirely overlooked by the Russian generals, who allowed their artillery to remain far in the rear during the crisis of the day.

Some of the mistakes committed by the Russians on the 20th reappeared on the 30th. They again attacked in two widely-separated columns, which were not in communication, and again the general reserve was too small. At the beginning of the battle Krudener had less than one sixth of his force under his hand, a great part of this small reserve was required, soon after the infantry advanced, to fill up gaps and meet unforeseen contingencies. A commander is only able to influence the course of a modern battle by means of the troops he has at his immediate disposal; when these are used up, he can no longer control events. As early as 4 p.m. Krudener was entirely in the hands of Veliaminov and Shakofskoi, and it was only Osman's want of cavalry and the exhaustion of the Turkish troops which saved him from complete disaster.

The tactics of the Russian infantry showed the same want of appreciation of the value of fire as on the 20th. Attempts were everywhere made to rush the Turkish positions with the bayonet before the enemy had been in any way shaken.

The Russian battalions in the firing line suffered much from the want of a mobile ammunition reserve. Great difficulty was experienced in getting supplies of ammunition across the broken country north of Radischevo to the firing lines of the 125th and 126th regiments. The want of entrenching tools was almost equally felt. Had the 126th regiment been as well supplied in this respect as were the Turkish battalions, they could have entrenched themselves on the ridge between points 13[1] and 15, and would in all probability have been able to withstand the counter-attacks which eventually drove them back. Shakofskoi could then have used this position to develop his further attack. The modern battle resolves itself into a number of successive fights for positions, and there is no more important aid to final victory than to fortify the first positions won. The possibilities of the entrenching tool in the attack are only now beginning to be understood.

The success which attended Skobelov's use of dismounted cavalry on the left flank shows the value of small bodies of mobile troops used to contain superior forces.

Covered by the 124th regiment Krudener succeeded in withdrawing his shattered forces, and took up a position on the line Karaagac-bolgarski-Poradim[2]; here he proceeded to entrench himself on the 31st. Osman had used up the whole of his reserve during the battle, and had no fresh troops with which to pursue. Indeed, he does not seem to have been aware of the completeness of his victory, probably because the darkness threw a veil over the disorder of the Russian retreat. He kept his weary men at work till close on midnight of the day of battle, in further strengthening the positions they had occupied during the day.

On July 31 the news of the battle of Plevna reached Nikopoli and Sistova, and created the greatest alarm. At the latter place a report that the Turks were approaching created a wild panic, and the bridges were blocked

[1] *See* Map III.   [2] *See* Map II.

for many hours by fugitive Bulgarians, sick, and wounded, and by camp followers, all hastening to place the river between themselves and the dreaded enemy. It is easy from this to imagine what would have been the effect of an offensive movement by Osman Pasha on the 31st. Napoleon declared that the whole art of war was to march, to fight, and to pursue. Pursuit is the most effective weapon of warfare and the most difficult to use. It can rarely be extemporized, and must therefore be provided for in the preliminary dispositions for battle. The problem consists in how to keep sufficient troops in hand to follow up such success as has been gained. After a modern battle the victors are usually as much exhausted as the vanquished and are inevitably in great confusion. It is difficult for a commander to realize at once the extent of the advantage he has won : he sees the exhaustion and confusion in his own ranks and cannot grasp the fact that the enemy must be in an even worse state. If a strong force of cavalry is at hand, a part at least will probably have had some rest during the infantry combat and be available for the first pursuit. But for a pursuit to be really effective infantry and artillery must follow hard upon the cavalry. This entails arrangements being made for the supply of the troops thus pushed forward with ammunition and food. Only a highly trained and practised staff can carry out this work in the confusion of a battle field. Osman had little cavalry, few trained staff officers, and neither the character nor the organization of his force were suited to sudden and unforseen efforts.

Krahmer, chapter xxii. *Défense de Plevna*, chapters i and ii.
Kuropatkin, vol. i, part i. Herbert, chapter vi and viii.

CHAPTER VI

THE TURKISH OFFENSIVE

Gourko's Operations beyond the Balkans—Suleyman's Move from Montenegro — Suleyman's Advance — Gourko's Retreat—Mehmet Ali—Situation of Russian and Turkish Armies on August 9—Comments—Russian Reinforcements—The Roumanian Army—Suleyman Attacks Shipka Pass—Mehmet Ali's Offensive—Action at Ajazlar—Action at Karahasankioj—Action at Kaseljevo—Situation of Western Army on August 22—Action at Pelisat

CHAPTER VI

THE TURKISH OFFENSIVE

GOURKO'S first care after capturing the Shipka [1] Pass was to place it in a state of defence. The works were immediately armed with the three mountain and five Krupp guns captured from the Turks, and were occupied by a Brigade of the 9th Division, upon the arrival of which Gourko moved his whole column, with the exception of the 30th Don Cossacks, who were still north of the mountains, to Kazanlik, where he gave it a short rest.

On July 22 the 9th Dragoons and a section of Horse Artillery were sent to occupy Eskizagra at the request of the Christian inhabitants. On July 23 information was received that Turkish reinforcements had arrived at Adrianople; Gourko therefore determined to cut the railways connecting that town with Philippopolis and Jenizagra. The 8th regiment of Dragoons, the 21st Don Cossacks, and a section of Horse Artillery, were ordered to destroy the railway station at Karabunar; [2] the 9th Dragoons, 20th Cossacks, and a section of Horse Artillery, were to do the same at Kajadzik; the 9th Hussars and two regiments of the Bulgarian Contingent

---

[1] *See* Map II.
[2] On the railway between Semenli and Jenizagra, not to be confused with Kurabunar on the Eskizagra-Jenizagra road.

were sent to occupy Eskizagra and reconnoitre towards Jenizagra. The destruction of the railway line was effected near both places, but neither of the first two detachments was able to destroy the stations to which they had been sent; both were found to be occupied by the enemy in strength.

The two parties fell back on Eskizagra with the information that the Turks were concentrating about the railway junction at Semenli. On the 25th it was discovered that Jenizagra was occupied by a force of about one Brigade, and on the 28th a reconnaissance ascertained that about two Turkish Brigades were in the neighbourhood of Semenli. Gourko had on that day at Eskizagra fifteen squadrons, twelve guns, and the Bulgarian Contingent; the 4th Rifle Brigade had been left at Kazanlik to cover his line of retreat, and the 1st Brigade of the 9th Division had arrived at Hainkioj, the 2nd Brigade of that division being in the Shipka pass.

A great change had taken place in the situation which confronted Gourko.

It will be remembered that the Sultan had decided, shortly after the Russians had crossed the Danube, to recall Suleyman Pasha's army from Montenegro.[1] The exact date on which the latter received his orders is uncertain, but about July 3 he was warned to be in readiness to move at short notice, and about July 9 the Turkish Government alarmed by Gourko's occupation of Tirnova issued orders that the army of Montenegro was to be transferred to Adrianople as rapidly as possible. On the 16th Suleyman began embarking at Antivari where a fleet of twenty transports had been

[1] *See* Map I.

collected. Three days later the first troops were disembarked at the mouth of the Maritza, and on July 26 the whole force of twenty-nine battalions, three batteries, and five squadrons was concentrated along the railway line between Hermanli and Karabunar.

This movement of Suleyman's army from Montenegro to Roumelia is one of the most striking examples in military history of the value of sea power to operations on land. The distance in a straight line from Antivari to Hermanli is 300 miles, the actual distance by sea and rail is 1,200. Thirty thousand men had been conveyed between these points without fatigue and without risk of interruption from the enemy, and had arrived at a moment when, if well and boldly handled, they could have changed the course of the campaign. This operation was made possible by the preponderence of the Turkish fleet; a single Russian cruiser unaccounted for in the Mediterranean would have confined Suleyman to Montenegro.

Gourko's position at Eskizagra on the 28th was precarious. Raouf Pasha had 18,000 men at Slivno, Jamboli, and Jenizagra. Suleyman had about 30,000 between Karabunar[1] and Semenli. Gourko was not, however, aware of the arrival of the whole of Suleyman's army in his front. He had received authority from Head Quarters to use the Brigade of the 9th Division which had been pushed through the Hainkioj Pass. Being a firm believer in the advantages of bold action he decided to call up the 4th Rifle Brigade from Kazanlik and the 1st Brigade of the 9th Division from Hainkioj. He recognized that the enemy's main strength was about

[1] *See* Map II.

Semenli, and hoped with the force at his disposal to crush the Turkish detachment at Jenizagra, and then be free to act against the flank of any Turkish movement from the direction of Semenli.

He moved his detachment on Jenizagra in three columns on the 29th. The left column consisting of five battalions of the 9th Division, a battery, and four sotnias, started from Hainkioj. The centre column was composed of the 4th Rifle Brigade, six sotnias, and sixteen guns. It moved from Kazanlik by Magliz, Kisla, and Balabanli. Gourko himself accompanied this column. Four battalions of the Bulgarian Contingent, three regiments of cavalry, and two batteries formed the right column which marched from Eskizagra by the main road. The left and centre columns effected their junction at Kavlikioj early on the 30th, but nothing had been heard of the right column. Without waiting for it to come up, Gourko advanced to attack the Turks who were occupying the town. The latter, who had five battalions and six guns, evacuated Jenizagra and took up a position east of the town, defending the line of railway. The Russians succeeded in driving them back about midday and capturing the station. About this time Gourko received information that the right column had been stopped eight miles out from Eskizagra by a superior force of the enemy. Leaving the 4th Rifle Brigade to observe the enemy who had retired from Jenizagra, he hurried back with the remainder, and halted for the night of the 30th at Kurabunar on the main road to Eskizagra. Here he heard that a strong force of Turks had engaged his right column which had retired to Eskizagra, and that the enemy were then at Dzuranli. This force was Raouf Pasha's main body, which had advanced from Jenizagra to join hands in an attack on Eskizagra with Suleyman, who was moving up from Semenli.

On July 27 Suleyman had met Raouf Pasha, and the two had agreed on a movement on Eskizagra in three columns to begin on the 29th, that is to say, the same day as that on which Gourko had decided to move on Jenizagra in three columns. Raouf moved on Eskizagra with twelve battalions, four batteries, and 700 cavalry, by the main road, and engaged the advanced guard of Gourko's right column near Kurabunar where he bivouacked after a slight skirmish. On the 30th the Russian right column fell back on Eskizagra, and was followed by Raouf, who reached Dzuranli. Suleyman, who had been reinforced from Adrianople, marched on the 29th with thirty-one battalions, four batteries, and 700 cavalry by Kurabunar and Arabadzi Kioj, which he reached on the 30th. Kouloussi Pasha, with seven battalions, one battery, and 150 cavalry, taken from the force which had retired on Philippopolis from the Shipka Pass in front of Gourko, reached Cirpan on the 30th. This force formed Suleyman's third column.

On the morning of the 31st Gourko advanced on Dzuranli and proceeded at once to attack the enemy there, in the expectation that the right column at Eskizagra would march to the sound of the guns and co-operate with him. The latter, however, being attacked by Suleyman, was with difficulty able to hold its ground. After hard fighting Gourko succeeded in repulsing the Turks opposed to him at Dzuranli, and established communication with his troops in Eskizagra. He learned that the latter were hard pressed, well nigh surrounded by the enemy in superior force, and that the town was in flames. He therefore ordered the evacuation of Eskizagra and the retreat of the whole force on Dalboka, where he bivouacked for the night.

This operation is one more example of the difficulty of combining the movement of columns that are not in communication. The left and centre columns had in their movement on Jenizagra passed out of the line of march of the Turks, and had left the right column to bear the brunt of the enemy's main attack. Only the magnificent bravery of the Bulgarian Contingent, which held on desperately to Eskizagra, Gourko's prompt return from Jenizagra and his unexpected attack on the Turkish rear at Dzuranli, saved the right column from annihilation.

On August 1 Gourko continued his retreat through the Dalboka Pass. On the 3rd he reached Hainkioj, where he halted. The 4th and 5th were occupied in reconnoitring towards Eskizagra and Jenizagra, and it was discovered that the enemy was moving in force from the former on the latter. On the 5th Gourko received instructions from Head Quarters that, in consequence of the second battle of Plevna, active operations were to be discontinued south of the Balkans, that the passes were to be held by the 9th Division, 4th Rifle Brigade, and the Bulgarian Contingent, and that he was to retire with the mounted troops on Tirnova. He reached Novi Nikup on the 8th with the cavalry. The 1st Brigade of the 9th Division were sent to hold the Hainkioj and Elena Passes; the Bulgarian Contingent the Shipka and Travna Passes; the 4th Rifle Brigade was brought back to Tirnova.

The total losses suffered by Gourko's column during his raid were thirty-four officers and 947 men. A very large number of horses had been lost or injured, and all were more or less exhausted. They required several weeks' rest at Novi Nikup before they were again able to take part in active operations.

Meantime, considerable changes were taking place within the Quadrilateral. Mehmet Ali had succeeded Abdul Kerim as Commander-in-Chief of the Turkish armies, and like his predecessor he had established his Head Quarters at Shumla,[1] and assumed direct command of the army of the Quadrilateral.

Mehmet Ali was of French extraction, but his family had for generations been settled in Germany. He had as a boy served in the mercantile marine, and finding himself at Constantinople had claimed the protection of a kinsman, who was serving in the Turkish army. Through the latter's influence he entered the Turkish Military School. He became a Mahomedan and threw in his lot entirely with the Turks. Having great abilities he rose rapidly, and at the age of fifty he was placed by the Sultan, whose confidence he enjoyed, in chief command of the Turkish armies. The situation in which he found himself was by no means easy. Mahomedans generally dislike a foreigner and despise a convert. Mehmet Ali soon found that there was a strong party at the Turkish Court intriguing against him, and that the Pashas of the old school were endeavouring to thwart him, either by direct disobedience or passive

[1] *See* Map I.

resistance to his orders. Suleyman Pasha in particular was a ringleader of the opposition to the new Commander-in-Chief. He was a Turk of the Turks, very ambitious, and very jealous of Mehmet Ali's appointment to the supreme command; there was, therefore, no loyal co-operation between the two generals.

Mehmet Ali first set himself to infuse some activity into the army of the Quadrilateral which had stagnated under the sleepy rule of Abdul Kerim. He organized the army into two corps, the first of which he established at Rasgrad, under Ahmed Eyoub Pasha;[1] the second, under Salik Pasha, was established at Eski Djuma.[2] His reason for selecting these places for occupation was that a good road ran from Rustchuk through Rasgrad and Eski Djuma, and thence by the Kazan Pass to Slivno. He hoped from these positions to secure Rustchuk by threatening the flank and rear of any body of troops operating against that fortress, and at the same time to keep open communication with Suleyman's army south of the Balkans which he intended to draw to him, and to menace the flank of any forward movement of the Russians from Tirnova.

The actual situation of the Turkish armies about August 9 was as follows:—

A division consisting of eight battalions of infantry, two batteries of artillery, and 600 sabres was in the Dobrudja in observation of the Russian XIVth Corps,

[1] *See* Appendix IV.
[2] The 2nd Corps was not completed until the Egyptian contingent arrived from Varna. This contingent did not all come in until August 26.

which had occupied the Tchernavoda-Kustendji line of railway. Varna was occupied by twelve battalions; Silistria by eight battalions, two batteries, and four squadrons, with a detachment of four battalions at Turtukai; Shumla was garrisoned by fourteen battalions; eighteen battalions were in Rustchuk. The 1st Corps of the Field army at Rasgrad consisted of forty-eight battalions, twenty-seven squadrons and thirteen batteries, about 45,000 men. The IInd Corps at Eski Dzuma was composed of twenty-seven battalions, twelve squadrons, and six batteries, 21,000 men. South of the Balkans, Suleyman had forty-three battalions, eight squadrons, and nine batteries, about 35,000 men in all, between Eskizagra and Jenizagra. In Plevna, Osman Pasha had forty-four battalions, twelve squadrons, and fifty-four guns, with a detachment of six battalions, a battery, and two squadrons at Lovcha. About 9,000 men were in Widin and on the Eastern frontier of Servia; 23,000 were between Sofia, Orkhanie, and Philippopolis. A general reserve of 30,000 men was in Constantinople.

After the second battle of Plevna the relations between Krudener and Shakofskoi, which had never been good, became somewhat strained. The troops of the XIth Corps who had taken part in the battle had been very severely handled. Early in August, Mehmet Ali's concentration of the IInd Corps about Eski Dzuma was discovered by the Russians, who feared that the Turks meant to advance through Osman Bazar on Tirnova. For these reasons it was decided at Head Quarters to move the 1st Brigade of the 32nd Division and the 1st Brigade of the

11th Cavalry Division from Poradim[1] to join the 35th Division in the neighbourhood of Dzuljunica, and to bring up the 16th Division of the IVth Corps, part of which it will be remembered had been employed under Zimmerman in the Danube Delta, to take their place at Plevna, the troops there being placed under General Sotov, Commander of the IVth Corps.

The situation of the Russian army on August 9 was then as follows. On the extreme left was the 12th Division with its Head Quarters at Pirgos, its outposts thrown towards Rustchuk. The 33rd Division continued the line along the Beli Lom, with its Head Quarters at Nisova. The 35th Division held from Kostanca on the Beli Lom to Polomarca, with the Head Quarters at Caseljevo. The 1st Division carried on the line to Cairkioj. The 32nd Division connected the latter with the 11th Division at Dzuljunica. The 14th Division held Tirnova and Selvi. The 9th Division with the 4th Rifle Brigade and the Bulgarian Contingent held the Balkan Passes from Elena to Selvi. The 30th Division was at Poradim; the 16th Division, on the march to reinforce the troops before Plevna, had reached Bolgareni; the 5th Division was at Karaagac-bolgarski, the 31st at Trestenikturski.

The position occupied by the Russian army was as remarkable as any to be found in the whole course of military history. The main army south of the Danube was strung out on an immense arc with a circumference of about 180 miles, the chord of the arc being formed by the Danube from Nikopoli to Pirgos. This huge outpost line covered nothing, unless it were the bridges

[1] *See* Map II.

over the Danube. There were no general reserves: everywhere the Russian armies were reduced to acting on the defensive, and there was no immediate prospect of dealing the enemy a decisive blow. It was impossible to withdraw from the extended position taken up, for this would have meant abandoning the Christian populations of those districts which had enthusiastically welcomed the Russian flag, to the savage revenge of the Moslem soldiery. It would also have meant a loss of prestige and *moral*, which the Russian leaders dared not face in view of the careless confidence with which they had entered on the war. Rarely has the neglect of the great principles of strategy led to more severe punishment. The Russian plan of campaign had put into the field, in that part of the theatre of war where the decisive results were to be obtained, a part only of the forces available for the war: even that part had, immediately the zone of serious operations was entered, been dispersed beyond hope of concentration. The result of neglecting the enemy's armies in the field, and aiming at the occupation of geographical positions, ended, as it always has ended, in the loss of the initiative. An offensive movement on the part of one of the enemy's armies had brought the whole of the Russian operations to a standstill, and the best that the Russians could hope for in the immediate future was to defeat the enemy in a position of his own choosing. The one substantial advantage that had been gained was the possession of the Balkan Passes.

Gourko's advance has often been called a bold strategic stroke, the one brilliant achievement of the Russian arms in the first phase of the campaign. To form Gourko's column, Skobelov I's advanced guard division was broken up, cavalry regiments were taken from the VIIIth and IXth Corps, and in all 31½ squadrons, out of about 87½ squadrons which were available at the time of the crossing of the Danube, were employed. Of the 56 squadrons left, 12 were almost entirely engaged on orderly and escort duties. The first task of the cavalry in war is reconnaissance. Its duty is to find out the numbers and position of the enemy's forces, and when the enemy is found never to leave him. The want of the large force of cavalry which was employed under Gourko was immediately felt in the other parts of the Russian army which were in contact with the enemy.

It has been shown how Ahmed Eyoub Pasha's movements from Shumla on Rustchuk across the front of the XIIth and XIIIth Corps was not discovered by the Czarevitch, and how the opportunity of dealing an effective blow at a part of the enemy's field force was thereby missed. More important still was the effect of the want of cavalry upon the operations of the western army. Krudener felt himself obliged to employ his mounted troops upon the lower Vid and the Osma, to cover his attack on Nikopoli; thus not a trooper was available to seek out Osman Pasha's army and watch its movements. Ignorance of the numbers of the Turks in Plevna and of their positions cost the Russians far more than they gained from Gourko's raid.

There is something romantic about a bold incursion of horsemen into a territory swarming with enemies, and a dashing ride round a hostile army appeals to the imagination more than almost any other feat in modern war. There is, however, little that is romantic in the warfare of the present day, and when tested by results cavalry raids appear an expedient of doubtful advantage. I do not mean that a bold pursuit by cavalry alone, such for instance as Drury Lowe's ride to Cairo after the battle of Tel-el-kebir, should be considered as a raid in this sense. Cavalry when engaged in this work is carrying out one of its essential duties. But to take cavalry away from the work of reconnaissance, and to send it where there is no immediate prospect of its being effectually supported, can rarely lead to any permanent result. Gourko's raid was evidently inspired by a study of the work of the American cavalry in the Civil War. Cavalry raids, as planned by Lee, were, however, never of long duration, and he never deprived himself of the use of his cavalry on the battlefield. Hooker in trying to copy without understanding Lee's method led directly to his own downfall at Chancellorsville. He detached Stoneman's cavalry to make a raid against the Confederate communications, and having thus deliberately deprived himself of his "eyes" was in complete ignorance of his enemy's movements and allowed his flank to be turned and surprised.

The greatest weakness perhaps in the Russian plan of campaign lay in its want of precision. This is a weakness which is always apparent when the plan of campaign aims at something other than the defeat of the enemy's armies in the field, for it is then constantly subject to modification in accordance with the enemy's movements, in other words the initiative gradually passes into the enemy's hands. The orders and counter orders sent to the Czarevitch, during his advance on Rustchuk and the anxiety to make good previous neglect and to push Krudener on to Plevna, after the fall of Nikopoli, are clear signs of the nervousness and hesitation which prevailed at Head Quarters. The Grand Duke Nicholas suffered greatly from a plethora of advisers. A number of Imperial and Royal personages with their suites, who surrounded the Czar and the Commander-in-Chief, constituted a Head Quarter Staff of unwieldy proportions; too many Archdukes had the same effect upon the Russian operations as too many cooks have upon broth.

After the second check at Plevna the Russian Head Quarters found themselves faced by the possibility of a winter campaign. The prospect was not encouraging. Already difficulties had arisen in the supply of food to the troops. Arrangements for provisioning the army were made with large private contractors, who were charged with the delivery of stores to the troops in the field. This arrangement naturally proved unsatisfactory. The contractors were not acquainted with the plans of the generals whose troops they had to supply, and did not know where and when to deliver their stores. It is easy to understand the anxiety at Russian Head Quarters to avoid adding to their difficulties by a campaign in the snows of a Bulgarian winter.

It was determined to make a great effort to bring the war to an early conclusion. The mobilization of the Guard and the Grenadier Corps of the 2nd, 3rd, 24th, and 26th Infantry Divisions of the line, and the 1st and 14th Cavalry Divisions of the line, was ordered early in August; but it would be many weeks before all these troops could take their place in the theatre of war. If the campaign was to be finished before severe weather set in it was necessary that the thorn which Osman Pasha had thrust into the Russian side should be at once removed. But there were no Russian troops immediately available to reinforce the Western Army; the menacing attitude of the Turks in the Quadrilateral made it impossible to reduce the Eastern Army; Suleyman's appearance south of the Balkans made it equally difficult to reduce the garrisons of the passes. It only remained for the Czar to swallow his pride and to crave the assistance of the little army of Roumania, which he had earlier treated with ill-disguised contempt.

The war party in the principality had grown in power since the beginning of the war. There was naturally strong sympathy between the Roumanians, who had but recently attained a virtual independence of Turkey, and the Christian inhabitants of Bulgaria. The feelings of the people had been roused by the senseless bombardment of their open towns by the Turkish fortresses along the Danube. The newly elected ruler of the State, Prince Charles, was a young man, a soldier by education, and a foreigner. He was eager to show his mettle by appearing in the field at the head of his army. There was, therefore, a strong and influential party in Roumania which was only waiting for a favourable opportunity to send their army across the Danube to take part in the war. Prince Charles had, however, very naturally resented the treatment he had received from Russian Headquarters, and he fully appreciated the difficult situation in which the Russian army was placed. He was, therefore, only disposed to give the services of his army to the Russians on his own terms. The Russians at first proposed that all the chief commands in the

Roumanian Army should be held by their officers. This was at once refused, and after some negotiation it was agreed at the end of August that Prince Charles should have the command of the Western Army, and direct the operations against Plevna, with General Sotov as his Chief of the Staff. The 2nd, 3rd, and 4th Divisions of the Roumanian Army were to join the Western Army, the 1st Division remaining about Kalifat in observation of the Turkish troops in Widin and the neighbourhood.

While these negotiations with the Roumanians were still in progress the Sultan had decided upon a general offensive. Mehmet Ali's plan of campaign was that Suleyman Pasha should join him by way of Slivno, and together with the Corps at Eski Dzuma should advance on Tirnova, and eventually join hands with Osman Pasha by way of Lovcha, while the Rasgrad Corps contained the Russian XIIth and XIIIth Corps. This plan had much in its favour; it at least insured concerted action on the part of a superior Turkish force. Unfortunately Mehmet Ali had not sufficient influence to get it adopted. Suleyman desired nothing less than to serve under the orders of the " Foreigner." After his success at Eskizagra he advanced in a leisurely manner, and did not reach Hainkioj till August 13: he then spent some days in reconnoitring the Balkan Passes. Meantime his friends were intriguing on his behalf at Constantinople. Finally under pretext that he was not provided with enough pack transport, and that the Eastern Passes were not practicable for vehicles, Suleyman was directed by the Sultan to attack the Shipka Pass. He reached Kazanlik on his return march on August 19, detaching a column on the way to make a feint against the Elena pass, and on the 20th made his preparations for battle. Twenty days of valuable time had thus been wasted in counter-marches. Had Suleyman promptly followed Gourko after his victory on July 31 one or more of the passes would inevitably have fallen into his hands, and the Russian armies south of the Danube could hardly have escaped a grave disaster.

The Russians had made good use of the respite allowed them. General Radetzky, Commander of the VIIIth Corps, was charged with the defence of the Balkans. On the 19th August his troops were disposed as follows:— the 36th regiment of the 9th Division, and five battalions of the Bulgarian Contingent, held the Shipka Pass; the 34th regiment and the 13th Dragoons were at Bebrova; the 33rd regiment held the Hainkioj Pass; the Head Quarters of the 9th Division and the 35th regiment were at Selvi, where were also the 55th and 56th regiments of the 14th Division; the remainder of the 14th Division, and the 4th Rifle Brigade, were in reserve at Tirnova; a battalion of the Bulgarian Legion held the Travna Pass.

On the 19th Radetzky received a report that the enemy had appeared in force at Kazanlik, and at the same time he heard that the detachment at Bebrova had been attacked. From his knowledge of Suleyman's movements he considered that the latter was probably the main attack. He therefore sent only the 35th regiment to reinforce the troops in the Shipka Pass, and he himself moved with the 4th Rifle Brigade to Elena, and ordered two battalions of the 14th Division to Zlatarica, through which place a branch road from Bebrova led to Tirnova. All the passes occupied by the Russians had been carefully prepared for defence, and on the 20th the arrival of the 35th regiment brought the garrison of the Shipka up to eleven battalions, with twenty-seven guns, including those captured from the Turks by Gourko.

On the 21st Suleyman began his attack. His method consisted in hurling strong columns successively against the Russian positions in the hope of discovering a weak point at which to penetrate. His attacks, which were purely frontal, were everywhere repulsed, but were renewed again on the 22nd and, after a second failure, on the 23rd. About 2 p.m. on that day the small Russian force, which was exhausted by its efforts, and had lost about one half of its effective strength, was on the point of giving way, when the first reinforcement hurried forward by Radetzky arrived, and the pass was saved. The latter had heard on the 20th, when on the march to Bebrova, that Suleyman's main army was preparing to attack the Shipka Pass. He at once recalled the 4th Rifle Brigade, which reached Prisova on the night of the 21st. The 2nd Brigade of the 14th Division which was at Seremet was ordered to follow the 4th Rifle Brigade, leaving one battalion in charge of the stores at Tirnova. The 2nd Division, under Prince Imeritinsky, part of the reinforcements which had been ordered from Russia after the second battle of Plevna, had been hurried forward to support the VIIIth Corps, and had reached Murad Bey on the night of the 21st. Radetzky ordered it to Selvi to relieve the 1st Brigade of the 14th Division, which was to reinforce the troops in the Shipka Pass. Radetzky had arrived at Gabrova on the night of the 22nd, and early on the 23rd, when on the march to the pass, he was met by an officer who reported the desperate condition of the Russian detachment. He at once ordered the Rifle Brigade to take off their packs and mounted some 250 of them on the horses of a Cossack detachment at Gabrova. The moral effect of the arrival of this small reinforcement, which reached the southern end of the pass soon after 2 p.m., saved the day for the Russians. The remainder of the Rifle Brigade came up on the evening of the 23rd, and were followed by the first troops of the 14th Division early next day. On the 24th Suleyman again renewed his attacks, but the arrival of the Russian reinforcements had placed the issue beyond doubt, and by the night of the 24th-25th, 20,000 Russians were in position. On the 25th when the battle was recommenced Radetzky was able to assume the offensive, and the Turks were driven from some heights which they had gained at the mouth of the pass.

On the 26th the Turkish efforts had become desultory, both sides were exhausted and had suffered very heavily. Suleyman had lost about 10,000 men in killed and wounded, nearly a quarter of his effective strength. The Russians had lost more than 100 officers and 3,500 men; General Derojinski, the Commander of the 2nd Brigade, 9th Division, had been killed. On the 27th Suleyman withdrew his shattered forces to Kazanlik, leaving detachments to hold such positions as he had been able to gain at the mouth of the pass. On the 28th one brigade of the 2nd Division was moved from Selvi to Tirnova; the 1st brigade of the 11th Division, which had been left at Giurgevo to observe the garrison of Rustchuk, and had been brought across the Danube when the need for reinforcements became urgent, reached Gabrova the same day. At the beginning of September the Russians thus had thirty-nine battalions in and about the Shipka Pass, and any immediate danger of its capture was averted.

Meantime in pursuance of the general plan of campaign Mehmet Ali had begun an offensive movement from the Quadrilateral on August 21. His army was on that day disposed as follows—Mustafa Zefi's brigade of the Rustchuk garrison watched the lower Lom with its left thrown back towards Kadikioj. It was in touch with the outposts of the 12th Russian infantry division. The advanced troops of Fuad Pasha's division of the 1st Corps held the right bank of the river Solenik, with their right thrown back to Pisanca. The headquarters of the division was at Eserce. The greater part of the cavalry of the 1st Corps and Assaf's division was at Rasgrad. The remaining division of the 1st Corps (Nedjib's) covered Rasgrad and was in touch with the cavalry of the XIIIth Russian Corps at Sadina and Spahalar. Salik's division of the IInd Corps, and an independent cavalry brigade covered Eski Dzuma, its advanced troops being in touch with the outposts of the 1st Russian Infantry division (XIIIth Corps), which had been rashly pushed forward to the Kara Lom, and had occupied the Kiricen hills. A second division was in process of formation, the 1st brigade, was at Sarnasuflar the 2nd brigade consisting of the Egyptian contingent (8 battalions and a battery) arrived on August 26, when the division was placed under Ismail Pasha. Prince Hassan, the commander of the Egyptian contingent, assumed the command of the IInd Corps on that day. South of the IInd Corps an independent brigade under Salim Pasha (ten battalions, five squadrons and three batteries) held Osman Bazar and contained the Russian 32nd and 11th divisions (less one brigade), which held the line from Zlatarica to Tulbeler.

Salik Pasha's Division of the IInd Corps became first engaged with a part of the Russian 1st Division on the 22nd, in the neighbourhood of Ajazlar. The Russian advanced troops were driven out of the Kiricen Hills, which commanded the valley of the Lom near Ajazlar. General Hahn, Commander of the XIIIth Corps, fearing that his right would be turned, ordered an attack in the afternoon to retake the lost positions. The Russians had only seven battalions, one squadron, and sixteen guns available, and by the 23rd the Turks were able to bring up the whole of Salik's Division, (16 battalions, three squadrons, four batteries). The Russians were repulsed with loss and had to retire from Ajazlar on Popkioj, where General Hahn had brought up the remaining brigade of the 1st Division and a brigade of the 35th Division, thus abandoning the left bank of the Kara Lom. It is interesting to note that the Russians had made no attempt to prepare the strong position in the Kiricen Hills for defence, though they had occupied it for some time, but that the Turks began to entrench themselves there immediately they had driven out the Russians.

Mehmet Ali, instead of following up this success, now proposed to attack the point of junction of the XIIth and XIIIth Corps, with the object of cutting off the latter from its line of retreat on Biela. He accordingly carried a reconnaissance in force on the 25th of August through Sadina towards Karahasankioj, and on the next day made a similar reconnaissance through Spahalar towards the same place. On the 27th, Fuad's division made a demonstration towards Kairkioj to occupy the attention of the XIIth's Corps. On the 28th the position on Mehmet Ali's left was as follows—One brigade of Salik's Division was on both banks of the Kara Lom opposite Sultankioj, the remaining brigade (Sabit Pasha) was opposite Haidarkioj. Nedjib Pasha's Division was about Spahalar with the cavalry of the 1st Corps, watching his right flank. Assaf Pasha's Division formed the reserve to the right on the Rasgrad-Eski-Dzuma road north of Spahalar. Ismail Pasha's Division formed the reserve to the centre and left near Sarnasuflar. General Hahn held Sultankioj with one brigade of the 1st division and a cavalry regiment. One regiment of the 2nd Brigade, 1st division, was at Haidarkioj. The remaining regiment and one regiment of the 35th Division formed the Corps reserve at Popkioj. The remainder of the 1st Brigade, 35th Division, held Polomarca and Gagovo. The 2nd Brigade and two cavalry regiments occupied Karahasankioj and Sadina, the cavalry connecting with the 12th Corps at Kostanca.

On the 29th Mehmet Ali moved Nedjib's Division and Sabit's brigade on Karahasankioj. The Russians made an obstinate defence but were overwhelmed by numbers and pushed back behind the Kara Lom. Simultaneously with the attack on Karahasankioj a brigade of Assaf's division drove the Russians out of Sadina and the cavalry of the 1st Corps, supported by a demonstration made by Fuad's division, secured Kostanca and Solenik. The arrival of Russian reinforcements from Polomarca and Popkioj checked the further advance of Nedjib's division. The 35th Russian division had to abandon the line of the Kara Lom, the left bank being commanded by the heights of Karahasankioj. It took up a position about Polomarca, the 1st division continuing to hold Popkioj. There is little doubt that if Mehmet Ali had put in his reserves he would have completely defeated the XIIIth Corps. Assaf and Ismail's divisions were hardly engaged thoughout the day; while Salik's 1st brigade did nothing beyond making a demonstration towards Popkioj.

Having thus secured the upper part of the Kara Lom and driven back the left of the XIIIth Corps, Mehmet Ali prepared to attack the right of the XIIth Corps, which was holding Kaseljevo and Ablava. With this object he made some modifications in the organization of his army. He had been recently joined by some battalions from Asia Minor, and with these and the reserve battalions of other divisions, a fresh division consisting of twelve battalions, six squadrons, and three batteries was formed. Sabit Pasha was promoted to the command of this division on August 30, and ordered to have it at Sadina on September 2. Nedjib Pasha received orders on August 30 to move his division to Turlak, on the Rasgrad-Rustchuk road, which he also was to reach on September 2. These movements were not completed until September 3, on which date Fuad's division reached Solenik.

Mehmet Ali's intention was that Fuad's Division should make a direct attack on Kaseljevo, and that Sabit's Division should attack the Russian right flank and threaten Ablava. While these operations were in progress Reschid's Brigade of Nedjib's Division was to make a wide turning movement round the Russian left, secure the bridge at Stroko and threaten the Russian line of retreat on Biela. To cover these operations the independent brigade of the Ist Corps and the garrison of Rustchuk were to keep the left of the XIIth Corps occupied, while Prince Hassan with the IInd Corps was directed to operate against the XIIIth Corps in the direction of Popkioj, and to manœuvre so as to separate it from the XIth Corps. Assaf's Division of the 1st Corps remained as a general reserve at Rasgrad.

On the Russian cavalry reporting that the Turks were moving from Karahasankioj, and from the direction of Rasgrad, on Kaseljevo, the garrison at that place was reinforced and brought up to a strength of five battalions, three squadrons, three sotnias, and twelve guns. This force was placed under the command of Major-General Arnoldi. Ablava was held by seven battalions, six squadrons, and thirty-four guns under Lieut.-General Driesen, these troops being the 12th Cavalry and 33rd Infantry divisions.

The country over which the Turks had to advance was difficult. Their movements were therefore slow, and Fuad Pasha was not ready to advance to the attack until the morning of September 5. The Russians held strongly entrenched positions which commanded the approaches, and their artillery was well posted. Their left was on the right bank of the Kara Lom, just north of Kaseljevo, their right on the left bank at Ablava. The ground was so cut up with ravines and water courses that the Turks were unable to find any suitable positions for their artillery, and Fuad's unsupported frontal attacks on Kaseljevo were again and again repulsed.

In the Turkish army at this time no combined orders were issued. The Commander-in-Chief merely informed each general what his troops were to do. Fuad Pasha was therefore unaware of the important rôle which had been allotted to Reschid's Brigade, and thinking the need for reinforcements urgent, he recalled it while it was on the march to Stroko. This was fortunate for the Russians, for the bridge at that place was only guarded by a weak detachment on the morning of the 5th, and when Sabit's attack was developed this bridge formed the only safe line of retreat for the detachment at Kaseljevo. Sabit's attack on Ablava did not begin before eleven o'clock, by which time Fuad had already been engaged for four hours. It compelled the Russians to abandon their first line of entrenchments and to fall back upon a second position which had also been prepared for defence. Here they held their own till about midday, when Mehmet Ali arrived and undertook the direction of operations. Under his orders a Brigade of Fuad's Division was sent to turn the Russian left wing, a Brigade of Sabit's Division was directed against their right, the remaining two Brigades attacking their front. Reschid's Brigade was again sent to secure the bridge at Stroko. This attack compelled the Russians to fall back on a third position on the Stroko road, and from this they were in turn driven about 3 p.m. and retired across the Lom, Reschid's Brigade arriving too late to cut off their retreat. Arnoldi's gallant little detachment had held at bay a force of about seven times their strength for close on nine hours; the Russians were beginning to learn the value of entrenchments to the defence.

While Mehmet Ali's main force had thus captured Kaseljevo, the Brigade of Sabit's Division, which had been detached against the Russian right flank, succeeded in crossing the Lom; and as it had not been engaged all day and was burning to take part in the battle, Ibrahim Pasha, its Commander, proceeded to attack alone the Russian position at Ablava. Mehmet Ali was, however, chary of supporting his hardy lieutenant; he appears throughout the day to have considered that he was dealing with very strong forces. General Driesen, who commanded at Ablava, realized that a retirement was necessary, but as he knew that there would be great difficulty in getting away the guns and transport over the broken country behind him, he decided to make a counter-attack to cover his retreat. With this attack he recaptured Ablava, which brought the action to a close. The Russian lost about fifty officers and 1,200 men, the Turks about 1,300.

While these operations were in progress Prince Hassan's column was advancing through Sarnasuflar and Haidarkioj on Popkioj, which was held by the 1st Division of the XIIIth Corps. Prince Hassan was the son of the Khedive of Egypt. A young man of twenty-three, with little military experience and no ability, he was a favourite of the Sultan, and as such Mehmet Ali was compelled to treat him with consideration and to give him a high command. He hoped that the Prince would have the good sense to take counsel with Salik Pasha who commanded one of his divisions, and was an energetic and able soldier. On September

6th Salik Pasha arranged a combined movement on Popkioj with his division and one of Ismail Pasha's brigades which was at Karahasankioj. The combination was successful, and the Russians, whose position at Popkioj was rendered untenable by the loss of Kaseljevo, were beginning to retire, when Prince Hassan arrived on the scene and stopped the advance of the Turks, for no other apparent reason than that the attack had not been devised by him. Mehmet Ali in despair of getting his orders carried out, and finding that there was no prospect of Suleyman's co-operating with him, and that want of transport and defective supply arrangements would not allow him to move far from his magazines, decided for the present to content himself with holding the Kara Lom. He established his force along that river from a point opposite Stroko to Ajazlar, and fixed his own Head Quarters at Sarnasuflar.

The Czarevitch had now determined to withdraw behind the Banica Lom. This movement was begun on the 7th and quietly carried out without interference from the enemy. By the 15th the army of Rustchuk, reinforced by the 26th Infantry Division which had recently arrived from Russia, had taken up an entrenched position with its left on Mecka, the centre near Banica, and the right at Cerkovna.

The Russian Western army had been re-organized, as has been already mentioned, after the second battle of Plevna; on August 22, it consisted of the IVth Corps, the IXth Corps, less two cavalry regiments not yet returned from Gourko's detachment, the 34th Don Cossack regiment and the Caucasian Cossack Brigade; twelve 24-pounder guns were on their way from Sistova; these had been ordered up as the 9-pounder had been found ineffective against the Turkish earthworks. The IVth Corps held the villages of Poradim and Pelisat, the IXth Corps held Karaagac-bolgarski and Trestenikturski. The 34th Don Cossacks, 4th Dragoons, and 4th Lancers watched the right flank, holding Trestenik, Ribino, and Verbica respectively. The 4th Hussars and the 9th Don Cossacks held Sgalevica and Bogot, while the left rear was covered by the Caucasian Cossack Brigade which held Katrica and watched the roads leading to Lovcha.

Osman had employed his time after his victory of July 30 in providing Plevna and Lovcha with stores of all kinds, in bringing up reinforcements, and completing the works of both places. On August 22 the garrison of Plevna comprised forty-nine battalions, twelve squadrons, and fifty-four guns; that of Lovcha, ten battalions, two squadrons, and six guns.

Osman, as well as the other Turkish commanders, had received the Sultan's orders for a general offensive. He therefore occupied himself in the organization of a field force independent of the garrison of the works he had constructed, and prepared to make a movement in the direction of Tirnova, so as to create a diversion in favour of Suleyman. The column thus formed was composed of nineteen battalions of infantry, three batteries, eighteen squadrons and about 100 irregular Circassian Cavalry. This force was organized in two brigades, under the command of Tahir Pasha and Emin Pasha. The column was about 11,000 strong, and was placed under the command of Hassan Sabri, Adil Pasha being given command of the troops left to garrison Plevna.

THE TURKISH OFFENSIVE

On the night of the 30th the mobile column was massed in the neighbourhood of the Ibrahim Redoubt, (14)[1] and at daybreak on the 31st moved out by the Pelisat road.

General Sotov was duly informed by his cavalry that a strong Turkish column was preparing to break out of Plevna. He appears to have been persuaded that Osman intended a movement on Nikopoli[2] to threaten the Russian communications. In accordance with the agreement with the Roumanians, the 3rd and 4th Roumanian Divisions had crossed the Danube—the former was at Magura, the latter at Bresljanica. Sotov, therefore, on the 30th September had ordered the 3rd Roumanian Division to Bres on the left bank of the Vid, and moved a brigade of the IXth Corps to Kojulovce, thus blocking all roads from Plevna to Nikopoli. He had further organized a special detachment, consisting of the 64th infantry regiment, one battalion of the 118th regiment, the Caucasian Cossack Brigade, with two Field and one Horse Artillery batteries, and placed it under the command of Major-General Skobelov, who had orders to occupy Kakrina, just north of the Lovcha-Selvi Road, and to prevent any attempt at interference on the part of the Lovcha garrison.

The Turkish cavalry moving towards Sgalevica and Pelisat discovered Russian entrenchments just east of those places. These were at once attacked by the Turks, and after a hard fight in which they were taken and re-taken they remained finally in the possession of the Turks, Sotov ordering a retirement of the left wing with the object of drawing on the enemy. The

[1] *See* Map III.   [2] *See* Map II.

Turkish column now came upon the main Russian works about Sgalevica. About this time Sotov appears to have realized that Osman's movement was directed against the south-west, and that no attempt was being made to break out in the direction of Nikopoli. He thereupon ordered a regiment of the 5th Division up to Poradim, and a Brigade of the same division, which was on the road to Grivitsa, to advance on Sgalevica and attack the Turkish left flank.

After the Turks had made two unsuccessful attempts to capture the Sgalevica position, Osman, who had discovered this Russian movement against his left flank, broke off the action and retired quietly on Plevna.

It is a little difficult to understand what was his object in this operation. The force employed was too strong for a reconnaissance and too weak to attempt to break through the Russian lines, or to effect any useful purpose if he had succeeded in this. The movement of this small force so far beyond the Turkish lines was very hazardous; it was only because Sotov had fixed in his mind the idea that Osman would attempt to break out to the north-east, and was occupied in providing for that contingency, that the Russian movement against the Turkish left flank was delayed too long, and did not therefore succeed in cutting off the column from Plevna.

The Turkish offensive had thus everywhere failed, and the Russians had succeeded to some extent in extricating themselves from the perilous position in which they were placed after their defeat of the 30th. The defect, which lead more than any other to this failure of the Turks, was one of organization. The control of modern armies is so complex a problem, that it is necessary to make special provision for it. Mehmet Ali, though nominally Commander-in-Chief of the Turkish forces, was in reality only the commander of the army in the Quadrilateral, which was indeed quite sufficient to occupy his entire attention. The Sultan should have nominated some Pasha to the command of the three main Turkish armies in the field. It is true that an attempt was made to direct these armies from Constantinople, but the Ministers in the capital were not in sufficiently close touch with the general situation to be able to exercise effective command. They had besides to consider the situation of their forces in the Drobrudja and in Asia Minor, and to arrange for the general maintenance and administration of all the armies in the field. A general charged only with the direction of the three main Turkish armies in the European theatre of war could hardly have failed to take advantage of the position of the Russian army in Bulgaria in the beginning of August. But the control of one man free to devote his whole attention to the problem was essential to success. We have recently seen how, with a wise appreciation of this fact, the Japanese Government appointed Marshal Oyama to command their three main armies as soon as they had each gained touch with the enemy.

See for *Gourko's and Suleyman's operations*: *La CavallerieRusse dans la guerre de* 1877-8; *La Guerre D'Orient*, part ii, chapter v, xii and xv. For *Mehmet Ali's Operations*: Valentine Baker chapter i–v.; *La Guerre D'Orient*, part ii, chapters xiii and xiv. For *Osman's Operations*: *Défense de Plevna*, chapter iii (ii); *Guerre D'Orient*, part ii, chapter xviii.

CHAPTER VII

THE CAPTURE OF LOVCHA BY THE RUSSIANS

Formation of Skobelov's Detachment—Description of Lovcha—Turkish Position at Lovcha—Skobelov's Proposals for Attack—Force Detailed for the Attack—Imeretinski's Orders for the Attack—Attack of the Right Column—Attack of the Left Column—Osman's March to relieve Lovcha—Comments.

CHAPTER VII

THE CAPTURE OF LOVCHA BY THE RUSSIANS

It will be remembered that one of Sotov's first acts on taking over command of the troops before Plevna was to form a special detachment to watch the Turkish garrison of Lovcha. The detachment consisted of the 64th infantry regiment from the 16th Division (three battalions), a battalion of the 118th infantry regiment from the 30th Division, the Causcasian Cossack Brigade, and an engineer detachment; a force of four battalions, two sotnias, and fourteen guns, 132 officers, 4,800 men strong. It was placed under the command of Major-General Skobelov, was first formed on August 22nd, and on the 24th reached Kakrina[1]. Skobelov at once took up an entrenched position there facing Lovcha, posted two sotnias of the 30th Don Cossacks at Demjanovo to watch the by-road leading through that place to Selvi, and established a Cossack post at Devetaki to maintain touch with the army before Plevna.

The formation of the detachment had been originally designed for the protection of the Western Army, but it soon became necessary also to charge it with the protection of the right flank of the troops holding the Balkan Passes. This duty had been performed by a

[1] *See* Map II.

detachment of the 9th Infantry Division which occupied Selvi. When Suleyman first attacked the Shipka Pass it was decided at Russian Headquarters to bring up the 2nd Infantry Division as soon as it arrived to Selvi, and to draw the troops of the 9th Division in to Gabrova ; but as the pressure of the Turkish attacks increased, it became necessary to call in the detachment at Selvi to reinforce the troops holding the Shipka Pass, and finally to bring the 2nd Infantry Division to Gabrova instead of to Selvi. This latter movement was ordered because the Russians had discovered that it would be possible for Suleyman to turn the right flank of their position on the Shipka Pass by way of Imitlija and Zelene Dveimvo. When Suleyman's first frontal attacks had failed, it was expected that he would attempt some movement of this kind. The Grand Duke Nicholas could, with the troops at his disposal, only very partially meet such a measure, for Suleyman was free to extend this turning movement by using the Rosalita and Trojan Passes, by the latter of which he could communicate directly with Osman through Lovcha. Very exaggerated views as to the strength of Osman's army prevailed at this time at Russian Headquarters, and the Grand Duke Nicholas was oppressed with the dread that Osman would attempt an advance on Tirnova by way of Lovcha, combined with a turning movement on the part of Suleyman's army.

Skobelov's little detachment isolated at Kakrina was the only force available to protect the Russian right from such an attack. It is not the least of Skobelov's brilliant achievements during this war that he never allowed himself to be overcome by the anxieties of this situation. He realized, as fully as did Stonewall Jackson in his memorable campaigns in the Shenandoah Valley, that the most effective weapon of a weak force acting on the defensive is to strike at the enemy wherever and whenever possible. Skobelov had passed August 25th and 26th in making a careful personal reconnaisance both of the Turkish position at Lovcha, and of the tracks which led from Selvi across the Balkans into the Tundja Valley. He satisfied himself that there was no probability of an offensive movement on the part of the Turks in Lovcha, and he reported to General Radetzky, who was charged with the defence of the Balkans, that he could prevent any movement on Selvi with the Caucasian Cossack Brigade, and the battalion of the 118th regiment, which he had posted in very carefully fortified positions, and he proposed with the remainder of his detachment to move by a little-used track through Bugol, and attack the left of Suleyman's army. But the Grand Duke Nicholas was too anxious for the safety of Selvi and of his right flank to hazard such a movement, and he refused his consent. On August 31, however, the failure of Suleyman's attacks and the arrival of reinforcements so far reassured the Russian Commander-in-Chief that he was prepared to receive more favourably another of Skobelov's proposals, namely, that the 2nd Division, and his own detachment, should attack Lovcha.

Lovcha lies on the Osma, and is at the junction of roads from Tirnova, from Plevna, and from Philippopolis and the Tundja Valley by way of the Trojan Pass. It is at a distance of about a day's march from Plevna, Selvi, and the Trojan Pass, and is the centre of a rich and fertile district. It will be remembered that Osman Pasha, when he first moved east from Widin, had intended to make Lovcha his first objective, but that he had been drawn northwards to Plevna by his orders to relieve Nikopoli. The possession of Lovcha was important to Osman, because it assured him direct communication, by way of the Trojan Pass, with the Turkish army in the Tundja Valley, and because it afforded him an opportunity to combine with Suleyman in an advance on Tirnova. It was also of importance to him as it covered his communications with Orkhanie and Sofia, whence the greater part of his reinforcements and supplies were drawn, against a Russian attack from the direction of Selvi. Finally the garrison at Lovcha was a standing menace to any force attacking Plevna from the south and south-east. It was equally of importance to the Russians to get possession of Lovcha to secure their right flank, to prevent direct communication between Osman and Suleyman, and as a step towards enterprises against the communications between Plevna and Sofia.

The town of Lovcha lies in a cup surrounded by two ranges of hills, between which flows the river Osma dividing the defence into two distinct sections. The western section consists of a succession of heights on the left bank of the river, bounded on the north and south by two streams which flow through narrow gorges from the village of Pridunsec, and from a point just south of the village of Gosnica, into the Osma. The eastern slopes of this series of heights drop sheer into the Osma; on the west the ground slopes gradually away in a succession of open ridges. The heights on the left bank of the Osma completely command those on the right, the key of the whole position being a spur just east-south-east of the village of Pordim. The eastern section consists of a detached hill south-east of the point marked **184** just south of the Lovcha-Selvi road, and of a range of three low hills covered with vineyards, running north from the Selvi road, and west of the stream which flows north from the v, in the word Lovcha into the Osma. Three bridges within the town connect the two sections of the defence.

At the end of August the garrison of Lovcha consisted of eight battalions, six guns, a squadron of regular cavalry, and about 1,200 Bashi-Bazouks, 6,000 men in all. The place was commanded by Rifaat Pasha. He had disposed of his garrison as follows :—one battalion held the hill just south of the Selvi road ; two and a half battalions occupied the hills north of the road. In the western section one and a half battalions and one gun held the line from Gosnica to Pordim, while three battalions and five guns held the spur just east-southeast of the latter village, which for convenience I shall call the Pordim hill. Both sections were strengthened by trenches and light earthworks, the Pordim hill being crowned by a strong redoubt, in which Rifaat Pasha established his headquarters. The weakness of Rifaat's dispositions was that the line of defence was too extended for the force available. It is a common temptation for a small force detailed to hold a town to occupy too much ground in the endeavour to cover all approaches from a hostile attack. In such a case it is nearly always preferable to hold the circumference merely with a line of outposts, and to limit the permanent defence to some point, which if held will prevent the enemy from occupying the town in question. In this case Rifaat Pasha was obliged to use his reserve to garrison the key to his defence, the Pordim hill. This can never be a satisfactory way of employing a reserve, which should never be tied to any one point in the line of defence, but should be held in some central position from which it can reinforce any threatened point, and be readily employed in its true rôle of delivering counter-attacks against the enemy's columns. Any damage which the Russians could have done to the town of Lovcha during a temporary occupation while attacking the Pordim hill, could not have injured the Turks in a military sense to any great extent. Lovcha was not of importance as a collection of houses but as a road junction, and as a point of passage over the river Osma.

The difficulty of such a system of defence as is here indicated consists usually in providing adequate protection for the reserves of ammunition and supplies, which cannot be left in a town which it is not intended to hold permanently. The heights which form the best tactical positions for defence are usually also the last places where a supply of water is to be found, more time is therefore required to prepare an adequate system of defence in some detached position, than to cover the existing water-supply and store-houses with a circle of posts. Rifaat Pasha had had, however, ample time to make all the arrangements that could have been necessary. It is a guiding principle of the defence that the position to be held must be suitable to the force which is to hold it, and this is a principle which it is often difficult to observe in practice. A commander should never allow himself to be induced to occupy permanently a position which, however strong it may appear, is too extended for his force. In defending a town a feeling of consideration for the inhabitants may often lead to an attempt to cover every possible avenue of approach. In such a case important private interests are often involved, and political and other influence are brought to bear upon the soldier. There is nearly always some one point, which we call the key of the position, which if held, will deny the enemy any permanent advantage from the occupation of other points in the line to be defended. No considerations should induce a commander to weaken his hold upon this point. To defend too much usually entails the loss of the whole.

The force destined for the attack on Lovcha consisted of the 2nd Infantry Division, under the command of Major-General Prince Imeretinski, which was ordered to march from Gabrova on August 31st, to join the 2nd Brigade of the 3rd Division, which reached Selvi on September 1st, and to effect a junction with Skobelov's detachment on September 2nd, when the whole was to attack Lovcha.

Imeretinski, who was to command the whole force, asked Skobelov to submit a plan for the attack. In reply Skobelov sent him the following general proposals:—

1. The first essential is a careful reconnaissance of the ground and of the enemy's dispositions.

2. The attack should be thoroughly prepared by artillery fire.

3. The advance should be gradual and progressive.

4. All positions occupied preparatory to the attack,

and those captured from the enemy, should be at once put in a state of defence.

5. A strong reserve should be kept in hand.

6. An endeavour should be made to cut the enemy's line of retreat, and the direction from which the enemy might receive reinforcements should be carefully watched.

These proposals are of interest, not because they were new in the year 1877, but because they clearly indicate the weak points in the Russian tactics up to this period of the campaign. The training of the Russian infantry had hitherto been in accordance with the principles of Suvarov, that the decisive factor in an attack was the charge with the bayonet. Up till now artillery preparation had been almost entirely neglected, and the infantry columns had rushed straight at their objective, without waiting to gain any fire-superiority over the defence. There is no one of the principles here laid down by Skobelov which had not been deduced by tacticians from the battles of the Franco-German War of 1870, and yet the lessons of Plevna were necessary to bring them home to the Russians; this is a striking example of how difficult it is for an army to model its tactics on the experiences of others.

Skobelov had personally reconnoitred the Turkish positions. He discovered that the weakest part of the defence was the western section between Pordim and Gosnica; there were, however, many objections to attacking this side. Such a measure would mean the abandonment of the line of retreat on Selvi, and would expose the Russians to the danger of being cut off by reinforcements arriving from Plevna. To attack in this way would be to stake everything on success; failure would mean complete disaster. The course of the campaign had not so far justified the Russians in accepting such risks. It was, however, discovered that though the hill at point 184 was strongly defended it was commanded at a range of about 2,000 yards by some heights just south of the Selvi road. If this hill were captured the remainder of the eastern section of the defence would be enfiladed, and the communications between the eastern and western sections seriously threatened. Skobelov therefore proposed to Imeretinski that the first attack should be directed against hill 184; that the high ground south of the Selvi road should be secured as soon as possible; that the attack should be prepared by a concentrated artillery fire from these heights; that while the main attack was being delivered, a holding attack should be made against the remainder of the eastern section; and that these operations should be covered by the cavalry, which should watch the Plevna road. He suggested that when the eastern section had been captured it should be placed in a state of defence, and used as an artillery position to prepare the attack on the Pordim hill, and that while the attack on that hill was in progress the cavalry should close in and endeavour to cut off the enemy's retreat.

These proposals were accepted by Imeretinski, who, however, decided that the attack should be made on September 3rd, and not on the 2nd as originally proposed.

Imeretinski had at his disposal about 20,000 infantry, 1,500 cavalry, and ninety-two guns. His command was composed of the 2nd Infantry Division, and the 2nd Infantry Brigade, the 2nd Brigade of the 3rd Division and two batteries of the 3rd Artillery Brigade, the 3rd Rifle Brigade, and a battery made up of the Turkish field guns captured at Nikopoli, two sotnias of the 30th Don Cossacks, one squadron of the Czar's cavalry escort, half a company of his infantry escort, and Skobelov's detachment. He ordered Skobelov to send the Caucasian Cossack Brigade on the 1st to Joglav, to watch the Plevna road and communicate with Sotov's army; while the remainder of the detachment was to move to the Pablikian springs, act as an advanced guard to the main body, and secure the high ground south-west of that point.

On September 1st the Caucasian Cossack Brigade reached Omarkioj and gained touch with the Russian army before Plevna, and with the main body of Skobelov's detachment through Prisjaka. The latter reached Pablikian, and after a slight skirmish drove the Turkish outposts from a height south of the Selvi road, where the Russians at once entrenched themselves. The 2nd Brigade of the 2nd Division was pushed on as far as the Sero springs, south of Kakrina. Imeretinski's main body halted at Selvi, the 3rd Rifle Brigade and the Nikopoli battery halting on the Gabrova-Selvi road.

On the evening of the 2nd Imeretinski issued the following orders for the attack :—

The detachment will advance to the attack of Lovcha to-morrow, September 3rd.

1. The right column consisting of the 3rd Rifle Brigade, half the Guard Escort Company, the Nikopoli battery, and 5th and 6th Batteries of the 2nd Artillery Brigade, total four battalions, half a company, twenty guns, under the orders of General Dobrovolski, com-

mander of the 3rd Rifle Brigade, will advance against the hills south-west of the village of Prisjaka and attack the enemy's left flank.

2. The left column, consisting of the 64th infantry regiment, one battalion of the 118th infantry regiment, one brigade of the 2nd Infantry Division, the escort squadron, one sotnia of the Kuban Cossacks, and one sotnia of Vladicaucas Cossacks, the 9-pounder batteries of the detachment, four batteries of the 2nd Artillery Brigade, total ten battalions, one squadron, two sotnias, and fifty-six guns, under the command of General Skobelov, will advance against the hills on either side of the Lovcha road.

3. The 2nd Brigade of the 2nd Infantry Division, and the 2nd Brigade of the 3rd Infantry Division, the 5th and 6th Batteries of the 3rd Artillery Brigade, total eleven battalions, sixteen guns, will be on the Lovcha road, and act as general reserve under the command of Major General Engman, commanding the 2nd Brigade 2nd Division.

4. Two sotnias of the 30th Don Cossack regiment will watch the Lovcha-Trojan road, and will send patrols to Mikre.

5. Colonel Tutolmin's detachment (six sotnias, six guns, Caucasian Cossack Brigade) will advance, as soon as the artillery opens fire, to the Lovcha-Plevna road, which they will block. They will maintain touch with Lieut.-General Sotov's force, watch the enemy's line of retreat on Mikre, and endeavour to gain touch with the patrols of the 30th Don Cossacks sent to that place.

6. The artillery will open fire at 5 a.m. All troops should be in their positions at that hour in accordance

with the orders of Major-Generals Skobelov, Dobrovolski and Engman.

7. If the enemy does not surrender after the first position has been captured the infantry will entrench themselves there, and the artillery will bombard the enemy's second position.

8. The Caucasian Cossack Brigade will watch the right flank, Major-General Skobelov's cavalry the left.

9. The advanced dressing-station will be on the road behind the reserve, the main dressing-station will be with the ammunition park.

10. The Second Line Transport, with the exception of the Field Hospitals and ammunition columns, will be parked with the ammunition park.

11. The two companies of the 12th infantry regiment now with the parks will act as escort to the 2nd Line Transport under the orders of Major Moltschanski.

12. I shall be on the Lovcha road near the artillery.

On receipt of these orders General Skobelov issued some tactical instructions which deserve to be given in full.

" The artillery will play the first part in the coming engagement. Battalion commanders will receive orders how to attack, and will be instructed to advance in such a way as not to interfere with the concentration of artillery fire. The infantry attack must be supported by fire whenever possible. Vigilance is absolutely essential. Fire must be specially maintained when the enemy's reserves show themselves, and still more when the attack meets any obstacle. Whenever the range admits the artillery should use shrapnel. The infantry must avoid confusion during the engagement, and must distinguish between the advance and the assault. Mutual support is a sacred duty, cost what it may. Ammunition must not be wasted; it must be remembered that the character of the ground makes ammunition supply difficult. I would once more remind the infantry of the importance of order and silence in the attack. Troops should only cheer when close to the enemy, and about to charge with the bayonet. I would impress upon all ranks that troops gallantly advancing suffer comparatively small losses, but that if they retire, particularly in disorder, they suffer heavily. Those of the above instructions which affect the infantry are to be read to every company."

The attack was begun by the artillery of Skobelov's column coming into action at 5 a.m. on the 3rd, on the hills south of the Selvi road, which he had seized with his detachment on the 1st. Soon afterwards the skirmishers of Dobrovolski's column made good the high ground south of Prisjaka, whence his artillery opened fire. Dobrovolski soon found that his troops, as they advanced down the western slopes of the Prisjaka ridge, were suffering from the artillery fire from the great redoubt on the Pordim hill, which his guns were unable to reach. The supports were moved forward to positions which gave them some cover from the Turkish guns, and this movement started a premature attack on the Turkish works in the northern part of the western section soon after 7 a.m. The Russian artillery, which had wasted some time in ineffectual efforts to reach the guns on the Pordim hill, had in no sense prepared the way for the infantry attack, which was repulsed with heavy loss. Dobrovolski asked for reinforcements, and three battalions were sent him from the reserve; but before these came up the Turks were reinforced by Rifaat Pasha from the Pordim redoubt. The Turks now issuing from their works made a counter-attack upon Dobrovolski's advanced troops and drove them back. But this attack was checked by two battalions of the 3rd Rifle Brigade who were in reserve, and after a sharp struggle the Turks began to fall back. Dobrovolski followed them up with the whole of his infantry, and secured the works in front of him before the Turks had time to rally. The right Russian column had, however, suffered very severely in this attack, losing 112 killed, 442 wounded, and the 3rd Rifle Brigade had to be withdrawn out of action, the 7th infantry regiment which had come up from the General Reserve undertaking the pursuit of the Turks across the river.

While this had been going on on the Russian right, the 9-pounder batteries had been engaged in a prolonged bombardment of the Turkish works on hill 184. It was not till 11.30 a.m. that Imeretinski sent word to Skobelov that it was time for the infantry to advance to the attack. The three battalions of the 64th infantry regiment advanced against hill 184, while the 1st Brigade of the 2nd Division moved at the same time against a height opposite this hill, and just north of the Selvi road. The fire of Skobelov's fifty-six guns was concentrated against these two points of attack, and was sustained until the last moment. The attack was completely successful, the Turks offering a comparatively feeble resistance, probably because they were by this time aware of Dobrovolski's attack on the northern works and were fearful that their retreat would be cut off.

THE CAPTURE OF LOVCHA

While the infantry attack against the western section was in progress, Tutolmin with the Caucasian Cossack Brigade was engaged in watching the Plevna road, and covering the attack against possible interruption from that direction. He moved forward to the Plevna road near Novoselo at dawn on the 3rd, and opened up communication with the 9th Don Cossack regiment of Sotov's army, which was at Slatina, and with Dobrovolski, by way of Prisjaka. As soon as he had received news that Dobrovolski's attack on the western section had succeeded he left detachments to maintain touch with Slatina, and to watch the main Plevna road, and also a track through the hills to Plevna which runs through Novoselo, Zalkova, and Laskar, and moved south to co-operate with the attack on the eastern section.

The 64th regiment following up the capture of hill 184 crossed the Osma, and secured the southern end of the town, the 7th regiment in the same way seizing the northern end. The leading battalions of the 1st Brigade 2nd Division which should have connected these two regiments had some difficulty in crossing the river, which was deep and unbridged in the part allotted them. A ford was eventually discovered, but as it was under fire from the Pordim redoubt the Russians lost heavily in crossing. By 2 p.m., however, the town was made good, and the Russians were in touch along the left bank of the Osma.

The Russian artillery was brought up to the captured Turkish positions on the right bank of the Osma, and some eighty guns prepared the way for the infantry attack on the eastern section, the batteries of the Caucasian Cossack Brigade co-operating from the north. By 3 p.m.

the latter had gained touch with the right of Dobrovolski's attack, and the Turkish position was surrounded on the north, east, and south by seventeen battalions and eleven squadrons, to meet which Rifaat Pasha had but five battalions, with the remnants of three others. About 3.30 p.m. Rifaat, seeng that he could not hope to hold his position for long, sent off his guns down the Mikre road, under escort of his Circassians. At 4 o'clock, when the Russians advanced to the assault of the Pordim redoubt, the Turks abandoned all their positions, and fell back into the hills west of Pordim and Gosnica, pursued by the Cossacks till dark. Though many stragglers were made prisoners the Russian cavalry did not succeed in cutting off the enemy's retreat, the rugged nature of the country and the darkness preventing an effective pursuit. Rifaat succeeded in bringing his guns and the remnants of his infantry into Plevna two days later, by side tracks through the mountains. The Turks lost more than 2,000 men in killed, wounded, and prisoners. The Russian losses amounted to 6 officers and 313 men killed, 33 officers and 1,112 men wounded and 52 missing.

On September 1 the guns of Skobelov's advanced guard had been heard at Plevna, and on the same day telegraphic communication with Lovcha was cut. Osman Pasha does not, however, appear to have attached any very great importance to this, nor to the first reports which he received from Rifaat Pasha. It was not until September 2 when he received a report from Rifaat giving details of the strength of the attacking force that he realized that Lovcha was in any danger. He then collected a column composed of twenty battalions of infantry, two squadrons of regular cavalry, one regiment of irregular cavalry, about 100 Circassian cavalry, and three batteries of artillery. But this column was not ready to start till midday on September 3. Osman accompanied the force himself, leaving Adil Pasha in command at Plevna.

After the Turks had passed Brestovetz some of the enemy were sighted east of the road in the direction of the village of Bogot. These were the 9th Don Cossacks of Sotov's force. Osman detached a flank guard to cover his left, and moved his main body by the mountain track through Laskar on Zalkova. But the track proved difficult, progress was slow, and before the latter place was reached night began to fall. Osman decided to bivouac just north of Zalkova.

Colonel Tutolmin had received information from the 9th Don Cossacks on the afternoon of the 3rd that a relieving column was on the march from Plevna. Imeretinski therefore issued orders during the night of the 3rd–4th to Skobelov, to collect his detachment as originally formed, and to take up a position covering Lovcha on the north.

Early on the 4th Skobelov took up a position behind a brook which flows into the Osma from the village of Pridunsec.

At dawn on the 4th Osman slowly continued his advance. His advanced troops soon came in contact with Tutolmin's Cossacks, and about midday Skobelov's position was discovered. The presence of Russian troops in force north of the town, and the fact that no firing could be heard in the neighbourhood of Lovcha, led Osman to suspect that he was too late. He therefore halted his column near the village Lisec, while he himself with a small escort rode by a bye track to a point whence he could view the town. Having convinced himself that the Russians were in undisputed possession he decided to halt where he was for the night and retire on Plevna next morning. He was confirmed in this decision by news from Plevna that the Russians were evidently preparing an attack on that place.

Starting at dawn on the 5th Osman retired through Miras to Peternica, and re-entered Widin early on the 6th by way of Ternina. This movement was cleverly designed both to avoid any interference from Sotov's force, and to deceive Imeretinski, who was convinced that Osman was endeavouring to outflank his left, and expended his energies on taking steps for the defence of Lovcha.

The incident of the capture of Lovcha has been dealt with at some length because it marks a turning-point in the campaign. The Russians had entered upon the war with a splendid contempt for field entrenchments. Courage and resolution were believed to be sufficient to enable infantry to capture the strongest positions. The failure of the attacks at Plevna against the despised earthworks, held by the even more despised Turk, had produced a sense of discouragement and despondency which led to the Russians holding all defensive positions in exaggerated respect. Earthworks were thought to be impregnable when occupied by troops with modern arms, until Lovcha taught the armies of the Czar that troops well handled and intelligent tactics could cope successfully with fortified positions. Imeretinski's orders and Skobelov's instructions sufficiently explain the principles on which the attack was carried out. There are, however, one or two points which call for comment.

Skobelov had suggested to Imeretinski that a containing attack should be made against the northern part of the western section, and that the main attack should be directed against hill 184. This proposal had been accepted by Imeretinski, a decision which was in accordance with the tactical situation. The ground east of hill 184 was covered from the fire of the Turkish guns in the Pordim redoubt, and was less easily reinforced than the northern works, which could, moreover, be enfiladed from that position. Still Imeretinski's orders contained no direct instruction to Dobrovolski that his attack was not to be pressed home, but the comparative strength of Skobelov's and of Dobrovolski's columns and the position of the general reserve make it quite clear which was to be the main attack. Dobrovolski does not appear to have appreciated his instructions, and finding himself in a difficult position he took the bull by the horns and engaged in a premature attack in which, though it was eventually successful, the 3rd Rifle Brigade was severely handled.

In almost every attack which is delivered there is a main attack against some part of the enemy's position and a containing attack against other parts. It is a disputed point as to how the instructions for these attacks should be conveyed in orders. There are many objections to the use of the terms "containing" or "holding" attack. Troops ordered to make a holding attack are usually anxious to avoid committing themselves, and such a term has a damping effect upon their energies. Since every available man will be taken for the main attack they will be in barely sufficient numbers to carry out their duties.

It is essential to the success of the main attack, whether it be in the form of a turning movement or of a direct attack upon some point in the enemy's front, that the enemy should be prevented from manœuvring to meet it. The object of a holding attack is to keep the largest possible number of the enemy tied to their positions with the least expenditure of force, so as to be in overwhelming strength at the decisive point. To carry out these duties successfully a holding attack must be conducted with energy and exert real pressure, or it will in its turn be contained by an inferior force, while the enemy will be free to move his superfluous troops to the point of danger. There is also the danger that valuable opportunities may be lost if the holding attack is apathetically carried out. It may well happen that the direction of the main attack may be discovered by the enemy at an early stage, and that to meet it he may unduly weaken his front at certain points and allow of the holding attack gaining valuable successes. The terms "holding" and "containing" attack have undoubtedly the effect of paralysing initiative, and it is, therefore, perhaps better to avoid using them. The alternative is to adopt Imeretinski's method, that is to apportion the strength of the various columns of attack to the objects they are required to achieve, and to leave their respective leaders a free hand to carry them out; the distribution of the troops will be a sufficient indication of the supreme commander's intention. This may occasionally lead, as at Lovcha, to a weak force compromising itself, but this is a risk which must be accepted, and is a lesser evil than a containing force not exercising sufficient influence upon the fortunes of the day. Dobrovolski's error lay rather in delivering his attack prematurely and without sufficient artillery preparation than in unduly pressing it home. He was enabled to make good his mistake because the Turks in their turn took a false step. Having checked Dobrovolski's first attack, they left their works and followed up the retreating Russians, only to be themselves checked and driven back by the attackers' supports and reserves, who pursued the Turks and secured their works before they were able to rally. This is a danger to which the defence is always exposed, and which must always be provided against. In allotting the garrisons of defensive positions, a firing line necessary to hold the works should be kept distinct from the reserves; the former should not be allowed to leave the works except to take part in a general offensive movement of the whole force; the latter should be used to deliver local counter-attacks and to follow up successes.

The slowness which so often before in the course of the campaign allowed golden opportunities to slip by, showed itself in the movements of Osman's column. If Osman had made up his mind to retain Lovcha a mobile force ready to start at the shortest notice should have been prepared in Plevna. The only alternative would have been to give up Lovcha altogether. It was too far from Plevna to be held as part of the defence of that place. The real value of Lovcha to Osman was that it enabled him to assume the offensive, and to strike a blow on the flank and rear of the Russians holding the Balkans.

Osman clearly showed that he considered that he could take a force of about twenty battalions from Plevna and still leave a sufficient garrison to hold that place and occupy Sotov. If instead of wasting his energies on the reconnaissance in force to Pelisat he had moved on Lovcha about August 26, and combining with the garrison of that place begun an advance on Tirnova, he would have compelled Suleyman to co-operate with him by way of the Rosalita Pass, and would have placed the Russians in a position of such difficulty that it is very doubtful whether they would have been able to retain their hold upon the Balkan Passes. Osman appears to have occupied Lovcha at first with a view to some such movement. But with that fatal disinclination to undertake a resolute offensive, which was characteristic of the Osmanli generals, he put off the hour for action until too late, and uselessly sacrificed the garrison of Lovcha.

Kuropatkin, vol i, part i. *Guerre D'Orient,* part ii. chapter xix. *Défense de Plevna,* chapter iii.

CHAPTER VIII

THE THIRD BATTLE OF PLEVNA

THE RUSSIAN REINFORCEMENTS—CONSIDERATIONS AS TO THEIR DISPOSAL—DISTRIBUTION OF THE WESTERN ARMY—ARRIVAL OF REINFORCEMENTS—DISTRIBUTION OF THE GARRISON OF PLEVNA—RUSSIAN PLAN OF ATTACK—THE PRELIMINARY BOMBARDMENT—IMERETINSKI'S OPERATIONS SOUTH OF PLEVNA—ORDERS FOR THE GENERAL ATTACK—MOVEMENTS OF THE TURKISH GARRISON—THE ATTACK ON THE SOUTHERN SECTION—THE ATTACK ON THE CENTRE SECTION—THE ATTACK ON THE NORTHERN SECTION—TURKISH COUNTER ATTACK IN THE SOUTHERN SECTION—THE RUSSIANS WITHDRAW—COMMENTS.

CHAPTER VIII

The Third Battle of Plevna

By the first week of September the Russians had passed the crisis in which they had been placed by the second battle of Plevna, and the sudden appearance of Suleyman's army south of the Balkans. All attempts to capture the Shipka Pass had been defeated, Osman Pasha's abortive offensive movement had been checked, Lovcha had been captured, and though the Western army had been compelled to give ground before Mehmet Ali's advance, the net result had been to cause a concentration of the Czarevitch's scattered forces, and to place them in a better strategic position.

A considerable part of the reinforcements ordered had arrived. Three Roumanian divisions, consisting of forty-two battalions, thirty-two squadrons, and eighteen batteries, had crossed the Danube. The 2nd, 3rd, and 26th Infantry Divisions and the 3rd Rifle Brigade had entered Bulgaria. The 24th Infantry Division was on its way, and the Guards and Grenadiers were expected by the middle of October. The Grand Duke Nicholas had now to decide how these reinforcements were to be disposed of. He had four courses open to him. He could remain on the defensive until the whole of his reinforcements had arrived, or he could reinforce either of his three armies, and assume the offensive with whichever of them he elected to support. The first alternative was dismissed because to remain for six weeks longer on the defensive would have been a confession of inferiority which might have had a serious effect upon the population of the Balkan States, would have allowed the Turks time to consolidate their defences and concentrate their scattered armies, and lastly it would have entailed a winter campaign amid the snows of the Balkans.

It remained then for the Grand Duke to decide with which of the three armies he should assume the offensive. He could bring the army of Rustchuk up to a strength of 100 battalions, 40 squadrons, and 400 guns. With this force there was a reasonable prospect of defeating Mehmet Ali in the field. This done he might cross into Eastern Roumelia by way of Slivno, and in conjunction with the army holding the Balkans advance against Suleyman Pasha. But there remained the probability that Mehmet Ali would decline an engagement in the open and would throw his army into either Rustchuk, Shumla,[1] or the entrenched camp at Rasgrad, and the Russians would have to deal with a second Plevna on their left flank. This was a prospect which the Grand Duke did not care to face, and this alternative was also dismissed.

If he were to reinforce the army holding the Balkans he could hope to defeat Suleyman, and by advancing on Adrianople directly threaten Constantinople. This course if successful promised to have a decisive influence on the campaign, but it entailed serious risks. The Turks were believed to have some sixty battalions in

[1] See Map I.

THE THIRD BATTLE OF PLEVNA 193

reserve at Constantinople, whence they could be railed rapidly to reinforce Suleyman. The command of the sea would allow the Turks to move the twelve battalions at Varna, with the probable addition of some detachments from Mehmet Ali's army, to Burghas, whence they would menace the Russian left flank. Finally Mehmet Ali might elect to contain the Czarevitch with a part of his force, and to march with his main body by Slivno against the Russian left and rear. His recollection of the serious situation in which he had been placed by his premature attempt to end the campaign by a dash through the Balkans, was too recent to allow the Grand Duke Nicholas to attempt a movement which appeared even more dangerous than his first advance from Sistova.

The remaining course was to reinforce the army before Plevna and to attempt to drive Osman from the position which threatened the Russian communications.

By the compact with Roumania the Grand Duke Nicholas was not free to employ the Roumanian reinforcements wherever he wished, but they could be used in an attack on Plevna. The Western army at this time numbered 42 battalions, 28 squadrons and sotnias, and 188 guns. After providing a suitable reserve for the army of Rustchuk the reinforcements available would, with the assistance of the Roumanian divisions, allow of the Western army being brought up to a strength of about 100 battalions, 90 squadrons and sotnias, and 400 guns. This force was considered sufficient for the capture of Plevna, and this important result once attained it was proposed to clear the Turks from Western Bulgaria, and to advance on Sofia. It was hoped that this movement would relieve and encourage the Christian population of Bulgaria, and would induce Servia, Macedonia, and perhaps Greece, to join in the struggle against the hated Moslem. It was then proposed to advance with the Western army from Sofia to Philippopolis, and it was expected that by this time the remaining reinforcements would have joined the army of the Balkans, and that the two armies would together crush Suleyman and advance on Adrianople and the Turkish capital. It is probable, however, that the reasons which led to the decision to reinforce the Western army and to assume the offensive against Osman were moral and political rather than strategical. There had been a general expectation throughout Europe at the beginning of the campaign that Russia would speedily crush " the sick man of Constantinople." The two Russian defeats at Plevna, and the unexpected check to the Russian advance which Osman's march from Widin had caused, were received first with amazement and then with delight by the enemies of Russia. Plevna had seriously affected Russian prestige, and the Grand Duke Nicholas held it to be his immediate duty to remove the blot from the Russian arms by driving Osman from that place at the earliest possible moment.

In criticizing the decision which had been formed at Russian Head Quarters it is necessary to bear in mind the great weight which the moral and political considerations mentioned above carried in the Russian councils. Still, however expedient it may have appeared to order another attack on Plevna, this decision is not one which would have been approved by a great commander.

The superiority of the Russian over the Turkish troops lay chiefly in their better march-discipline and better power of manœuvre, in short the Russian army was more mobile than the Turkish army. The whole course of the war up to September 1877 had shown that the Turks were masters of the art of applying field-fortification to battle tactics, and that the organization, equipment, and character of the Turkish infantry was more adapted to the dogged defence of prepared positions than to any other kind of warfare. From the time when the two armies had first come in contact the Turks had gained no successes either by manœuvre, or by action in the open field, with the exception of the small advantage won by Mehmet Ali against some detachments of the scattered army of Rustchuk. The decision to attack Osman Pasha behind his entrenchments at Plevna meant that the Grand Duke Nicholas had deliberately determined to forego the tactical advantages which the superior mobility of his troops would give him in an open battlefield, and had elected to meet the enemy under conditions which were the most favourable to the Turks. Nor could it be hoped that a success gained at Plevna would have any immediately decisive influence upon the course of the campaign as a whole. It was not to be expected that the Sultan would be brought to his knees until his capital was threatened. Even if Osman were driven from Plevna, and an advance on Sofia were successful, it would be many weeks before Western Bulgaria could be cleared of the enemy, and a serious invasion of Eastern Roumelia undertaken. It will be remembered that one of the objects of resuming the offensive as early as possible was to obviate the necessity of a winter campaign. It is difficult to see how an offensive movement of the Western army, even if successful, could have been expected to attain this result. Once the Russians had sufficient force at hand to enable them to meet the various offensive movements of the Turkish armies they were strategically in a better position than the Turks. Detachments could be moved from any one of the Russian armies to reinforce any other quicker than a corresponding movement could be carried out by the Turks; that is to say the Russians had the strategic advantage of interior lines. The Russian army in the Balkans could be reinforced before Suleyman's army could be strengthened by detachments either from Plevna or from the army of the Quadrilateral. In spite of his repeated failures to force the Shipka Pass, Suleyman had not been seriously reinforced from Constantinople. It was, therefore, clear that the Sultan was anxious not to let go his hold upon his last reserves. The alarm which Gourko's appearance south of the Balkans had created in Constantinople was known at the Russian Head Quarters. The Grand Duke Nicholas, therefore, might have expected that, if the army of the Balkans could be reinforced sufficiently to give it a reasonable prospect of success against Suleyman's army, an advance into Roumelia would cause the Sultan to withdraw considerable detachments from the armies in Bulgaria to cover Constantinople. The defeat of Suleyman in the field would, in all probability, have had the effect of relieving pressure upon the Russian flanks as successfully as the defeat of either Osman Pasha or Mehmet Ali.

The tactical advantages of an advance against Suleyman were not less than the strategical. The command of the Balkan passes allowed the Russians to issue forth at their pleasure, and attack Suleyman in the open.

There was a prospect that by successful manœuvring they could force Suleyman to stand when and where they wished, to cover his communications with Constantinople: a very different prospect to that offered by an attack upon the elaborated works which surrounded Plevna, or upon the fortresses of the Quadrilateral. Therefore, provided sufficient force could be assembled, an advance on Adrianople afforded greater hopes of success than an offensive movement against either Osman Pasha or Mehmet Ali. A bold and resolute commander determined to make sacrifices for the attainment of a great result would certainly have found means to collect a sufficient force for the purpose. Three Roumanian Divisions and the IVth Corps might well have been held capable of containing the Turks in Plevna, when the ease with which Osman's movement on Pelisat was checked is taken into consideration. Similarly the XIth, XIIth, and XIIIth Corps were capable of checking any forward movement on the part of the Turkish army in the Quadrilateral until the effect of an advance into Eastern Roumelia had made itself felt. The VIIIth Corps, the 4th Rifle Brigade, and the Bulgarian contingent were already holding the Balkans. By September 15 these could be reinforced by the IXth Corps, transferred from Plevna, and by the 2nd, 3rd, and 24th Infantry Divisions, and the 3rd Rifle Brigade, of the reinforcements which had recently arrived. In addition the whole of the cavalry which had taken part in Gourko's raid was available. Thus ninety-eight battalions of infantry, with a sufficient body of cavalry and artillery, could have been put in the field against Suleyman. Russian Head Quarters had arrived at an approximately correct estimate of Suleyman's strength, which was placed at fifty battalions. At this period of the campaign the Russian battalions were about half as strong again as the Turkish. The Russians would therefore have had a reasonable chance of defeating Suleyman in the field even if he were considerably reinforced from Constantinople. If detachments were moved from the army of the Quadrilateral to Varna and thence by sea to Burghas, with the object of threatening the flank of the Russian advance, corresponding detachments could be moved even more rapidly from the XIth Corps, and could check this movement by in turn threatening the Turkish flank from the Balkans. There were certainly risks in such a plan, but they were not greater than would have been accepted by a determined leader. The trying period through which the Russian armies had passed had, however, made the Grand Duke Nicholas unwilling to run any risks which might be avoided.

It may be thought that to advocate an advance upon Adrianople is to run counter to the principles of strategy which were discussed when dealing with the original Russian plan of campaign. It was then said that it was not sound strategy to rely upon the effect of a sudden dash through the Balkans before the enemy's main army had been met and defeated. The two cases are, however, very different. Sistova is some fourteen marches from Adrianople, and between these two towns lies a difficult range of mountains. It was possible for either of the Turkish armies north of the Balkans seriously to endanger the Russian communications by a successful advance before the Russians could menace the Turkish capital to a corresponding degree. Shipka is not more than seven marches distant from Adrianople, and a blow at that place could not fail to cause the most lively alarm at Constantinople. The Russian communications could be sufficiently protected by the army of Rustchuk on the one flank, and the Western army on the other, the Roumanians taking the place of the IXth Corps. In this instance, though nominally the main Turkish army was that under the command of Mehmet Ali, strategically the main army was that covering the place of most vital importance to the Turks, Constantinople.

On September 1 the Western army consisted of the 16th Infantry Division less the 64th regiment with Skobelov, the 30th Infantry Division less one battalion of the 118th regiment with Skobelov, the 16th Artillery Brigade, less one battery with Skobelov, the 30th Artillery Brigade, three regiments and two Horse Artillery batteries of the 4th Cavalry Division. The above formed the IVth Corps. Of the IXth Corps there were the 5th Infantry Division less the 19th regiment, which still garrisoned Nikopoli, the 31st Infantry Division, the 5th Artillery Brigade, the 31st Artillery Brigade less one battery, two regiments of the 9th Cavalry Division, and the 34th Don Cosssacks. The army thus consisted of 42 battalions, 16 squadrons, 12 sotnias, and 188 guns, a total of about 40,000 men. The IXth Corps was about Trestenik-turski[1] and Kar-aagac-bolgarski, the IVth Corps about Poradim and Pelisat, the cavalry holding the line Bresljanica-Bogot.

Sotov had occupied himself since he took over command in making preparations for another attack upon Plevna, and in strengthening the positions held by his army with a view to meeting any advance on the part of the Turks,

[1] *See* Map II.

which they might undertake before the arrival of the Russian reinforcements made it possible to resume the offensive. Fascines, gabions, and scaling-ladders were constructed, the troops were exercised in escalading whenever possible, and artillery positions to the south and east of the town were carefully reconnoitred.

Meantime the reinforcements meant for the Western army were on the move. Of the four Divisions of the Roumanian field army three, the 2nd, 3rd, and 4th, were to join the Russians before Plevna, the 1st Division remaining on the Roumanian bank of the Danube in the neighbourhood of Kalifat,[1] to watch the Turks on the eastern frontier of Servia. The 4th Roumanian Division had begun to cross the Danube as early as August 17th, and was garrisoning Nikopoli and protecting the Russian communications between that place and Plevna. On August 25th the 2nd and 3rd Roumanian Divisions began a bridge over the Danube at Karabia,[2] which was completed on the 31st. The 3rd Division had all crossed on the 29th, and on the 30th had moved to Bres, at Sotov's request, with the object of preventing Osman moving on Nikopoli by the left bank of the Vid. Meanwhile on the 29th Prince Charles of Roumania had received orders from Russian Head Quarters to march as soon as possible with the 2nd and 3rd Divisions, cross the Vid, effect a junction with the 4th Roumanian Division, and join the right flank of the Western army, when he was to take command of the troops before Plevna, with Sotov as his Chief of the Staff. The 2nd Roumanian Division had crossed the Danube by 8 p.m. on September 3rd, and marching by night over difficult and sandy

---

[1] *See* Map I. [2] *See* Map II.

THE THIRD BATTLE OF PLEVNA

tracks, by Gigen, joined the 3rd division at Bres. The two divisions reached Golenci on the Vid at 8 a.m. on the 2nd, where they halted. On the 3rd the 2nd, 3rd, and 4th Divisions united at Muselimselo on the Osma. At 5 p.m. on the 4th the march was resumed by Debrova, Mecka, to Kojulovce. The column halted here on the 6th, when orders were received to move to Trestenikturski. Though the distance was only three and a half miles the column lost its way in the dark, and did not reach its destination till 3 a.m. on the 7th, when the 3rd Division took up a position on the extreme right of the Western Army, the 4th Division connecting it with the IXth Corps, while the 2nd Division formed the reserve to the Roumanian contingent in rear of the other two. This march of the Roumanian contingent must be considered a very risky operation. Osman Pasha could hardly have failed to be aware that the Roumanian troops had crossed the Danube, and it was highly imprudent to engage in night marches in a difficult country without any flank guard. The correct course would appear to have been to move the 4th Division to a defensive position somewhere in the neighbourhood of Bresljanica, and to march the 2nd and 3rd Divisions behind it to their rendezvous. Osman's preoccupation with Lovcha saved the march of the Roumanians from interruption, but the fact that he would engage in a tardy and futile attempt to save the garrison of that place could not have been known at the time the Roumanians began their march.

Next to the Roumanian contingent the most important reinforcement destined for the army before Plevna consisted of Prince Imeretinski's column which had captured Lovcha. Osman's relieving column having withdrawn, Imeretinski began his march to Plevna on September 6. He left the 11th and 12th regiments of the 2nd Brigade of the 3rd Infantry Division, two batteries, and three sotnias of Cossacks to garrison Lovcha, one battalion of the 12th regiment being detached to hold Selvi, and cover the communications with Tirnova. The column reached Bogot on the night of the 5th without incident, and on the 6th the 64th infantry regiment, the 1st battalion of the 118th regiment, and two batteries of the 16th Artillery Brigade, rejoined the IVth Corps. The remainder of the force, consisting of the 2nd Infantry Division, the 3rd Rifle Brigade, the Caucasian Cossack Brigade (less one sotnia at Lovcha), and nine batteries, a total of sixteen battalions, eleven sotnias, and eighty-two guns, took up a position under the command of Imeretinski behind the left wing of the Western army, near Tucenitsa.

On September 3rd the 9th Dragoons, 9th Hussars, 8th Dragoons and two Horse Artillery batteries, which had formed part of Gourko's column, and which had been resting at Novinikup since August 6, joined the Western army. Seven sotnias and a Horse Artillery battery of Tschernosubov's Don Cossack Brigade (21st and 26th Don Cossacks), the 9th infantry regiment, and 1 battery of the 3rd Artillery Brigade (both of the 3rd Infantry Division) also joined on this day.[1] On the 4th a siege park of twenty guns came up from Giurgevo. These reinforcements brought the strength of the

[1] The 9th Infantry regiment and the battery did not actually join the army before Plevna. They were halted at Bulgureni by Sotov's order to guard the communications.

Western army up to 107 battalions, 61 squadrons, 30 sotnias, and 444 guns, or about 100,000 men.

Osman had employed much of his time since the second battle of Plevna in bringing up reinforcements, and stores of all kinds. On September 6th his army consisted of 45 battalions of infantry, 11 squadrons of cavalry, 70 field-guns, and some 300 Circassian Cavalry. These were formed into three Divisions, each of twelve battalions, and a general reserve of nine battalions. The works in existence at the time of the third battle are shown on the plan of Plevna.[1] North of the Grivitsa brook they were substantially the same as those that existed at the second battle, though they had been much improved and strengthened. In the southern and south-eastern sections, which had been shown in the battle of July 30th to be the weakest part of the line of defence, it will be noticed that a number of new works had been thrown up, particularly in the neighbourhood of the Green Hills—a tribute to the success of Skobelov's attack during the second battle. Immediately on his return from Lovcha Osman was informed of the arrival of Russian reinforcements, and of the evident intention of the enemy to attack shortly. He disposed of his troops as follows :—Adil Pasha's Division held the northern section, north of the Grivitsa, two battalions and six guns occupying the works about Opanetz ; seven battalions and nine guns held the Janik Bair ; two battalions and two guns the advance work at point 3 ; the Grivitsa No. I. Redoubt (8) was held by one battalion and two guns, Grivitsa No. 2 Redoubt (7) by two battalions and four guns (fourteen battalions, twenty

[1] See Map III.

three guns); Adil Pasha's Division being reinforced by two battalions from the general reserve to strengthen the garrisons of the Grivitsa redoubts. Adil Pasha had his headquarters at point **5**, which was in signalling communication with Osman's headquarters at point **9**, the Grivitsa No. 2 Redoubt was in telegraphic communication with the latter. On the south-east Atouf Pasha, who had established his headquarters in the work which bore his name (**11**), held the line from point **13** through **14**, **15**, **11**, to **16**, and also the redoubt called the Arab Redoubt (**12**) (twelve battalions and eighteen guns). Three battalions and four guns under Tahir Pasha held the works between point **16** and the valley of the Toultchenitza. The works at points **18** and **19**, which subsequently became famous as the Skobelov redoubts, were also under Tahir's command, and were actually occupied by two battalions and two guns under Riza Bey. Junous Bey was in charge of the works at points **20**, **21**, **22** and **23**, which were held by five battalions and five guns. In the south-eastern section a second line of defence was formed by the works at points **10** and **33**, which was held by the reserve under Rifaat Pasha (seven battalions and fourteen guns). One battalion and one gun held the works at point **32** commanding the bridge over the Vid.

Sotov's plan of operations was to make his main attack upon the south-eastern and southern sections of the Turkish defences. This attack was to be covered by a prolonged bombardment from artillery positions which he had selected south and north-east of the village of Radischevo. The infantry were to advance under cover of darkness and seize the artillery positions referred to, and cover them by a line of lightly held posts which were

THE THIRD BATTLE OF PLEVNA

to be entrenched. It was proposed that the bombardment should last several days, that under cover of it the infantry should gradually work their way nearer to the Turkish defences, and that a general assault should take place when the latter had been seriously damaged and their occupants shaken by artillery fire. With this intention the following preliminary dispositions were ordered on the evening of September 6th. The IXth Corps under General Krudener (less its cavalry, the 20th infantry regiment, and two batteries of the 31st Artillery Brigade), were to move to a line extending from a point about one and a half miles east of the village of Grivitsa, on the Plevna-Rustchuk road, to the Plevna-Pelisat road. Krudener's command thus consisted of eighteen battalions and nine batteries (seventy-two guns). The IVth Corps under General Krylov, formerly commander of the IVth Cavalry division, who had succeeded Sotov, was to move to the high ground just south-east of the village of Radischevo. The 119th and 120th infantry regiments and 2 batteries of the 30th Artillery Brigade were detached from this Corps, which consisted of eighteen battalions and ten batteries (eighty guns). Imeretinski's detachment of sixteen battalions and ten batteries (seventy-six guns) was ordered to Tucenitsa.[1] The 4th and 3rd Roumanian Divisions, in that order from left to right, were ordered to extend the left of the IXth Corps north of the Rustchuk road, the 2nd Roumanian Division being in reserve behind the other two on the Bresljanica road. The 9th Cavalry Division (twelve squadrons, six sotnias, and twelve guns), under

[1] *See* Map II.

General Lockarev, was ordered to cover the right flank of the IXth Corps and maintain connection with the 4th Roumanian Division. The 1st Brigade of the 4th Cavalry Division (eight squadrons, six guns), under General Leontiev, was ordered to cover the left of the IVth Corps and keep touch with Imeretinski's detachment. The Caucasian Cossack Brigade and the Don Cossack Brigade (eighteen sotnias and twelve guns) were ordered to cover the extreme left flank on the Lovcha road. The cavalry of the 4th Roumanian Division was ordered to Verbitsa to cover the extreme right flank. The 9th infantry regiment and one battery, both of the 3rd Infantry Division, were ordered to hold the bridge over the Osma at Bulgureni. The general reserve consisted of the 20th, 119th and 120th infantry regiments, the 4th Hussars, the 9th Hussars, and five batteries of artillery, in all nine battalions, eight squadrons and thirty-eight guns, and was to take post just west of the village of Pelisat; the siege park of twenty guns was to follow the IXth Corps and occupy a position behind it.

These movements were carried out as ordered, with the exception that the 2nd and 3rd Roumanian Divisions were late at their rendezvous, as has been explained. During the night of the 6th-7th the whole advanced, covered by skirmishers, to within gunshot of the Turkish works.[1] The construction of epaulments on the artillery positions previously selected was at once begun, and trenches were thrown up in front of them for the infantry charged with the protection of the guns. At dawn on the 7th the advanced Russian and Rouma-

[1] *See* Map III.

nian infantry were holding a line from a point about one and a half miles north of the village of Grivitsa on the Verbitsa road, through the villages of Grivitsa and Radischevo, to the Toultchenitza brook. Three batteries of the 4th Roumanian Division had taken up a position on the high ground about 2,500 yards north-east of the Grivitsa redoubts. Three 9-pounder batteries of the 31st Division came into action on the slopes in the angle between the Grivitsa-Rustchuk and Grivitsa-Sgalevica roads. One of the siege batteries, consisting of eight 24-pounder guns, took up a position behind and above the latter; three 9-pounder batteries of the 5th Division came into action on the ridge (E) running due south from the village of Grivitsa. The remaining battery of the siege artillery, consisting of four long-range steel guns and eight 24-pounders, opened fire from the ridge just east of the junction of the Plevna-Pelisat and Grivitsa-Pelisat roads. Three 9-pounder batteries of the 30th Division came into action east-north-east of Radischevo (G), and three batteries of the 16th Division on the slopes above, and to the south of that village (H). The siege artillery gave the signal for the opening of the bombardment. It began at daylight and lasted until dark, without intermission and without noteworthy incident. In the course of the morning one battery of the 3rd Roumanian Division arrived, and extended the right of the line of guns of the 4th Roumanian Division. During this day the fire of some fifty guns was concentrated against the Grivitsa No. 1 Redoubt (8), thirty against the Ibrahim Redoubt (14), and twenty against the Atouf Redoubt (11). Tschernosubov's Cossacks had a skirmish with Circassian Cavalry on the extreme left flank and drove them from the village of Brestovetz back to the heights about Krischin, but withdrew at night to a bivouac near the village of Bogot. About midday, when it became evident that the 4th Roumanian Division and the IXth Corps could keep touch without the assistance of the cavalry, Lockarev's Brigade was ordered to Ribino to join the eleven squadrons of Roumanian cavalry covering the right flank. Lockarev was directed to cross the Vid on the 8th, and to seize the village of Dolna-Dubniak, in order to cut the enemy's communications with Sofia. Lockarev reached Ribino at 8 p.m. on the 7th; towards evening Prince Charles and Sotov decided to continue the bombardment the next day. Orders were sent to Imeretinski to move down to the Lovcha-Plevna road and to seize the ridge east of Krischin (*J*). The Turks throughout the 7th kept up an intermittent fire in reply to the Russian guns, but no movements of any importance took place within the line of works. During the night the Russian artillery fired at intervals, with the object of preventing the Turks from making good the damage done during the day; but in this they were entirely unsuccessful, for at daylight on the 8th it was discovered that not only was any damage that had been done repaired, but that many of the works had been considerably improved.

The bombardment was resumed at 5 a.m. on the 8th, and again it was continued until dusk. The number of Russian guns in action was gradually increased throughout the day by the addition of the 4-pounder batteries, and by the arrival of more Roumanian artillery. Two other batteries of the 3rd Roumanian

THE THIRD BATTLE OF PLEVNA 209

Division had arrived during the night of the 7th-8th, and were joined at daybreak by three more batteries of the 4th Division. Fifty-four guns were thus in action on the ridge north-east of the village of Grivitsa. The 9-pounder batteries of the 5th division, IXth Corps, reinforced by some of its 4-pounder batteries, in the course of the day advanced nearer the Turkish defences, and took up positions on the ridge (*F*) south of Grivitsa village, alongside the batteries of the 5th division. The 9-pounder batteries of the IVth Corps were also reinforced by some of its 4-pounder batteries. In all 226 Russian guns were in action this day.

Imeretinski's detachment, which had been strengthened by the addition of Tschernosubov's Cossack Brigade, and thus numbered eighteen sotnias, sixteen battalions and eighty-eight guns, started at daybreak on the 8th from the village of Tucenitsa.[1] Imeretinski divided his command into two parts. The advanced detachment under Skobelov consisted of the 5th and 8th infantry regiments, the 9th and 10th Rifle battalions, three sotnias of Don Cossacks, and thirty-six guns. The remainder of the infantry, one sotnia, and forty guns followed under command of General Dobrovolski. The Caucasian Cossack Brigade, the rest of the Don Cossack Brigade, and two batteries (fourteen sotnias and twelve guns) were under the command of Tschernosubov.

The Cossacks advanced and drove the Circassians from Brestovetz[2] and the ridge *I*, Skobelov following in support occupied the village of Brestovetz and the ridge *M*, threw out outposts and halted. Tschernosubov

[1] *See* Map II.   [2] *See* Map III.

was directed to cover the left flank, and extended a chain of posts down to the Vid. While these operations were in progress epaulments were thrown up on ridge M and were occupied by twenty guns which opened fire against the Turks on the ridge east of the village of Krischin (J). Imeretinski's object was to secure this ridge, but as it was not desired to push the attack further this day he decided to wait till the afternoon before advancing. He considered that the approach of darkness would prevent the Turks from attempting to recapture the position, and that his troops could more easily entrench themselves under cover of night. Accordingly Skobelov did not receive his orders to advance until 3 p.m. At that hour the 5th infantry regiment moved to the attack of the ridge J, its flanks covered by the Cossacks. The Turks had only lightly occupied this ridge and their infantry had suffered considerably from the bombardment of the Russian guns at M. The 5th regiment captured the ridge soon after 4 o'clock without great difficulty. They then came under infantry and artillery fire from point **23**, and artillery fire from the works **18** and **19**. In spite of the fact that ridge J was the objective of the attack, the 5th regiment having secured it, made no attempt to entrench themselves; this was probably because the defective method of carrying entrenching tools in the Russian regiments made it very difficult to get them to the firing line when required. The 5th regiment suffered severely in its exposed position. Thinking it better to advance than to remain where they were, they engaged in a premature attack on the works **18** and **19**. They succeeded in getting as far as the brook below these redoubts, but here they were attacked in front by Turkish infantry and taken in flank by fire from works 20 and 21. The regiment lost all order and was driven back in confusion, a remnant only being rallied by Skobelov himself, who hurried up part of the 8th regiment to ridge *J* in its support. Here he maintained himself till dark, but hearing during the night from Imeretinski that it had been decided not to make any general attack on the 9th but to continue the bombardment, he retired to the ridge *I*, where he entrenched himself. The Russians had gained nothing by this premature attack, which cost them over 900 killed and wounded. The primary cause of the failure appears undoubtedly to have been the neglect to make proper provision for entrenching the ridge east of Krischin as soon as it was captured.

On the right flank Lockarev, whose force with the addition of the Roumanian cavalry consisted of twenty-eight squadrons, six sotnias, and eighteen guns, succeeded in occupying Dolna-Dubniak after a slight skirmish with Turkish cavalry. During the night the Russian guns again fired at intervals, but again at daybreak the Turks were found to have made good any damage caused by the bombardment.

Prince Charles having decided to resume the bombardment on the 9th, the Russian guns opened fire at daybreak and continued with little alteration all through the day.

On the morning of the 9th Skobelov was holding the ridge *I* from the Toultchenitza river to the village of Brestovetz, his flanks covered by Cossacks pushed somewhat in advance. The number of guns on the ridge *M* had been increased to twenty-eight and were protected by the 9th Rifle battalion. The 10th Rifle battalion and the 7th regiment, which had relieved the 5th, formed Skobelov's immediate reserve behind his right wing. Dobrovolski's detachment, with the 5th regiment in place of the 7th, formed the general reserve behind the ridge M. In the morning the ridge J was seen to be occupied by Turkish infantry. This was a part of Junous Bey's command from works **21, 22** and **23**. They advanced and drove the Cossack outposts into the outskirts of Brestovetz; but on the Cossacks being supported by Skobelov's infantry the Turks retired on Krischin. Junous Bey had reported to Osman the presence of a considerable body of infantry behind Brestovetz. The latter thereupon sent Emin Pasha with three battalions to reinforce this section of the defence. Emin advanced to the valley between the ridges J and I, but did not press his attack, and, as Skobelov was anxious to avoid again committing himself prematurely, no very serious engagement took place. Emin finding his men exposed to the Russian artillery fire withdrew in the afternoon to the northern slopes of ridge J and took up a position with his right on redoubt **23**. Towards evening he was reinforced by two battalions, and during the night by three others. With these eight battalions he bivouacked between points L and K, covered by a line of outposts. In the evening Sotov sent the 1st Brigade of the 16th Division to support Imeretinski. They bivouacked on the Toultchenitza behind Skobelov's right. Lockarev occupied himself on the 9th in sending patrols to all the villages in his vicinity on the left bank of the Vid, but beyond a few skirmishes with Bashi-Bazouks nothing happened on this side.

THE THIRD BATTLE OF PLEVNA 213

Emin Pasha had been ordered by Osman to seize and hold the ridge *I*. He accordingly advanced towards it at daylight on the 10th, but finding that it was occupied in force he reported to Osman that the position was too advanced to be held permanently, and he contented himself with occupying the ridge *J* with a line of skirmishers and holding six battalions in reserve on the spurs *L* and *K*. During the night of the 9th–10th Imeretinski had received orders from Sotov that these spurs were to be seized next day. Skobelov therefore advanced to the attack about midday. Supported by the 1st Brigade of the 16th Division, and covered by artillery fire from the ridge *M*, and by three batteries which Skobelov had sent to the western end of the ridge *G* in front of Radischevo, his infantry had little difficulty in driving Emin's skirmishers back from the ridge *J*. Skobelov now saw that spurs *L* and *K* were held in considerable force, and that even if he succeeded in driving the Turks from them his troops would be under effective fire from the semi-circle of Turkish works to the south of Plevna. He wisely concluded that any attempt to capture these spurs on the 10th would bring on a premature engagement similar to that of the 8th. He therefore determined to make no further advance but to entrench himself on ridge *J*. This he succeeded in doing, the Turks attempting no further attack.

Elsewhere the bombardment continued as before. There were 228 guns in action on the 10th, exclusive of the two horse-artillery batteries with Lockarev. The Russian artillery had, however, begun to feel the strain of the prolonged bombardment. Ammunition began to run short, and certain of the batteries, particularly those in the neighbourhood of Radischevo, experienced great difficulty in getting up fresh supplies. A number of guns, especially in the 4-pounder batteries, which had been firing at distances beyond their range, were damaged, and had to be taken out of action. In two or three cases fires were seen to break out in the Turkish works, and magazines were blown up, but with these exceptions the amount of damage done was not great and was always repaired without difficulty. During the day Prince Charles and Sotov decided that the assault should take place on the 11th. The Czar and the Grand Duke Nicholas with their suites arrived to witness the attack, but they did not interfere in any way with the commander of the Western Army, who on the evening of the 10th issued the following orders.

" The fortifications of Plevna will be stormed to-morrow, September 11—

1. All batteries will at daybreak open fire on the Turkish works, and keep up the hottest fire possible until 8 a.m. At 9 a.m. the batteries will cease fire simultaneously. At 11 a hot fire will be resumed, and continued till 1 p.m. Batteries will cease fire from 1 till 2.30, and at 2.30 it will be renewed and only discontinued by those batteries whose fire is masked by the attack.

2. The attack will begin at 3 p.m.

(a) The Roumanian Army will attack the northern works. One infantry brigade of the IVth Corps with two 4-pounder batteries will support this attack and cover the left flank of the Roumanian Army. Two battalions of this brigade will attack the northern works from the south-west simultaneously with the Roumanians.

(b) Two regiments of the IXth Corps will cover the batteries on the ridge between Grivitsa and Radischevo. Two regiments with three 4-pounder batteries will form the reserve and be posted in front of Radischevo on the right bank of the stream.

(c) The 9th regiment 3rd Infantry Division with the battery attached to it will be posted on the left wing of the twelve gun siege battery.

(d) The G. O. C. of the IVth Corps will attack the works in front of the batteries on his left with the 2nd Brigade of the 16th Division, supported by the 1st Brigade of the 30th Division. The general reserve of three infantry regiments and three batteries will follow this column.

(e) The G. O. C. Western Army will be with the general reserve.

(f) General Skobelov's detachment, consisting of the 1st Brigade of the 16th Division, the 3rd Rifle Brigade, and one regiment of the 2nd Infantry Division with one 9-pounder and one 4-pounder battery will attack the works covering Plevna near the Lovcha road.

(g) The remainder of the 2nd Infantry Division under the command of Major-General Imeretinski will support General Skobelov's attack and cover his left flank.

(h) The 1st Brigade of the 4th Cavalry Division, with the Horse Artillery battery and the Don Cossack and Caucasian regiments attached to it, will cover the left flank of the army, and advance towards the Sofia road, in the direction of Dolna-Dubniak, where it will gain touch with General Lockarev's Cavalry.

(i) General Lockarev's cavalry will act energetically

against any Turkish troops on the left bank of the Vid, and will get touch with the 1st Brigade of 4th Cavalry Division.

(*k*) The Roumanian Cavalry Brigade under Col. Rasnovan will cover the right flank of the Roumanian Army. The 4th Hussars will remain on the Plevna-Rustchuk road, and maintain touch between the IXth Corps and the Roumanian Army. The 8th Hussars with one Horse Artillery battery will join the general reserve.

(*l*) Instructions as to dress, transport, dressing-stations, field-hospitals, and rations, already issued will hold good. The dressing-stations for the troops on the Lovcha road will be arranged for by Major-General Imeretinski. The field-hospital of the 16th Infantry Division is placed at his disposal. Any further orders will be issued on the battlefield. Each Corps will send three mounted officers to Head Quarters."

In explanation of these orders it may be mentioned that the northern works referred to in 2 (*a*) were the Grivitsa redoubts, and that the works opposite the IVth Corps referred to in 2 (*d*) were the Omar Bey redoubt (**16**). The disposition of the Western Army in accordance with these orders was as follows. Eight Roumanian squadrons covered the extreme right flank. Three Roumanian divisions, one brigade of the 5th Russian Division, and two batteries (forty-eight battalions and sixteen guns), were to attack the Grivitsa Redoubts. The 4th Hussars (four squadrons) were to connect this attack with the IXth Corps. Of the remainder of the IXth Corps two regiments of the 31st Infantry Division were to cover the artillery in position on ridge *F*, and two regiments of the 31st Infantry Division and three batteries formed the Corps Reserve; total twelve battalions and twenty-four guns. Of the IVth Corps, the 2nd Brigade of the 16th Infantry Division and the 1st Brigade of the 30th Infantry Division (twelve battalions) were to attack the Omar Bey redoubt (**16**). The 1st Brigade of the 16th Infantry Division, the 2nd Infantry Division, and the 3rd Rifle Brigade (a total of twenty-two battalions), were to attack the works at **18** and **19**. The 2nd Brigade of the 30th Division and one regiment of the 5th Division, the 4th Hussars, and three batteries formed the general reserve (nine battalions, four squadrons and twenty-two guns). Eight squadrons, eighteen sotnias, and eighteen guns covered the left flank; twenty-eight squadrons, six sotnias, and eighteen guns operated against the enemy's communications. One regiment of the 3rd Infantry Division and one battery were brought up from Bulgureni,[1] and covered the Russian line of retreat through Sgalevica. The artillery employed in the bombardment remained in the positions already described.

It had become evident to Osman that a general attack could not be long delayed, but beyond relieving the troops, which had been most tried by fresh battalions, and strengthening the southern section by the reinforcements sent to Emin Pasha, he made no great change in the dispositions already recorded.

Up till the 10th the weather had been bright and pleasant, but on that day the sky clouded over and rain fell at intervals; it poured throughout the night of the 10th–11th. The ground became so soft as to make the movement of troops difficult in many places, and dawn

[1] *See* **Map II.**

of the 11th found the whole battlefield shrouded in a dense mist.

During the night of the 10th–11th Osman had sent three more battalions, which he had withdrawn from the northern section to reinforce Emin Pasha, so that on the morning of the 11th eleven battalions were holding the northern slopes of the Green Hills.[1] One battalion had been also sent to reinforce the garrisons of the redoubts **18** and **19**. This brought the garrisons of the works in the southern section on the 11th up to eight battalions and eight guns. Osman Pasha was at first anxious that Emin should assume the offensive and drive the Russians from ridge *J*. It is not easy to understand why Osman had not included the ridge *J* in his line of defence. Two redoubts on this hill would have served to connect the centre and southern sections of the defence. As it was, eleven of the nineteen battalions allotted to the southern section had to fight in the open. Emin Pasha used the three battalions sent him to prolong his left, and occupied a line extending from the Lovcha-Plevna road along the spurs *K* and *L* to the redoubts north of Krischin.

The battle of the 11th may be divided into three parts : the attack on the southern section, the attack on the central section, and the attack on the northern section of the Turkish defences. As in point of time the attacks were delivered in the order named, it is convenient to deal with them in that sequence.

Attack on the Southern Section For the attack upon the nineteen Turkish battalions and eleven guns which were holding this section Skobelov had thirteen battalions and twenty-four guns, namely the 61st and 62nd

[1] *See* **Map III.**

regiments of the 16th Infantry Division, the 9th, 10th, 11th, and 12th Rifle battalions and the 7th regiment of the 2nd Infantry Division. To support his attack Imeretinski had nine battalions and sixty guns, while Leontiev's brigade which was to co-operate consisted of eight squadrons, eight sotnias and eighteen guns. At daybreak Skobelov's artillery opened fire from ridge J against the Junous Bey redoubt 23 and the works at 18 and 19. Skobelov collected his infantry upon and in rear of ridge J. The objective allotted to him in the general assault was the works 18 and 19, and he decided that if he was to attack those works at 3 p.m., he must before that hour be in possession of the spur K. Accordingly he ordered the 61st regiment and the 10th Rifle battalion to advance at 10 a.m., seize this spur, entrench themselves upon it, and hold it until 3 p.m. The country between the ridges K and J was covered with vineyards, and in this part of the field it was difficult at any time for infantry to see far. On the morning of the 11th the denseness of the mist, added to the close nature of the country, made it hard to see more than a few yards. The 61st regiment succeeded in passing the three Turkish battalions on Emin's left in the fog and in surprising his right, which they drove back in a confusion which involved also the battalions sent to its support. The Russians thus secured the ridge K with little trouble, but in the fog the advanced companies were not aware that they had reached their objective, and pushing on, they arrived at the slopes below works 18 and 19. It was now 11 a.m. and the fog began to lift. Emin rallied his troops and began a counter-attack. At this time the whole of the 61st regiment and the 12th Rifle battalion were deployed in more or less disorder along the northern and western slopes of ridge K. Skobelov sent forward the 9th Rifle battalion to reinforce his firing line, and brought up the 62nd regiment to the southern slopes of ridge K in support. In accordance with Sotov's orders all fire was to cease at 11 a.m., but it was clearly impossible for Skobelov to leave the situation as it was at that hour. His men were exposed to fire from the Turkish infantry in their front, and to artillery and infantry fire from the works on their flank. He accordingly reinforced his artillery on ridge J with a battery, and decided to make an effort to drive the Turks definitely from the Green Hills. With this object he ordered the 62nd regiment to attack, and these troops meeting Emin's counter-attack in front and flank drove the Turks back into their works. Skobelov reformed the 61st regiment and the 9th and 10th Rifle battalions, and with them and the 62nd regiment held the vineyards until 3 p.m., though much harassed by the Turkish fire from the works on his left flank. While this had been going on Leontiev, in accordance with his orders to cover the left flank of the attack, brought his Horse Artillery into action against the Turkish redoubts **22** and **23**, and dismounting three sotnias of Cossacks he drove the Turkish outposts out of Krischin and engaged in a holding attack on the Junous Bey redoubt (**23**), keeping 4 sotnias in hand in the valley below Krischin to take in flank any attack which might issue from the Turkish works against Skobelov's left. Two sotnias covered the right flank in the Toultchenitza ravine, while the remainder of the cavalry covered the left towards the Vid.

THE THIRD BATTLE OF PLEVNA

It was now past 1 o'clock and Skobelov began his preparations for the assault. He disposed the 9th and 10th Rifle battalions on his right, the 61st on his centre, and the 62nd on his left, all in the first line. In second line, behind ridge K, were posted the 7th regiment and the 11th and 12th Rifle battalions. Thirteen guns, all that were serviceable of three batteries, were brought forward to ridge K to support the attack. Twenty-four guns of Imeretinski's detachment assisted with their fire from ridge J, behind which the remainder of the detachment was placed in reserve. At 3 p.m. Skobelov's first line advanced to the attack of redoubts **18** and **19**. They succeeded in getting within 400 yards of the Turkish works, but could get no further. Skobelov thereupon threw in his second line, which carried the attack onwards a little, but the Russians were still unable to drive the Turks from their positions. At this moment Emin Pasha in attempting a counter-attack was wounded, and owing to some confusion in orders the Turkish battalions in the open began to retire. Skobelov at once himself went forward to the firing line and ordered the assault, which he led against the work **19**. A small party of Russians got round in rear of this work which was open in the gorge. The garrison mistaking them in the fog for a much larger body, fled. It was now about 4.30 p.m., the Russians were in great confusion and suffered much from fire from work **18**. Skobelov, however, succeeded in getting a garrison for the redoubt by 5 p.m., and hurried back to ridge K to bring up reinforcements to make good the success gained. In his absence Rifaat Pasha, who had succeeded to the command, rallied his troops and made a counter-attack against the redoubt

19. This attack, however, failed, and the Russians, following up the flying Turks, with the assistance of the fire of two batteries which Skobelov had directed against work **18**, and of parts of the 6th and 7th regiments, drove the Turks out of that work.

While this attack was going on Leontiev's cavalry and the 8th regiment were engaged in masking the Turkish redoubts **20, 21, 22,** and **23,** and they succeeded in preventing their garrisons from interfering with the Russian occupation of the captured positions except by artillery fire. At night-fall the Russians were in possession of the whole of the Green Hills, the works **18** and **19,** and had isolated the redoubts north of Krischin from the rest of the Turkish defences.

The Attack on the Central Section

At 7 a.m. the Russian batteries in the centre opened fire from their former positions between the Plevna-Rustchuk and Plevna-Bogot roads. The fog greatly interfered with them and they were unable to observe their fire. At 9 a.m. the batteries ceased fire, and began again at 11 a.m. The troops of the IVth Corps, consisting of the 63rd and 64th regiments of the 2nd Brigade of the 16th Infantry Division, and the 117th and 118th regiments of the 1st Brigade of the 30th Infantry Division, were getting into position in readiness for the attack. The 63rd and 64th regiments were to attack the Omar Bey Redoubt (**16**), and the works between it and the Toultchenitza, respectively. By 11.30 a.m. these regiments were in position on the spur *G* in front of Radischevo, with the 117th and 118th regiments behind them in support. Shortly before midday, when the fog had cleared somewhat, some Turkish troops were seen to be moving near the works in front. This and the noise of Skobelov's attack on ridge K led to the supposition that the Turks were attempting an offensive movement. One battalion of the 63rd regiment was ordered forward to cover the guns on the spur G, but the reason for this movement was apparently not explained to the troops, and before they could be stopped the whole of the 63rd regiment, followed by the 117th, started a premature attack against the Omar redoubt. Neither regiment was able to get further than to within about 500 yards of the Turkish trenches. Here they remained hotly engaged for about an hour, when, having lost more than 30 per cent. of their strength, and a large proportion of officers having been hit, they retired on Radischevo, where they were rallied about 2.30 p.m.

In spite of the fact that half the force originally destined for the attack on the centre section was out of action before the hour fixed for the general assault, no effort appears to have been made to replace the 63rd and 117th regiments by fresh troops from the reserve, or from the 31st Division. At 3 p.m. the 64th regiment advanced against the trenches between the Omar redoubt and the Toultchenitza, and the 118th regiment against the Omar redoubt itself. This attack met with no better success than the preceding one, and by 4 p.m. it had been repulsed with heavy loss. No attempt was made throughout the day to move the artillery nearer to the Turkish works to support more effectually the infantry advance, nor were the regiments sent forward supported in time from the reserves. The afternoon was spent in delivering a series of isolated assaults, each fresh advance being begun after the former had failed.

About 4.30 p.m. the 123rd and 124th regiments of the 31st Division, which was covering the guns on the ridge *F*, were brought up and launched against the Turkish works. This attack also failed, and was followed by an attempt on the part of the 20th regiment from the general reserve, which also ended in failure. It was by this time after 6.30 p.m., and it was decided to do nothing further as darkness was coming on. The Turks had six battalions and six guns manning the works attacked, and late in the day these troops were reinforced by a battalion from redoubt No. **12**, so that the Turkish infantry was about equal to that of each of the successive Russian attacks. Between the Suluklia and the Grivitsa one brigade of the 31st Division was employed in containing the Turks in the Ibrahim Bey (**14**) and adjoining redoubts, but no serious attack was attempted here.

The Attack on the Northern Section The fog on the morning of the 11th affected the Russian troops in the neighbourhood of Grivitsa more than in any other part of the field. Between eighty and ninety guns in position north and south of the Rustchuk road were charged with preparing the way for the assault on the Grivitsa No. 1 redoubt (**8**). The orders regulating the hours at which the batteries were to open and cease fire appear to have been for the most part disregarded. In particular the Roumanian and Russian batteries did not co-operate, the fire was irregular and spasmodic, and comparatively ineffective. The Turks had connected the two Grivitsa redoubts by lines of shelter trenches, three lines of which had also been constructed on spur *C* in front of redoubt **8**, and also to the west of the redoubt near *D*. The two redoubts were about 200 yards apart.

Owing to the character of the ground the redoubt 7 could alone be seen from the north where the 3rd Roumanian Division was posted, while the redoubt 8 could alone be seen from the east where was the 4th Roumanian Division, and from the south-east where was the 1st Brigade of the 5th Russian Division. It was intended that these troops in three columns should attack the Grivitsa No. 2 redoubt (8) simultaneously. But while the Russian Headquarter Staff can hardly have been unaware of the fact that there were two redoubts, it did not occur to them to see that the troops had this information. In particular the 3rd Roumanian Division, which had but recently come up and since its arrival had been in the neighbourhood of Verbitsa, would naturally be ignorant that there were two works above the village of Grivitsa.

At 3 p.m. the 4th Roumanian Division advanced against the eastern face of the redoubt 8, with the 1st Brigade in two lines and the 2nd Brigade in reserve. The 1st Brigade succeeded in capturing the advanced trenches, but could get no further till reinforced by the 2nd Brigade, when the Roumanians pressing forward with great gallantry reached the ditch of the redoubt. They were, however, unable to get any further, and retired into the Turkish shelter trenches which they had captured on spur C. It was now 5 p.m. and there were no signs of either the 3rd Roumanian Division or the 1st Brigade of the Russian 5th Division. The engagement for a time came to a standstill, and profiting by the pause the Turks reinforced the garrison of the redoubt by one battalion.

The 3rd Roumanian Division assembled in the valley of the Bukova stream and advanced to the attack at

3 p.m. Here, too, one brigade formed the first two lines, the 2nd Brigade being in reserve. One regiment of the 1st Brigade advanced against redoubt **6** and the trenches west of the Grivitsa No. 2 redoubt, with the object of preventing the garrisons of the former assisting the Turks in the latter. The remaining regiment and one Rifle battalion advanced against the northern face of redoubt **7**. But the attack was not supported and was repulsed with heavy loss. The 2nd Brigade lost its way in the fog and arrived too late to be of any assistance. The 2nd Roumanian Division, which formed the general reserve in this part of the battlefield, did not take any part in either attack.

Meanwhile the 1st Brigade of the Russian 5th Division had moved forward through the village of Grivitsa at 3 p.m. and taken up a position on a spur below the Grivitsa No. **1** redoubt. The fog in the valley of the Grivitsa having lifted somewhat, the brigade came under fire both from the trenches near point D and from the redoubts **13** and **14**. General Rodionov, who commanded the brigade, seems to have considered that his orders to cover the left flank of the Roumanians necessitated his keeping his whole brigade in observation of these works. He therefore took no part in the first attack on the Grivitsa No. 1 redoubt. He did not gain touch with the 3rd Roumanian Division until after 5 p.m. when the latter had already been repulsed. At 5.30 p.m. he determined to assault the redoubt, the 17th regiment advancing directly against the southern face, two battalions of the 18th against the western face, while the remaining battalion kept the Turks in the trenches at D occupied. The troops of the 3rd Roumanian Division on seeing Rodionov's advance charged out from the trenches they had captured against the eastern face of the redoubt. This simultaneous attack was successful, and after a sharp struggle Russians and Roumanians together poured over the parapet and either bayonetted the defenders or drove them from the work, which was in undisputed possession of the Russians by 6.30 p.m. At 7 p.m. General Schildner-Schuldner, the commander of the 5th Russian Division, arrived and took over command from Rodionov, who had been wounded. Osman was at this time entirely occupied with the difficult situation in which he was placed by the loss of redoubts **18** and **19**, and as the loss of the Grivitsa No.1 redoubt was of minor importance so long as the Grivitsa No. 2 redoubt remained in his hands, no reinforcements were sent to this part of the defence and no attempt to recapture the lost work was made.

Prince Charles's orders had not placed the troops allotted to the attack on the northern section under one command, an omission which had serious consequences. There was no proper co-operation between the artillery and the infantry and between the various columns of attack. The general reserve was hardly employed at all, and the reserve of the 3rd Roumanian Division was wasted. Had the attacks been simultaneous, and the reserves been put into the fight at the proper moment, there is little doubt but that both the Grivitsa works would have fallen into the hands of the Russians; for Osman had been compelled to withdraw every man who could be spared from the northern section to meet the pressure to the south of Plevna, and four Turkish battalions and six guns had to meet the attacks of thirty-one Russian and Roumanian battalions supported by the fire of eighty guns.

In the day's fighting the losses were as follows. In the northern section the Roumanians lost 58 officers and 2,511 men killed and wounded, the Russians 19 officers and 1,019 men. In the centre the losses amounted to 115 officers, 4,319 men; in the southern section 97 officers and about 3,800 men, though as the action here did not cease on the 11th, the exact number that fell on that day could not be determined. As the net result of these losses the Russians had possession of the Grivitsa No. 1 redoubt, which was of comparatively little value as it was commanded by the Grivitsa No. 2 redoubt, and also of the redoubts 18 and 19. The latter success was of real importance; the works were on the outskirts of the town of Plevna, and while they were in Russian hands any direct communication between the southern section of the defences and the other Turkish positions was impossible. Osman therefore decided to make a great effort to drive the Russians back from these works.

Junous Bey had five battalions more or less intact in and about works 21, 22 and 23, while Riza Bey had rallied the remnants of some eight battalions, all that was left of Emin's command, in the neighbourhood of redoubt 20. Mehmet Nasif Bey held spur *C* between the work 18 and the Toultchenitza with three weak battalions and some refugees from the garrisons of the works 18 and 19. The artillery ammunition in all the works to the north of Krischin was almost exhausted, and there was no immediate prospect of getting more while the Russians commanded the communications between these redoubts and Plevna. During the night Mehmet Nasif's battalions were withdrawn, and joined the reserve at point 9, where they were supplied with food and ammunition. Five

THE THIRD BATTLE OF PLEVNA

fresh battalions were moved up the valley of the Keremetchi to the neighbourhood of work 20, where they arrived at daybreak.

Skobelov and Imeretinski were no less busy than the Turks during the night, and made every possible effort to secure their troops in the positions they had gained. That some organization was required may be gathered from the fact that the two captured redoubts and the trenches adjoining them were manned by detachments from the 61st, 62nd, 6th, 7th and 8th infantry regiments, and from the 9th, 10th, 11th and 12th Rifle battalions. During the night the gorge of redoubt 19 was closed by a rough trench and a breastwork of stones. Water and ammunition were brought up to the troops, and two guns were dragged into redoubt 19. On spur K Skobelov succeeded in collecting about 1,000 men, stragglers from almost every battalion which had been engaged, and after getting them into some sort of order, he disposed them on spurs L and K, to meet in flank any attack from the redoubt 20 against the captured works. Imeretinski had posted three battalions (5th regiment) and four batteries on ridge J and in the village of Krischin to cover Skobelov's rear. During the night three and a half sotnias of dismounted Cossacks were sent by Imeretinski to reinforce Skobelov on ridge K. The remainder of the cavalry bivouacked at Brestovetz. At daybreak on the 12th twelve guns, all that were serviceable in three batteries, were brought forward from ridge J to ridge K. This was the situation when the Turks began their efforts to recapture the redoubts.

At 7 a.m. the Turkish reinforcements which had arrived at redoubt 20 advanced against the Russians in redoubt 19 ; but the guns in the Turkish redoubts were so short of ammunition that they could give them little assistance, and being taken in flank by rifle and artillery fire from ridges L and K they were unable to get nearer than 400 yards from that work. Here they kept up a hot fire upon the garrison for about an hour, when they were compelled to withdraw. Soon after 9 o'clock a supply of artillery ammunition which Osman had sent round by the Keremetchi Valley reached redoubts 21 and 22, and their guns were able to keep up a sustained fire upon the Russians on spur L and on redoubt 19. Encouraged by this the Turks resumed the offensive at 10.30, and advancing with great gallantry they reached the trenches in front of the latter work. The Russian garrison was actually beginning to withdraw, when for some unknown reason Tahir Pasha, who commanded the attack, sounded the retire.

About this time Imeretinski and Skobelov received a message from Sotov instructing them if possible to hold on to their positions till dusk, and then to retire on Tucenitsa ; the message stated that it was not intended to resume the attack. Both generals had sent urgent requests to Headquarters for reinforcements, but this reply showed that there was very little prospect of their obtaining them. Their men were almost exhausted, but they still determined to maintain themselves in the positions they occupied. Meanwhile Osman had decided on another effort to recapture the redoubts. Tewfik Bey was given command of three battalions, which were withdrawn from works 16 and 17 as the Russians showed no signs of an offensive in that direction, the three battalions under Mehmet Nasi, and the troops in the neighbourhood of work 20 which had taken part in the previous attack. These he formed into two columns, one of which he ordered to advance from the town against the northern sides of the two captured works, and to make during its attack as much noise and as great a show of force as possible; the other was collected on the Namasguiah Hills and concealed among the vineyards. Soon after three o'clock the first column advanced from the town and began its attack. When this had been well developed, and had attracted the attention of the defenders, the second column rushed forward. This charge was successful and redoubt 19 was carried. Part of the garrison fled towards work 18, and the Turks following close upon them entered the redoubt at their heels, and it too, after a short and sharp struggle, was recaptured.

While this attack was in progress the 118th infantry regiment from the IVth Corps arrived on ridge J to reinforce Skobelov. The latter brought it forward to spur K, where it was able to cover the retreat of the hard-pressed garrisons of works 18 and 19. This brought the fighting to a close, both sides being too utterly exhausted to attempt anything further.

In other parts of the field little was done beyond a bombardment, particularly of Grivitsa No. 2 redoubt. The Czar, the Grand-duke Nicholas and Sotov had witnessed the failure of the centre attack, and this so impressed them that they decided that any further offensive was out of the question. They apparently also attached great importance to the capture of the Grivitsa No. 1 redoubt, and were bitterly disappointed to find that it was practically neutralized by the No. 2 redoubt.

So absorbed were they in the events in this part of the field that they took no steps to confirm the really important success gained by Skobelov; had the latter been energetically supported early on the 12th by parts of the IVth and IXth Corps it can hardly be doubted but that a permanent foothold in Osman's line of defence would have been gained.

On the 13th and 14th the Russians were gradually withdrawn, Imeretinski's command moving back to Bogot[1] on the left, while the line was continued thence through Pelisat, Sgalevica, Verbitsa, to Ribino on the Vid, the Grivitsa No. 1 redoubt and the heights above Radischevo being held as advanced posts. Beyond a desultory bombardment and some fighting in the neighbourhood of the Grivitsa redoubts, active operations ceased.

The failure of the Russian attack was primarily due to the want of control of the operations by Prince Charles and Sotov. As in the previous attacks on Plevna, this want of control was due to the reserve being too small. The general reserve should be strong, rarely less than a quarter of the force. The Russian reserve at the third battle of Plevna was less than a tenth of the whole force. The position allotted to it was very remarkable; it was directed to follow the weakest of the three attacks and that which was destined to assault the strongest part of the enemy's line. Judging from the distribution of the troops the main attack was apparently intended to be that against the Grivitsa redoubts, but no arrangements were made by which Prince Charles or Sotov could exercise any directing

[1] *See* **Map II.**

influence in that part of the field. As has been pointed out no general was placed in command of all the troops engaged in the northern attack, and in consequence no less than three Roumanian brigades were wasted. Without in any way interfering with the arrangements for the attack as laid down in Sotov's order the general reserve might well have consisted of the whole of the 31st Division, one brigade of the 5th Division, and the 2nd Roumanian Division. One regiment of the 5th Division, and that of the 3rd Division which was uselessly employed in rear of the army, would have amply sufficed to cover the batteries south of the Rustchuk road. With such a force under his hand the commander of the Western Army would have been in a position to follow up effectively either the success gained by Skobelov, or that obtained in the northern section. As it was, the reserve was frittered away in endeavouring to extricate the troops employed in the centre attacks, and exercised no decisive influence on the course of the battle. Much importance was attached to the prolonged artillery bombardment; this shows a complete misconception of the purposes for which field-artillery should be used. Field guns are intended to subdue the fire of the enemy so as to enable the infantry to advance. For this it is necessary that there should be the closest co-operation between the two arms. During a bombardment, or as it is more usually called the artillery preparation for an attack, the enemy's infantry are naturally kept under cover until they are compelled to come out to meet the infantry attack; hence if the artillery preparation is to be effective the enemy must be kept in expectation of an infantry advance at any moment ; if any long interval is left between the artillery bombardment and the advance of the infantry the artillery ammunition has been merely thrown away. The most effective artillery bombardment is that which increases in intensity up to the moment of assault, and to attain this result the artillery must in the majority of cases move forward in support of the infantry. During the third battle of Plevna damage done by the artillery was not only made good in the night, but the Turkish works were actually strengthened, until on September 11 they were in a better condition to meet attack than they had been at the beginning of the battle. On the other hand the Russian artillery fire on the 11th was weaker than on any other day. This was in part due to the fog ; but even more to the fact that many batteries had run short of ammunition, and that a considerable number of guns were injured in consequence of the excessive strain which had been put upon them. It was only in the southern attack that there was any effective co-operation between the artillery and the infantry ; in no other part of the field did the batteries which had taken part in the bombardment move forward to support the infantry.

The Russian losses during the third battle from September 11 to 13 amounted to about 300 officers and 12,500 men killed and wounded ; of these 126 officers and 5,332 men, or nearly one half of the whole, belonged to Imeretinski's command. The Turkish losses amounted to about 4,000, and of these about 3,000 fell in the southern section.

Kuropatkin, vol i, parts ii, iii, and iv. *Défense de Plevna,* chapter iv. *Guerre D'Orient,* part ii, chapter xxi and xxii. Herbert, chapter x.

CHAPTER IX

EVENTS IN THE THEATRE OF WAR FROM THE THIRD BATTLE OF PLEVNA TO THE FALL OF MEHMET ALI

Mehmet Ali's Advance to the Banica Lom — Position of the Army of the Quadrilateral on September 16 — Mehmet Ali's Difficulties — Attack on Verboca — Mehmet Ali's Recall — Second Attack on the Shipka Pass — Political Situation after Third Battle of Plevna — Position of Western Army on September 18 — Appointment of Todleben — Arrival of Convoy at Plevna — Osman Proposes to Evacuate Plevna — Gourko's Operations against Osman's Communications — Completion of the Investment.

CHAPTER IX

Events in the Theatre of War from Third Battle of Plevna to the Fall of Mehmet Ali

Operations in the Quadrilateral

The Czarevitch had decided after the actions at Kaseljevo and Popkioj [1] to withdraw the army of Rustchuk to the plateau between the Banica Lom and the Jantra. This movement was quietly carried out with little interruption from the Turks. The line selected for occupation ran from the Danube near Mecka through Trestenik and Banica to Cerkovna, where the XIIIth Corps touched the left of the XIth Corps. The headquarters of the army of Rustchuk were fixed at Dol Monastir, those of the XIIth Corps were at Ablanova, those of the XIIIth Corps at Koprivca. This line was at once entrenched as the troops arrived in their positions, which they had all reached by September 15.

Mehmet Ali had halted his forces on the 8th, on the line of the Kara Lom, which he held from Stroko to Ajazlar; the army of the North, as the 1st Corps was now called, under Ahmed Eyoub, formed the right wing; the army of the South, or IInd Corps, under Prince Hassan, the left wing. Mehmet Ali established his headquarters at Sarnasuflar, where he could keep an eye

[1] *See* Map II.

on Prince Hassan, in whom he had no great confidence. After five days of inaction, Mehmet Ali, acting on the advice of Valentine Baker Pasha, an English officer who had been employed in the Gendarmerie in Turkey, and who was attached as a Major-General to the Army of the South, decided to attempt a further advance. His plan was to attack the point of junction of the XIIIth and XIth Corps, and to isolate and defeat the 32nd Division of the latter, while the army of the North made a demonstration against the Russian left and centre. With this object he issued orders to the army of the South to advance in three columns, crossing the Kara Lom at Karahasankioj, Haidarkioj, and Sultankioj, and to move by Popkioj on Kovacica and Vodica. The army of the North was ordered to march by Stroko and Ablava on Banica and to communicate with the army of the South through Jenidzesi.

This movement was begun on the afternoon of September 12th, but was delayed by bad weather. It was continued on the 13th without gaining touch with the enemy, except on the right of the army of the South, where Salik's Division drove back the Russians after a skirmish near Vodica. On the 15th Assaf Pasha, whose division formed the left of the Northern army and the centre of the whole Turkish line, advancing from Ablava by Sinankioj, came into contact with the advanced troops of the Russians holding Banica. The Russians were in force at this place, having there the greater part of the 33rd Division, a brigade of the 12th Division, and the 26th Division, which had recently come up to reinforce the army of Rustchuk. They at once proceeded to make a counter-attack. Assaf Pasha took up a defensive position on a line of hills due south of Sinankioj, and managed to hold his own until he was joined by Sabit Pasha's Division. The Russians then withdrew into their positions behind the Banica Lom. The forward movement of the Russians had, however, the effect of making Mehmet Ali give up any idea of a vigorous offensive. He drew in Sabit's Division to the army of the South and halted behind a line of outposts which extended from Osikova, through Vodica to Karatas.

Mehmet Ali's army on the 16th September occupied the following positions. On the right, Fuad's Division of the army of the North held from Stroko through Cernica, where it was in touch with the outposts of the Russian XIIth Corps, to Ostrica; Assaf's Division extended from Sinankioj to Osikova; Sabit's Division was at Jenidzesi, where Ahmed Eyoub had his head-quarters; Salik's Division occupied from Osikova to Vodica, Ismail's Division from Vodica to Karatas. Nedjib's Division remained at Kaseljevo, while Mustafa Zefi's Brigade watched the extreme right flank, extending as far as Kadikioj. Salim's detached Brigade, covering Osman Bazar, was near point 518 on the Osman Bazar-Kesarovo Road, in touch with the outposts of the Russian XIth Corps. The positions thus occupied by Mehmet Ali are a sufficient indication of his intentions. Had he had any fixed idea of making a resolute advance he would most certainly have concentrated the greater part of his army and screened his concentration by a lightly held line of outposts. Circumstances had given him the advantage of the initiative, and he was in a position to throw superior force against some one part of the Czarevitch's necessarily extended line; but to do this successfully it was essential for him to be able to manœuvre rapidly, and this was impossible with his troops scattered over such a wide front. The truth of the matter was that Mehmet Ali had completely lost heart, he despaired of loyal co-operation from his subordinates, and his attention was turned more to the intrigues, which he knew to be going on in the palaces of the Golden Horn, than to the affairs of his army. He knew that Suleyman's party was gaining the ascendency in the Sultan's Councils. Every Pasha in the army had, as a matter of necessity, some friend at Court, and they were perfectly informed of the decline of Mehmet Ali's favour with the Sultan. This encouraged them in their insubordination, and made any effective command of the army almost impossible.

The Council of War at Constantinople was by this time informed of the result of the third battle of Plevna, and the Sultan being anxious to take advantage of the embarrassment in which the Russians were placed owing to the failure of their attack, sent imperative orders to Mehmet Ali and Suleyman to assume a vigorous offensive. No attempt was, however, made to ensure that the armies under these generals should operate on any combined plan. Each was left to carry out his instructions in his own way, though by this time it must have been clear, even at Constantinople, that no co-operation could be expected from the rival commanders without the intervention of superior authority. Mehmet Ali appears by this time to have given up all hope of getting Ahmed Eyoub to act with energy. He therefore decided to advance on Draganovo with the army of the South, of which he had practically assumed the command himself. On the 17th and 18th the Russian outposts were driven over the river and Cerkovna was occupied by the Turks; the 19th was spent in reconnoitring the Russian position. This extended from the ridge north-west of Verboka to Cairkioj. The Russian cavalry held the line of the brook in front of this and prevented the Turks making any accurate reconnaissance of the main position. The slowness of Mehmet Ali's movements had, however, given the Russians ample warning of the intended attack, and they had collected portions of the 1st Division of the XIIIth Corps, and of the 26th Division and the 32nd Division of the XIth Corps, in all twelve battalions, eight squadrons, and forty guns, under the command of General Tatischev.

On the 20th Mehmet Ali assembled ten battalions of the army of the South at Cerkovna for the attack, which was delivered the next day, but, being made against a superior force entrenched in a strong position, it was foredoomed to failure, and was repulsed with a loss of 2,400 killed and wounded, the Russians losing about 500. On the 22nd and 23rd the Turks remained in position facing the Russian line, but on the 24th Mehmet Ali, suspecting from some movements of the Russian troops that the latter were about to assume the offensive, decided to fall back behind the Kara Lom. Meanwhile, on September 19, while under the conviction that he had only a small body of cavalry opposed to him at Cairkioj, and intending to make his main attack on Draganovo some days later, he had ordered Selim Pasha with a detachment of about 2,000 men, chiefly irregular cavalry, to make a demonstration towards Elena, with the object of containing the right of the Russian XIth Corps. An indecisive engagement took place on September 24th some five miles east of Elena at Maren, and the Turks subsequently fell back on Osman Bazar.

The Turkish retirement to their old positions behind the Kara Lom was carried out quietly, and their retreat was not molested by the Russians; but the failure at Cairkioj was the final blow to Mehmet Ali's prestige, and on October 2 Suleyman Pasha arrived with an order from the Sultan giving him the chief command, and directing Mehmet Ali to return to Constantinople.

Valentine Baker, chapter vi. to xiii. *Guerre d'Orient*, part ii, chapters xiii and xiv.

The Second Attack on the Shipka Pass

At the beginning of September Radetzky's troops holding the Balkans were disposed as follows. The VIIIth Corps less one brigade, the 4th Rifle Brigade, and the Bulgarian contingent less one battalion, twenty-five battalions in all, held the Shipka Pass; one regiment of the 1st Brigade of the 11th Division held Zelene Dveimvo; one battalion of the Bulgarian contingent watched the Travna Pass, while one brigade of the VIIIth Corps and the remaining regiment of the 1st brigade of the 11th Division (nine battalions in all), were in reserve at Gabrova. The most southerly point held by the Russians was the San Nicholas Mountain, and their flanks were thrown sharply back towards Zelene Dveimvo and Jantra. The Turks held a semi-circular position on the heights at the southern end of the pass round San Nicholas, with their supports in the village of Shipka and the main body at Kazanlik.

Up to September 13th Suleyman contented himself with a desultory bombardment of the Russian position. This period was spent by both sides in fortifying their positions and in repairing the losses caused by the severe fighting. At the end of the month of August Suleyman was reinforced by contingents from Roumelia and Albania, which brought his strength up to about 40,000 men, and in the second week in September he also received several batteries of mortars and heavy artillery. These he established on the heights at the southern end of the pass, and on the 13th he began a bombardment of the Russian works on San Nicholas, which lasted until the 17th. Meanwhile, he had received from Constantinople the orders which have been already referred to directing him to assume the offensive. Osman's success at Plevna had inspired the Sultan's advisers with the belief that the moment had come when a vigorous advance would drive the Russians into the Danube. The terrible losses caused by Suleyman's frontal attacks in the first attempt to capture the Shipka Pass had taught them nothing, and Suleyman was directed to renew his efforts at the first opportunity. He required little urging, and made arrangements for an immediate advance. He had, however, learnt the futility of hurling masses of troops straight on the Russian trenches, and determined to endeavour to surprise the Russians during the night of September 16-17. For this he selected a body of 3,500 volunteers, which he divided into three columns. The first of these under Redjib Pasha was to attack the mountain on the east side, the second under Salih Pasha was to attack the southern side, while the third under Vessel Pasha was to advance against the western face.

Each of these commanders had six battalions under his orders to support his volunteers. The three columns started at 3.30 on the morning of the 17th. Redjib Pasha's column, which had the shortest distance to go, reached the slopes of the mountain first, but was discovered by the Russian outposts and checked. The top of San Nicholas is in the form of a rough plateau; after a sharp engagement Redjib's column succeeded in reaching the south-eastern edge of this plateau, but could get no further. Salih and Vessel's columns, however, surprised the Russian outposts and established themselves on the southern and western sides of the plateau.

Suleyman at daybreak, seeing his troops on the mountain, was convinced that he had captured the Shipka Pass, and despatched a telegram to that effect to Constantinople. The Russians still, however, held the northern edge and prevented any advance. Salih and Vessel Pasha therefore brought up their supports to assist their volunteers, but Redjib finding that his volunteers were checked, and apparently considering that the surprise had failed, left his six battalions at the foot of the mountain and made no attempt to support the other columns. By 8 a.m. Radetzky had arrived on the scene of action with reinforcements, and any chance of a successful surprise was gone. Seeing that Redjib Pasha was making no attempt to move, Radetzky directed a vigorous counter-attack against Salih and Vessel's columns. By 9 a.m. the Russians had regained possession of the plateau. The action still continued for some hours, the Turkish volunteers fighting with dogged bravery on the slopes of the mountain. By 4 p.m. the Russians were again masters of the whole of San Nicholas, and the Turks drew off with the loss of over 3,000 men. This was Suleyman's last attempt to capture the pass. He established his troops in their old positions round San Nicholas, and confined himself to a blockade of the southern end of the pass. At the end of the month he was appointed to the chief command of the forces in the field and departed to relieve Mehmet Ali. At the beginning of October the cold weather set in, and the Turks being ill-provided with warm clothing were obliged to withdraw their men into the villages at the mouth of the pass, while the Russians busied themselves with providing huts for the garrisons of the Balkan passes and with improving the roads so as to ensure that their men should be well supplied during the winter months.

Guerre d'Orient, part ii. chapter xv.

The Preparations for the Investment of Plevna by the Russians and the Revictualling of Plevna by the Turks.

The failure of the third attack on Plevna produced a feeling of depression in the Russian ranks which amounted almost to dismay. The repeated failures of the Russian attacks had created an impression in Europe which Russian Statesmen regarded with the gravest appehension. Russian stock was falling daily on the Continental Bourses, and Russian paper money was 35 per cent. below its face value. This greatly increased the cost of raising loans for carrying on the war, and combined with a growing unwillingness among Continental bankers to undertake the flotation of Russian war loans, caused the financiers of St. Petersburg to report to Russian Headquarters at the seat of war, that a further failure would involve serious financial difficulties. The unexpected successes of the Turks had, moreover, greatly encouraged the enemies of Russia in Continental States, induced waverers to hold their hand and to await the further progress of events, and weakened the influence of the advocates of Russia. In Austria and Hungary in particular the Russophil party was in the ascendant at the beginning of the war, and the Austrian Government had adopted a peremptory tone in treating with Turkey about the insurgent states on the Austro-Hungarian frontier. Since the failure of the Russians before Plevna the attitude of the Dual Monarchy had completely changed. The many sympathizers with, and friends of Turkey, among the Czechs had begun to make their influence felt, and the tone of the despatches from Vienna to Constantinople had become more friendly. The Russian Government expected that Turkey would induce Austria at the least to exercise a benevolent neutrality on her behalf, by allowing Austrian troops to enter Bosnia and Herzogovina, and the Austrian Government to arrange some form of settlement for those distressed provinces. It was feared that Austria would join with England in bringing pressure to bear upon the Czar to conclude an unsatisfactory peace with the Sultan. Further, as long as the Russian arms were under a cloud no active assistance could be expected from the Christian States of the Balkans. Servia, which in the spring had been openly negotiating with Russia as to the part she should take in the campaign, now showed no desire to participate in the struggle. Apart from these considerations of high finance and politics the military situation called for the exercise of the utmost prudence. The *moral* of the Western army was far from satisfactory. Sotov was inclined to exaggerate the extent of his failure, and to overestimate the power of offence and strength of the Turks in Plevna. Even if a fourth attack upon Plevna were successful a winter campaign appeared now to be inevitable; there was, therefore, no object in hurrying matters so as to compel the Sultan to sue for peace before the cold weather set in. These considerations induced the Russian Headquarters to suspend for the present any active offensive operations. It was decided that the armies of Rustchuk and of the Balkans should remain rigidly on the defensive, and that the Western army should be concentrated in a defensive position east of Plevna pending the arrival of reinforcements, that the whole of the latter should be brought up to Plevna, and that on their arrival that town should be strictly blockaded and starved into submission.

The Western army accordingly took up the following positions on September 15.[1] The Roumanian contingent filled their former position on the right flank, with their left on Grivitsa No. 1 redoubt, which they garrisoned; the IXth corps held from that point to the Plevna-Pelisat road; the IVth Corps from the Pelisat road to the Toultchenitza; the 2nd Division and 3rd Rifle Brigade took post in rear of the IVth Corps, and formed the general reserve of the army; the 9th Cavalry Division covered the left flank and watched the Lovcha road; while a special Cavalry Division composed of twelve cavalry regiments and four horse

[1] *See* Map III.

artillery batteries were placed under General Krylov to operate on the left bank of the Vid, and intercept Osman's communications with Sofia. The Western army at once began to entrench itself in its main positions. On September 18 Prince Charles who was elated by the share which the Roumanians had taken in gaining the only permanent success achieved by the Western Army, the capture of the Grivitsa No. 1 redoubt, persuaded the Grand Duke Nicholas to allow the Roumanian contingent to attempt the capture of the Grivitsa No. 2 redoubt. The attack was easily repulsed by the Turks, and the failure confirmed the Russian Headquarters in their decision to try no further assaults. With the exception of this incident little of interest took place east of Plevna during the remainder of the month. The Russian Headquarters were busied with preparations for a winter campaign. It was decided as far as possible to billet the troops in various villages, supplemented by huts. Arrangements were also made for replacing the field hospitals by stationary hospitals in huts. Permanent depôts were established and immense quantities of stores and warm clothing ordered from Russia. The most difficult problem to be solved was that of transport. The roads of Bulgaria had proved none too good during the summer months, and even if, as was contemplated, the armies were to remain stationary for some time the mud and snows of autumn and winter would make supply a very difficult matter. It was, therefore, decided to begin at once to improve the main communications; a line of railway from Bendery to Galatz[1] was already under construction, and it was determined to begin two others, one

[1] See Map I.

from Fratesti to Simnitsa, the other from Sistova by Biela to Tirnova.

A re-arrangement of the higher commands also took place. The veteran hero of the siege of Sebastopol, Todleben, was recalled from retirement to conduct the blockade of Plevna, While Prince Charles of Roumania nominally remained in charge of the Western army the conduct of operations was really left entirely to Todleben, who arrived and took over his duties on September 24. Sotov gave up his position as Chief of the Staff of the Western army and resumed command of the IVth Corps. Krylov who had commanded the corps during the third battle was given command of the cavalry on the left bank of the Vid. Imeretinski became Chief of the Staff of the Western Army. Skobelov was given the command of the 16th Division. Gourko, who had returned to St. Petersburg to superintend the mobilization of the Division of Guard Cavalry which he commanded, was on his arrival placed in command of all the cavalry of the Western army. In the army of Rustchuk General Hahn, who was held responsible for the defeats of Ajaslar, Karahasankioj, and Popkioj, was removed from the command of the XIIIth Corps and was succeeded by Prince Dondoukov Korsakov, Shakofskoi was also removed from the command of the XIth Corps and replaced by Baron Dellinghausen. The 26th Infantry Division, which had joined the army of Rustchuk on the arrival of reinforcements at the beginning of September, now joined the XIth Corps to replace the 32nd Division of that Corps, which was incorporated with the XIIIth Corps. In order to raise the spirits and *moral* of the army a large number of promotions and decorations were distributed amongst those who had distinguished themselves.

Of the reinforcements expected, the Guard Rifle brigade reached Bulgaria about the middle of September, and was followed by the 2nd Division of the Guard Cavalry, the 1st, 2nd and 3rd Divisions of the Guard Infantry, the 2nd and 3rd Grenadier Divisions and the 24th Infantry Division. With the exception of the latter, which crossed the Danube in the first week of October, and was sent to the Shipka Pass to relieve the advanced troops of the VIIIth Corps, all these reinforcements were destined for the Western army.

While the Russians were thus occupied with preparations for the blockade of Plevna, and for a winter campaign, Osman was no less busy with arrangements for provisioning Plevna and repairing the losses which his troops had suffered. After the capture of Lovcha, he had asked for a reinforcement of twenty-five battalions, and undertook if these were furnished him to re-occupy that town. Seventeen battalions, one regiment of cavalry and two batteries were gradually collected at Orkhanie by September 17, and though it was now too late to think of recapturing Lovcha it was decided to use these troops to escort a large convoy of supplies and ammunition to Plevna. The troops collected for this purpose were placed under the command of Ahmed Hifzi Pasha, who had been wounded at the first battle of Plevna, but had recovered. The column was organized in three brigades, under Hakki Pasha, Edhem Pasha, and Veli Bey, the first two consisting of six battalions, the other of five. Ahmed Hifzi started from Orkhanie on September 18, and reached Telish on the 20th after a slight skirmish with an advanced party of Krylov's cavalry.

Krylov's command consisted of Tchernosubov's and Tutolmin's Cossack Brigades, the 4th Lancers, 4th Hussars, and 4th Dragoons of the 4th Cavalry Division, and the Roumanian cavalry, in all about 4,000 sabres. Part of this force had crossed to the left bank of the Vid on September 15, but the main body did not assemble at Dolna Dubniak till September 19. Krylov's attention was at first occupied in reconnoitring along the Widin road and in the direction of Rahova, it having been reported that there were Turkish forces in that direction. This rumour proved unfounded, and on the 20th patrols were sent towards Telish. It was these patrols which met the Turkish convoy. On the 21st as Ahmed was about to resume his march it was reported that a strong force of cavalry was in his front on the Plevna road. This was Tutolmin's Cavalry Brigade which had been sent towards Telish by Krylov, when he learnt that there was a considerable body of Turks at that place. Ahmed, thinking that this cavalry was probably the advanced guard of a strong force, deployed his troops and brought his artillery into action. Tutolmin, in face of the enemy's superior numbers, fell back on Dolna Dubniak, but by this time the day was so far spent that Ahmed decided to remain that night at Telish. On the 22nd Krylov assembled his cavalry at Dolna Dubniak to oppose the march of the convoy. But here he was engaged in rear by a column consisting of six squadrons, six battalions and four guns, under Atouf Pasha, which Osman had sent out from Plevna to assist in bringing in the convoy. Threatened in front and rear by strong bodies of infantry, Krylov drew off, and Ahmed entered Plevna on the 23rd.

On September 23rd, Krylov fell back on Ribino[1] in accordance with orders from Prince Charles, which directed him to cover the right flank and to reconnoitre along the Widin road and towards Rahova. The next five days were spent in extended reconnaissances in those directions, which resulted in little but a few skirmishes with Bashi-Bazouks. On October 1, Krylov had assembled his main body at Trestenik with detachments at Bivolar, at Gorna and Dolna Metrapolje, and with patrols pushed forward along the Sofia road. Meantime Osman, who foresaw that the object of the Russians was to cut his communications and to establish a blockade of Plevna, was availing himself of every opportunity of obtaining supplies of food and forage. The reinforcements which had arrived under Ahmed Hifzi were formed into a mobile column on September 27, and employed in collecting supplies from the villages on the right bank of the Vid south-west of Plevna. These expeditions resulted in a number of skirmishes with the Russian cavalry, who were unable, however, to prevent the Turks accomplishing their tasks.

On October 6 Chefket Pasha, the commandant of Orkhanie, had collected at that place a second convoy of 500 wagons destined for Osman Pasha. Chefket organized an escort for the convoy composed of two regiments of cavalry, two batteries of artillery, and fifteen battalions. He reached Telish[2] without incident on the 7th, and having left a large proportion of his

---

[1] *See* Map II.   [2] *See* Map I.

escort to hold that place, entered Plevna on October 8 with the assistance of Ahmed Hifzi's column which went out to Dolna Dubniak to meet him. Chefket Pasha and Osman now had a consultation as to the methods to be adopted for securing the communications between Plevna and Sofia. Osman was too good a soldier to allow himself to be shut in without protest. He was well aware that his army had fully accomplished its mission in bringing the whole offensive campaign of the Russians to a standstill, and in drawing against himself an army more than twice as numerous as his own. He knew that the time for taking advantage of the situation which he had created had been allowed to slip by, and if he were to remain indefinitely at Plevna the Russians would gradually accumulate overwhelming force against him, and that the inevitable end would be the starvation or capture of his army. He had therefore applied to Constantinople soon after the third battle of Plevna for permission to fall back by Orkhanie on the Etropol Balkans, where he would have freedom of manœuvre and could co-operate with one or other of the remaining Turkish armies. The answer he received from Constantinople was that Plevna had acquired too much importance to be abandoned, and that it must be held at all costs. It is difficult to conceive a more unjustifiable answer to the request of a gallant commander. The importance which Plevna had acquired was due to the menacing position of Osman's army, which from that place was a constant danger to the Russian right flank and to their communications. Once the Russians were able to accumulate sufficient force to make an offensive movement by Osman Pasha impossible the importance of Plevna was gone. To order Plevna to be held because it had proved to be a strategically important point under quite different conditions was to sacrifice uselessly a brave leader and a gallant army. The only possible defence of the policy of holding on to Plevna at any cost is that it was intended to take advantage of the fact that the Russians were concentrating the greater part of their strength against that place, and to throw every available Turkish soldier against one of the other Russian armies, and by overwhelming it compel the Russians to give up their operations against Plevna. But any such resolute action as this was far from the thoughts of the Sultan's advisers. The Turkish successes at Plevna had enhanced the position of Turkey in the eyes of Europe, and for that reason Plevna was to be held to the last. This decision, together with the enterprises of the Russian cavalry on the left bank of the Vid, and his knowledge that Russian reinforcements were daily arriving in Bulgaria, caused Osman the gravest anxiety. His command when he entered Plevna was a field army, carrying with it supplies for a few days only; Plevna itself was a small country town with few resources. To obtain provisions and reserves of stores, when in the presence of the enemy, sufficient to enable an army of 40,000 men to stand a siege, was a very serious undertaking. It was, therefore, of vital importance to Osman that his communications with Sofia should be kept open to the last possible moment. He arranged with Chefket for the establishment of a number of fortified posts along the route. By the middle of October the garrision of Plevna consisted of fifty-nine battalions, seventeen squadrons, and sixty-six guns.

Dolna Dubniak was occupied by five battalions and two guns; Gorna Dubniak by six battalions, four squadrons, and four guns; Telish by seven battalions and four guns. These posts with their garrisons were under Osman's direct command. From Telish to Orkhanie the line of communications was under the command of Chefket, who returned to the latter place on October 9 to arrange for the despatch of further convoys to Plevna. He had at his disposal twenty-three battalions, twelve squadrons, and twelve guns, these were disposed at Orkhanie and at two posts between it and Telish.

While making arrangements for the provisioning of Plevna, Osman did not neglect the repair and extension of his fortifications. He divided the circumference, which was about twenty miles in extent, into five sections.[1] No. 1 section extended from Bukova to the Grivitsa No 2. redoubt, and was in charge of Adil Pasha. No. 2 section extended from the Grivitsa brook to the Toultchenitza. The 3rd section extended from the Toultchenitza to point **22** north of Krischin. This section was extended and improved by a chain of works, running along ridge *J*, and connecting point **17** with the redoubt at point **23**. The 4th section ran from the redoubt at point **22** along the ridge, which runs south-east from Blasivas to the works commanding the bridge over the Vid at point **32**. The defence of this section was completed by the construction of a chain of redoubts connected by shelter-trenches along the Blasivas ridge. The 5th section consisted of the works about Opanetz, which were connected with No. 1 section by lines of trenches running towards Bukova. The enceinte of Plevna was thus

[1] *See* **Map I.**

completed and Osman was in a condition to meet an attack on any side.

Todleben had been appointed assistant to the commander of the Western army on October 4, and had been given command of all the Russian troops before Plevna. He agreed in the proposal that no further attempt should be made to assault the Turkish position, but that Osman should be blockaded. He also decided not to extend the line held by the Western army until the arrival of the expected reinforcements. At this time Todleben estimated Osman's strength as high as 80,000 men, a total which exceeded the effective strength of the Western army. Osman's effective at the beginning of October was actually about 50,000. On it becoming known at Russian Headquarters that Suleymen Pasha had succeeded Mehmet Ali, and had taken over command of the Turkish forces in the Quadrilateral, it was expected that the Turks in that quarter would at once begin an offensive movement. Suleyman's fiery attacks upon the Shipka Pass had earned him a reputation for enterprise and boldness, and fears were entertained that he would break through the extended position occupied by the army of Rustchuk. It was therefore intended by Russian Headquarters that the 2nd Guard Division, from the reinforcements which were arriving in Bulgaria, should be used as a general reserve for that army. This proposal did not suit Todleben's views. He urged that Plevna should be the chief objective of the Russian armies in Bulgaria, and professed himself unable to complete the blockade unless every available man was sent to reinforce the Western army. As it was found that Suleyman showed no signs of an immediate advance the Grand Duke Nicholas finally consented, and the 2nd Guard Infantry Division reached Poradim [1] on October 20th

The first measure necessary for the blockade of Plevna was to cut the communications between Plevna and Sofia, and to complete the circle of investment by the occupation of the left bank of the Vid. Krylov's cavalry had proved quite unable to prevent the entrance of convoys into Plevna. It was therefore decided to organize a strong force of all arms, chiefly composed of the reinforcements recently arrived, and to place it under the command of General Gourko, who was to be entrusted with the task of capturing the Turkish posts established on the Sofia road. Accordingly on October 21 the following troops were placed under Gourko's command :—the 2nd Guard Cavalry Division, Krylov's Cavalry Division, the 1st and 2nd Guard Infantry Divisions, the Guard Rifle Brigade, one regiment of the 3rd Guard Infantry Division, and an engineer battalion ; a total of sixty squadrons, forty battalions, and 146 guns. It was decided that this corps should attack Gorna Dubniak [2] on October 24, and that to cover this movement, and to prevent Osman from detaching troops to assist the posts on his line of communication, a demonstration should be made by the remainder of the western Army against the Turkish works at Plevna.

Todleben had waited for the arrival of reinforcements before attempting finally to close the Plevna-Lovcha road and invest the town on the southern side. He determined that this operation should be carried out simultaneously with Gourko's movement, both to cover

[1] *See* Map II. [2] *See* Map I.

the latter and to give greater effect to the intended demonstration against Plevna. The barring of the Plevna-Lovcha road was intrusted to General Sotov, who was given the 16th Infantry Division, one brigade of the 30th Infantry Division, three regiments of the 3rd Guard Infantry Division, three battalions of the 3rd Rifle Brigade, an engineer battalion and 184 guns. On October 24 all the Russian batteries around Plevna began a bombardment of the Turkish works, which was continued throughout the day, and the hills south of Brestovetz were occupied by Skobelov with the 16th Infantry Division, the 3rd Rifle Brigade, and one regiment of the 3rd Guard Infantry Division. Meantime, during the previous night, Gourko had crossed the Vid above Medeven by three fords, and he attacked Gorna Dubniak on the morning of the 24th. The garrison of that place consisted only of six battalions, four squadrons, and four guns. This little force defended itself with such gallantry that, though it was surrounded on all sides by immensely superior numbers, the post was not captured until after dark, with a loss to the Russians of over 3,000 killed and wounded. On October 25 the whole of the 3rd Guard Division was, at Gourko's request, moved to the neighbourhood of Medeven with the object of taking in flank any movement from Plevna against his rear. On that and the four following days the bombardment of the works round Plevna was continued. On the 28th Gourko captured Telish. He left a garrison entrenched in that place to check any movement of the Turks from the direction of Orkhanie, and at once moved back towards Dolna Dubniak. Veli Pasha held that place with five battalions, he had reported to Osman that heavy firing had been heard in the direction of Gorna Dubniak on the 23rd, that it had ceased on the 25th, and that he had been unable to communicate with the garrison. The Russian bombardment, the occupation of the hills about Brestovetz, and the constant movement of troops to the south of Plevna, induced Osman to believe that the Russians were about to deliver another general assault. He was confirmed in this belief by his knowledge that they had recently been heavily reinforced. He therefore decided to call in Veli Pasha, who evacuated Dolna Dubniak on the night of the 27th–28th. It was accordingly occupied by Gourko without opposition on November 1. Thus Plevna was for the first time completely isolated, and from that day the blockade was established.

Kuropatkin, vol. ii, part v. *Défense de Plevna*, chapter v. *Guerre d'Orient*, part ii, chapters xxiv and xxv.

CHAPTER X

THE FALL OF PLEVNA

ORGANIZATION OF A COVERING FORCE—DISTRIBUTION OF THE INVESTING FORCE—OSMAN'S PREPARATIONS FOR A SORTIE—SULEYMAN AS COMMANDER-IN-CHIEF—DISTRIBUTION OF THE FORCES IN THE QUADRILATERAL—SULEYMAN'S ADVANCE—ACTION AT MECKA—SULEYMAN'S ADVANCE ON ELENA—COMMENTS—GOURKO'S OPERATIONS WEST OF PLEVNA—MEHMET ALI AT ARABKONAK—OSMAN'S SORTIE FROM PLEVNA—OSMAN'S SURRENDER—STRATEGICAL LESSONS OF PLEVNA—KUROPATKIN'S TACTICAL DEDUCTIONS FROM BATTLES OF PLEVNA—FINAL PHASE OF THE CAMPAIGN.

CHAPTER X

THE FALL OF PLEVNA

The Investment of Plevna DURING the first fortnight of November few events of importance occurred round Plevna. Gourko holding the left bank of the Vid effectually prevented any further supplies or reinforcements being introduced into the town. The Russian batteries kept up a desultory bombardment of the Turkish works, and from time to time skirmishes took place between the troops holding the advanced trenches. But the only serious operation attempted by the besieging army was the occupation by Skobelov of the first ridge of the Green Hills (ridge *I*),[1] which was successfully carried out on November 9th.

During the first days of this month information reached Russian Headquarters that the Turks were assembling troops between Orkhanie[2] and Sofia, and that Mehmet Ali had been appointed to the command by the Sultan, with the express object of relieving Osman Pasha. In order to secure the blockade from interruption it was necessary to organize a covering force. The Grand Duke Nicholas decided that this should be made up from the troops under Gourko's command. But it was determined to await the arrival of the last of the reinforcements, the 2nd Grenadier

[1] *See* Map III. [2] *See* Map I.

Division, before sending off Gourko on this duty. The 2nd Grenadier Division reached Plevna on November 14th, and relieved the 1st Guard Infantry Division in its position on the left bank of the Vid. The same day the covering force was finally organized. It consisted of—

The 2nd Guard Cavalry Division,
The Astrachan and Kasan Dragoon Regiments,
The Caucasian and Don Cossack Brigades,
The 1st and 2nd Guard Infantry Divisions,
The Guard Rifle Brigade,
The Guard Engineer Battalion,

and in addition the 2nd Brigade of the 3rd Infantry Division, and the 3rd Artillery Brigade from the garrison of Lovcha. Gourko's command thus comprised 43 battalions, 32 squadrons, 18 sotnias, and 174 guns. It left the army before Plevna on its new mission on November 15th. All the remaining troops round Plevna were now placed under the nominal command of Prince Charles of Roumania, actually the executive power was in the hands of Todleben. He had at his disposal—

The 2nd, 3rd, and 4th Roumanian Divisions,
The 3rd Guard Infantry Division,
The 2nd Grenadier Division,
The 3rd Grenadier Division,
The 4th Army Corps (the 2nd, 16th, and 30th Infantry Divisions and 4th Cavalry Division),
The IXth Army Corps (the 5th[1] and 31st Divisions and 9th Cavalry Division),
The 3rd Rifle Brigade,
The 2nd Engineer Brigade,

Besides the divisions which had recently arrived from Russia strong drafts had joined the regiments of the

[1] Except the 19th Regiment at Nikopoli.

IVth and IXth Corps, which were thus made up to something approaching their normal establishment. The army received the name of the Blockading army of Plevna. Its strength about the middle of November was 120,000 men and 522 guns. The arrangements for the blockade were reorganized on Gourko's departure. Todleben divided the whole circumference into six sections. The first section stretched[1] from the Vid at Bivolar to the Grivitsa No. 1 redoubt; it was held by the 2nd and 3rd Roumanian Divisions, under the command of General Tschernat. The 2nd section ran from the Grivitsa redoubt to the Plevna-Pelisat road; it was occupied by the IXth Corps under General Krudener. The 3rd section carried on the line as far as the Toultchenitza ravine, and was under the command of General Sotov, who had at his disposal the 2nd Infantry Division, the 12th Rifle battalion, and the 30th Artillery Brigade. The 4th section extended from the Toultchenitza ravine, just east of Brestovetz, to the stream immediately north of Kartouschaven. This section was held by the 16th Infantry Division, the 30th Infantry Division, less its Artillery Brigade, the 9th, 10th, and 11th Rifle battalions, the 9th Cossack regiment and the 2nd Artillery Brigade. It was commanded by Skobelov. The 5th section extended from the brook north of Kartouschaven to the Vid at Ternina. It was under the command of Lieut.-General Katalei, who had under him the 3rd Guard Infantry Division, with two squadrons of Guard Cossacks, and the 10th Don Cossack battery. The 6th section ran from the Vid at Ternina in front of Dolna Dubniak, and Dolna Metrapolje to the Vid again at Bivolar. This

[1] *See* **Map III.**

section was occupied by the 2nd and 3rd Grenadier Divisions, the 4th Roumanian Division, the 9th Cavalry Division, the 4th Don Cossacks, one Roumanian Cavalry regiment, and eight Horse Artillery batteries. The remainder of the cavalry was used to keep touch with Gourko, and on the line of communications.

The whole front thus occupied was prepared for defence, shelter-trenches strengthened at intervals by redoubts being constructed along the inner line of investment, while batteries and gun emplacements were erected in rear. In many places a second line of works was also formed. The advanced line of trenches was on a circumference of thirty-five miles, and the reserves of the various sections were on an outer circle of about sixty miles. It was known to the Russians that Osman had in Plevna, at the time that the blockade was made effective, supplies for about one month. It could not be supposed that Osman would allow himself to be starved into surrender without making some effort to break out. As there were no roads worthy of the name running parallel to the circle of investment, and the country round Plevna is very broken, the problem of arranging for the rapid concentration of sufficient force to meet such an attempt presented great difficulties, and Todleben at once set himself to face them. Plans were prepared to meet an attempt of the Turks to break out in any possible direction. The best routes by which reinforcements could move were reconnoitred, the numerous streams and gullies which they had to cross were bridged, existing tracks were improved and new roads made, posts and other distinguishing marks were erected along the lines of march to obviate mistakes at night. Officers were carefully selected to act as guides to the various columns, and they were ordered to make sketches of every road by which the troops, to which they were attached, might have to move, in order that they should be thoroughly acquainted with their duties. The times reinforcements would take to reach any given section were carefully worked out, and were checked by experimental marches of reinforcements along the selected routes. Telegraphic communication was established between the various sections and Headquarters, and a number of observation posts and signalling stations was provided in each section.

Meanwhile in Plevna the state of affairs was becoming desperate. About the middle of November it was necessary to put the men on half-rations, and even this allowance had shortly afterwards to be reduced. By the 27th Osman estimated that even with the utmost economy his supplies could not last much more than a fortnight. There was no forage for the animals, no medicine or bandages for the sick and wounded, the men's clothing was in rags, there was barely sufficient fuel for cooking and the cold was becoming intense. Osman was unable to obtain intelligence of any movement for his relief. He therefore summoned a Council of War on December 1, at which it was decided to attempt to break through the line of investment.

Osman had little choice as to the direction in which he would make his sortie. He calculated that the necessary preparations would take him at least a week. As he had about fourteen days supplies available he could only reckon on being able to take about six days supplies with him from Plevna. If he were to succeed in breaking out to the south or south-east he would have to deal with Russian forces other than those which were investing him, and the operations which such a measure would involve would, in the most favourable circumstances, take more than a week. If he were to break out to the north he would almost certainly be hemmed in between the lower Vid and the Danube. There remained only the western side to consider. If he were successful in breaking through between Dolna Dubniak and Dolna Metrapolje, he might hope to reach the Isker[1] in one march, and by using that river to cover his flank there was some prospect of his being able to move on Sofia, and to get into touch with the relieving army, which was assembling in the Etropol Balkans. The Russian defences on the left bank of the Vid were the most recently constructed, and were less formidable than those in any other section of the investment. The Vid would make it more difficult for the Russians to reinforce this section rapidly than any other. The flat ground[2] between the junction of the Grivitsa and the Vid formed a convenient place in which he could assemble his army, and the works at Opanetz, and near the permanent bridge over the Vid, would with some extension enable his rearguard to hold off a very superior force. Osman therefore decided to make his sortie to the west. He calculated that he would be ready to move about December 8th or 9th.

The reinforcements which had reached Plevna before the Russian investment was complete had brought up the total number of Osman's battalions to seventy-six. Losses in action and sickness had, however, greatly

[1] *See* Map I.   [2] *See* Map III.

reduced the strength of certain of these battalions, and some of them had an effective strength of not much over 200 men. It was one of the great defects in the organization of the Turkish Army that there was no system of drafts for replacing casualties. A large part of the reinforcements which Osman had received consisted of battalions of Mustafis. In order to equalize the strength of his battalions and to insure that the Mustafi battalions should have a stiffening of seasoned soldiers, to fit them for the desperate enterprise he was about to undertake, the weakest battalions were broken up, and the army was formed into fifty-seven battalions. These were divided into seven brigades, made up into two Divisions. The 1st Division consisted of four brigades, the first three of eight battalions, the fourth of nine battalions; it was placed under the command of Tahir Pasha. The 2nd Division was composed of three brigades, each of eight battalions, and was under the command of Adil Pasha. All the reserves of clothing were issued to the troops, and as far as the supply would admit the Snider rifles of the Mustafis were exchanged for Martinis. Additional bridges were thrown over the Vid and works were constructed to be manned by the rearguard covering the retirement across the river.

Kuropatkin, vol. ii, part vi. *Défense de Plevna*, chapter vi.

Turkish Efforts to relieve Plevna While both armies at Plevna were thus preparing for the final catastrophe, which had been rendered inevitable by the Sultan's refusal to allow Osman to evacuate his positions early in October, the Turkish armies elsewhere in the theatre of war were making efforts for the relief of Plevna. Reinforcements were hurried up to Sofia, but time was required before these could be in a fit condition to take the field. Heavy falls of snow in the Balkans made it difficult for the army at Shipka to resume active operations. In the first instance, therefore, everything depended upon Suleyman, and much was expected of him. The rapidity with which he had carried out the transfer of his force from Montenegro to Roumelia and his fierce frontal attacks on the Shipka Pass had gained him a reputation for energy and determination. The news of his appointment to the supreme command of the armies of the Quadrilateral had been enough to make the Grand Duke Nicholas detain the 2nd Grenadier Division, which had been destined for the blockading army of Plevna, to form a general reserve to the Czarevitch's army. But it was soon discovered that the command of the armies of the Quadrilateral demanded very different qualities from those which Suleyman had shown as commander of the army he had brought from Montenegro. This force was organized as a fighting unit, and had been engaged in active operations for many months before it was called upon to meet the Russians. In that case Suleyman and his subordinate commanders knew each other, and some degree of mutual confidence existed between them. The railway had enabled the whole army to be concentrated at Hermanli,[1] almost within striking distance of the enemy. The problems involved in its command did not, therefore, require any very exceptional tact, power of organization, or knowledge of strategy. The case of the armies of the Quadrilateral was very different.

[1] *See* Map II.

In the first place they occupied an immense front, stretching from the Danube near Rustchuk to the Balkans at Slivno. The higher commanders distrusted each other and the Commander-in-Chief, and were perpetually engaged in intrigues in their own interest. A large part of the force was employed in garrisoning the fortresses, and was not equipped to take the field for long periods. It was, therefore, no easy matter to concentrate such a command and deal a rapid and decisive blow at the enemy. Suleyman proved himself to be no more capable of grappling with the problem than Mehmet Ali. On taking over command he made certain minor changes in organization, but for some time he did not materially alter the dispositions which had been made by his predecessor.

By the middle of October the army of the Danube, as the Turkish army of the Quadrilateral was now called, was distributed as follows. The garrison of Rustchuk, under the command of Kaisserli Ahmed Pasha, consisted of seven battalions and the fortress artillery, together with a brigade, under Mustafa Zefi Pasha, composed of eight battalions, five squadrons and a battery. The total force at Rustchuk was thus about 14,000 strong. The main field army was organized into four Infantry and one Cavalry Divisions. The 1st Division was commanded by Fuad Pasha, the 2nd Division by Assaf Pasha, the 3rd Division by Nedjib Pasha, the 4th Division by Sabit Pasha, the Cavalry by Kerim Pasha. It consisted of about 40,000 bayonets, 3,000 sabres, and 111 guns. The headquarters of Sabit and Assaf's Divisions were established in an entrenched camp at Kadikioj; their advanced troops held the line of the Beli Lom from Besarbova to Solenik. Nedjib and Fuad's Divisions were at Rasgrad, one brigade of the former being at Turlak to connect with Kadikioj. The advanced troops held from Solenik to the Kiricen Hills on the Kara Lom opposite Ajaslar. Eski Dzuma was occupied by a detached corps under Salik Pasha, which consisted of twenty-three battalions, five batteries, and twelve squadrons, about 15,000 men in all. This was the old 2nd Corps, less the Egyptian contingent, Prince Hassan having withdrawn to Varna in a huff at Suleyman's appointment to the chief command. Salim Pasha's independent brigade occupied Osman Bazar, it consisted of nine battalions and a battery, or about 5,000 men—this number is not included in Salik Pasha's command. One battalion held Kasan and one battalion Slivno. Besides this some 30,000 men were distributed among the garrisons of Turtukai, Varna Silistria, and Shumla.

At this time the army of the Czarevitch was disposed as follows. The XIIth Corps held from the Danube, near Mecka, to Damogila, the 12th Division occupying Mecka and Trestenik, the 33rd Division Damogila and Obretenik. The infantry outposts of the corps held a line through Pirgos and Han Gul Cisme to the Damogila-Stroko road, the cavalry of the corps held the Kara Lom as far south as Stroko. The XIIIth Corps held from Stroko to Cerkovna, the 35th Division was about Buzovca and Sinankioj, the 32nd Division, detached from the XIth Corps held Koprivca and Osicova, the 1st Division held Cerkovna, the cavalry of the corps watched the Kara Lom from Stroko to Opaka, and their posts ran south-south-west from that place to Kovacica. Of the

XIth Corps the 26th Division was at Cairkioj, the 11th Division had one brigade at Dzuljunica, the other at Novoselo and Zlatarica. The cavalry of the XIth Corps held from Tulbeler, where they connected with the XIIIth Corps, to Bebrova. A detachment from the 9th Division of Radetzky's command occupied Elena and Maren where they connected with the Czarevitch's army.

The whole of the month of October, and the greater part of November, passed without Suleyman attempting any serious operation, a number of reconnaissances were undertaken, which resulted in nothing more than affairs of outposts and cavalry skirmishes. The Grand Duke Nicholas finding that Suleyman did not display more energy than Mehmet Ali withdrew the 2nd Grenadier Division to reinforce the troops before Plevna. Towards the end of November the Sultan's advisers, who were impatient at Suleyman's inactivity, and by this time had begun to realize that the troops collected at Sofia could not be formed into an effective field force in time, caused stringent orders to be sent to Suleyman that he should at once do something to assist Osman Pasha. Suleyman had discovered that the Russians had bridged the Danube at Batin, and that the Czarevitch's line of communications with Roumania ran across this bridge. He arrived at the conclusion, as the result of his reconnaissances, that the Russians were in no great strength immediately south of the Danube; he therefore decided to attack the Czarevitch's left flank, and endeavour to destroy the bridge at Batin. For this he proposed to employ Assaf and Sabit's Divisions under the command of the former. Asim Pasha with the 1st Brigade of Sabit's Division was to cross the Lom at Besarbova and attack Pirgos. Ibrahim Pasha, with the 2nd Brigade of Assaf's Division, was to move by Krasna on Mecka; a third column consisting of the 2nd Brigade of Assaf's Division was to cross at Ciftlik and attack Trestenik. Hassan Pasha with the 2nd Brigade of Sabit's Division formed the reserve.

The main position of the XIIth Corps ran east of Mecka, Trestenik, and Damogila, following roughly the line of the brook which flows into the Danube between Mecka and Pirgos. The three Turkish columns crossed the Lom at 8 a.m. on November 26, driving in the Russian cavalry post on the line of that river. The Russian line of defence gradually receded from the Lom as it ran from north to south, Pirgos being much nearer that river than Trestenik. As the three Turkish columns of attack advanced at the same time the attacks were consequently delivered in succession, the northern column having a shorter distance to go than the centre column, and the centre column than the southern. The northern column under Asim succeeded in capturing Pirgos, which was only held as a supporting point to the outpost line of the 12th Division. The Russians fell back on the main position immediately north of Mecka. Asim's attack had merely the effect of putting the Russians everywhere on the alert, and when Ibrahim's column came up and began its attack on Mecka it was repulsed without difficulty. Meanwhile the 3rd column began its attack on the Russian positions north-east of Trestenik. It was delayed for some time by a strong outpost position on the high ground south of Han Gul Cisme, but having carried this it was able to join hands with Ibrahim's column which had fallen back in a south-easterly direction. The two columns thereupon advanced simultaneously and succeeded in piercing the Russian line between Mecka and Trestenik. This occurred about midday, up to which time the brunt of the attack had been borne by the Russian 12th Division, the 1st Brigade of which held Mecka, and the 2nd Brigade Trestenik. Soon after midday the 1st Brigade of the 33rd Russian Division reached Trestenik from Obretenik, and the Grand Duke Vladimir, who commanded the XIIth Corps, ordered a counter-attack.

While these events were taking place to the south Asim Pasha on the north had collected his brigade after the capture of Pirgos and proceeded to attack the Russian works to the north of Mecka. Before this movement took place Ibrahim's attack on Mecka from the east had been repulsed, and the Russians were able to employ the greater part of the brigade at Mecka to meet Asim, who was driven back with heavy loss. Thus about the time that the counter-attack from Trestenik was begun it was possible to detach a regiment from Mecka, which took Ibrahim's column in flank. Assaf Pasha who was with Hassan's brigade on the high ground south of Han Gul Cisme then ordered a general retirement behind the Lom, which was executed in good order under cover of Hassan's column, which had hardly been engaged. The Turks lost about 1,200 men in these attacks, the Russians some 700, chiefly about Trestenik.

Without taking the garrisons of the various towns and fortresses of the Quadrilateral into account Suleyman could dispose of about 75,000 men, yet he had made this attack, which he meant to be a serious effort to drive the Russians back, with not more than 25,000 men; the remaining two-thirds of his army was not even employed in any effective effort to keep the Russians from reinforcing the part of their line selected for attack. The engagement which did take place shows the same want of careful arrangement and cohesion which had marked all previous efforts of the army of the Quadrilateral.

Having thus failed in his attempt upon the Russian extreme left, Suleyman now determined to try to break through the Czarevitch's right. With this object he assembled at the end of November the greater part of Fuad's Division, and Salik's Corps from Eski Dzuma, at Osman Bazar. The Russians had on their right flank at Elena two infantry regiments of the 9th Division (VIIIth Corps) and one cavalry regiment, with advanced posts at Maren; the 4th Rifle Brigade, attached to the VIIIth Corps, was in reserve at Tirnova; the 1st Brigade of the 11th Division was at Zlatarica, with advanced posts at Kesarova, Kozlubeg, and Novoselo; the 2nd Brigade of the 11th Division was in reserve at Dragicevo, and Merdan. The greater part of the 13th Cavalry Division was distributed amongst the advanced posts in this section. The country between Elena and Osman Bazar is very mountainous and difficult for mounted men; this accounts for the fact that the Russian cavalry failed to discover that the Turks were attempting anything more than a reconnaissance in force, such as had frequently taken place during the month of November. Suleyman had altogether collected about 30,000 men for this effort. The main column about 20,000 strong moved on Ahmedli, the 2nd Column was directed on Zlatarica. Suleyman's object was to advance with his main column on Elena, take the Russians holding the Shipka Pass in flank, join hands with Raouf Pasha, who was in command at Shipka, and advance with him on Tirnova. He reached Ahmedli on December 3, and at daybreak on the 4th began an attack upon the Russian outposts at Bebrova and Maren. This attack was carried out with such dash by the Turks that they drove the Russian advanced troops back in confusion, and by mid-day they were engaged with the Russians holding Elena. Elena lies in a gorge, and the position was a difficult one to defend. Suleyman divided his force for the attack into three columns, the centre column advancing direct along the Bebrova road, while the remaining two moved through the mountains north and south of the town, with the object of intercepting the Russian line of retreat on Tirnova. General Dombrovski, who commanded the brigade of the 9th Division which was holding Elena, discovered these movements, and fearing that he and his whole command would be captured, as the Turks were evidently in greatly superior force, he decided to evacuate Elena and to fall back upon a more defensible position at Jakovci, about three miles down the Tirnova road. The retirement was executed in good order, but the Russians, having lost a large number of horses and the road being very difficult, were obliged to abandon eleven guns. Dombrovski managed to reach the position at Jakovci and to maintain himself there till dark, but his losses had been very heavy, about 1,800 men killed and wounded.

Meantime the northern Turkish column had succeeded about 2 p.m. in gaining possession of Zlatarica, the Russians falling back on Dragicevo, where they prevented any further advance of the Turks.

Suleyman being in possession of Elena and Zlatarica had apparently only to press his advantage to gain Tirnova; once there he would have taken the VIIIth Corps, holding the Balkans, in reverse, and completely turned the line of the Jantra; the Russian armies would then have been in great danger, and it would in all probability have been necessary for them to abandon the blockade of Plevna just at the moment when they were about to reap the fruits of their toil. Had Suleyman pressed his attack early on the 5th the Russians could not have opposed sufficient troops to stop his advance. But he was wanting in resolution at the critical moment, and wasted time in trying to get into communication with Raouf Pasha at Shipka, so that on the morning of the 5th practically nothing was attempted. During the night of the 4th-5th Prince Sviatapolk Mirski, commander of the 9th Division, who had arrived at Jakovci with a battalion of the 2nd Brigade of the 9th Division, was reinforced by the 4th Rifle Brigade from Tirnova, and during the course of the 5th the 2nd Brigade of the 11th Division also came up; so that by the afternoon of the 5th the Russians at Jakovci were in a position to hold their own for some time at least.

On the 5th the right Turkish column occupied Minde and pushed the advanced Russian troops back as far as Merdan, but made no serious attack. During the night of the 5th-6th the 1st Brigade of the 26th Division reached Seremet from Cairkioj, and the 2nd Brigade of this Division, which was relieved at Vodica and Cerkovna by troops of the XIIIth Corps, reached Dzuljunica. These reinforcements enabled the Russians to re-occupy Minde and Zlatarica, the Turks retiring to Mahalesi. The movements of Russian reinforcements from the north, which threatened his right flank, and the fact that Raouf Pasha was not in a condition to move, appear to have paralyzed Suleyman, and nothing further was attempted. By December 8 one battalion of the 9th Division from the Hainkioj Pass, and the remainder of the infantry of the Division from Gabrova, had reached Jakovci, and two battalions of the 3rd Division from Lovcha had reached Tirnova; so that on that day the Russians had on the line between Zlatarica and Jakovci, and in reserve between those places and Tirnova, the whole of the infantry of the XIth Corps and of the 9th Infantry Division, together with the 4th Rifle Brigade and two battalions of the 3rd Division; the artillery lost at Elena had been replaced by batteries taken from the 14th and 24th Divisions of the VIIIth Corps. Suleyman showed no sign of further activity, and General Dellinghausen at Tirnova reported to Russian headquarters that no further reinforcements were required.

Suleyman's second attempt had thus ended in failure. It had had however greater prospects of success than his previous effort. He had assembled at Osman Bazar sufficient force to carry out his intention provided the remainder of his army co-operated with him by keeping the Russians employed along their whole front. Little or nothing was done to insure this either from Eski Dzuma or Rasgrad, so that the Czarevitch was able to denude his centre to reinforce his threatened right flank. Suleyman appears to have expected much from the co-operation of Raouf Pasha, but he must have known that the force at Shipka had been greatly reduced to make up the army assembling at Sofia, and that those who were left at Shipka had suffered much from cold and exposure, so that Raouf could, at the beginning of December, only put about 12,000 effectives in the field. Further, the snow was lying so thick on the mountains about the Shipka Pass that even a demonstration against the Russian positions was difficult. But the alarm which the capture of Elena caused the Russians, and the fact that four days passed before they could assemble sufficient reinforcements to make themselves secure, shows that once at least Suleyman had struck his blow at the right point. As has been said there is little doubt that if he had persevered in his attack on December 5th he would have been able to seize Tirnova, which must have placed the Russians in the greatest difficulty; and there is equally little doubt that had such an attack been made by the Turks in the month of August, before the Russian reinforcements had arrived, and while it was still possible for the army at Shipka actively to co-operate in the movement, the Russians would have suffered a grave disaster.

Valentine Baker, chapters xv to xviii. *Guerre D'Orient*, part ii, chapter xxx.

Gourko's Operations West of Plevna

Gourko was not a man to consider that the duty of covering the siege of Plevna against any enterprises of the Turks from the west could be satisfactorily carried out by passively occupying a defensive position. He determined to drive the Turks in Western Bulgaria south of the Balkans, and if possible to secure the passes through those mountains. Even during the first fortnight of November, while the bulk of his command was still employed in blockading Plevna on the west, he used his cavalry, the detachments he had left to garrison Telish [1] and Gorna Dubniak, and the garrison of Lovcha, which was placed under his command, in clearing the country to the west and north-west of Plevna. On November 2nd a detachment from the garrison of Lovcha drove a party of Turks from Teteven, and secured that place with trifling loss. By the first week in November his cavalry had cleared the country as far west as the Isker up to the Lovcha-Sofia road, and on November 9th had seized Vratza. On November 14th, as has already been mentioned, the positions occupied by Gourko's troops west of Plevna were taken over by the Grenadier Corps, and Gourko was able to move west with his whole force.

The Grand Duke Nicholas had been induced to make so considerable a detachment from the army blockading Plevna by the news that the Turks were making great efforts to assemble a relieving force at Sofia. Mehmet Ali, who had returned to Constantinople after handing over the command of the Turkish armies to Suleyman, suddenly received orders from the Sultan to proceed to Sofia, and there organize an army to relieve Osman Pasha. By the middle of November a considerable portion of the army from Shipka had joined him, and he had received twelve battalions from Asia Minor, so that with the troops he had been able to collect in Sofia and

[1] *See* Map I.

its neighbourhood he had a force of 20,000 bayonets, 2,000 sabres, and thirty-six guns. This he formed into two Divisions under Chakir Pasha and Redjib Pasha, with a cavalry brigade and a reserve brigade under Valentine Baker Pasha, who had followed him to Constantinople on his removal from the command of the armies of the Quadrilateral. With the exception of Chakir Pasha's Division, which had joined him more or less complete from Shipka, this apparently imposing force was little more than an agglomeration of units, the supply and transport arrangements were woefully defective, and a great part of the force was lacking in those constituents which make an army of an assembly of armed men. Mehmet Ali concentrated the greater part of his army at Arab Konak, and held Orkhanie, Etropol, and Slatitza with detachments. Mehmet Ali recognized that his force was not in a condition to meet Gourko in the open. He therefore occupied himself chiefly in preparing the Balkan Passes for defence, and made no serious effort to oppose the advance of the Russians at Orkhanie and Etropol. As these towns command the issues from Sofia into Western Bulgaria it is clear that Mehmet Ali had no intention of making any immediate attempt to relieve Osman; practically the whole of his efforts were directed to covering Sofia. Thus on November 24 Gourko drove the Turkish detachment from Etropol without difficulty, and soon after the Turks evacuated Orkhanie, falling back upon Arab Konak. This success encouraged Gourko to believe that he could secure the Arab Konak Pass and advance on Sofia. By December 1st he had made good the northern end of the pass without difficulty. Mehmet Ali had, however, fortified an extremely strong position about Arab Konak, and after several attempts to break through, Gourko decided on December 5th that the Turkish positions were too strong to be forced, and as he had received news from Plevna that Osman was not expected to hold out much longer, he decided to hold the northern ends of the passes and to wait for reinforcements. On December 4th Mehmet Ali was recalled by the Sultan to Constantinople to prepare the capital for defence, and Chakir Pasha assumed command of the troops at Arab Konak.

When once involved among the foothills of the Balkans, Gourko found that his strong force of cavalry was of little use to him; he therefore employed it in further clearing the scattered detachments of Turks who were still in Western Bulgaria. Meanwhile on November 21 a contingent of Roumanian troops crossed the Danube and attacked Rahova; after a short engagement the Turkish garrison abandoned that place and retired on Widin, which by the first week in December was the only place the Turks still held in Western Bulgaria.

The Fall of Plevna Osman had decided to begin his sortie during the night of the 9th-10th December. On the evening of the 9th and during the ensuing night a thick fog enveloped the Turkish works. This assisted Osman in the difficult task of evacuating his positions unobserved by the Russians. He had, as has been mentioned, ordered fire from the works to be gradually slackened during the 6th, 7th, and 8th, and on the 9th not a round was fired from any of the Turkish positions. This was done that the suspicions of the Russians should not be roused by any sudden silence in the works as they were abandoned. Elaborate orders were issued for the assembly of the two Divisions which were to form the fighting force in the sortie. The outer lines of works, the Grivitsa No. 2 Redoubt[1] (**7**), the Tchoroum (**13**), Ibrahim (**14**), Omar (**16**), Toultchenitza (**17**), and the Krischin Redoubts, were first evacuated; the troops from these, together with the general reserve, formed the 1st Division under Tahir Pasha. The movement was begun at 6.35 p.m. on the 9th. The 1st Division assembled quietly and without incident on the flat ground between the Grivitsa and the Vid, and by 5 a.m. on the 10th the whole had crossed to the left bank of the latter river. The convoy then began to pass; it consisted of about 1,000 vehicles and some 3,000 pack animals. By 8 a.m. the greater part of the 1st Division was deployed on the left bank of the Vid. Owing to the fog and the late winter dawn the movement was not discovered by the Russians until after that hour, when they at once opened fire. By this time not more than half the convoy had crossed the river and the bridges were blocked by a mass of vehicles and transport animals, which were thrown into ever-increasing confusion as the fog gradually lifted and the Russian artillery fire began to take effect among them. Osman had allowed himself to be persuaded by the Mahomedans of Plevna to permit them and their families to accompany his force; their fear of being left to the tender mercies of the Bulgarian inhabitants was so great that they announced their intention of following the army, with or without permission. Some 150 families with all their goods and

[1] *See* **Map III.**

chattels, loaded on whatever vehicles or animals they could obtain, added not a little to the congestion and confusion at the bridges.

The attack of the 1st Division was directed generally along the line of the Gorna-Metrapolje road. The 6th Section of the Russian blockading line, which comprised the left bank of the Vid, was held by the Grenadier Corps, and the 4th Roumanian Division (forty-four battalions). They held two lines; the first was occupied by sixteen battalions, and ran east of Dolna Dubniak to Dolna Metrapolje, roughly along the line of the 100-metre contour. The second line was occupied by twenty-eight battalions in reserve, and followed generally the line of the 150-metre contour, from Dolna Dubniak towards Gorna Metrapolje, and thence to the Vid just north of Bivolar. The brunt of the Turkish attack was borne by six battalions of the 3rd Grenadier Division; it was delivered with such dash that the Turks succeeded in piercing the first Russian line of defence, and driving the Russians back on to their second position. The works which had been captured were however all open to the rear, and the Turks found themselves exposed to a heavy artillery fire from the second Russian position, and to enfilade fire from batteries in the neighbourhood of Dolna Dubniak. It was impossible for the 1st Division to remain where it was, and the 2nd Division had not yet begun to cross the Vid. Osman therefore decided to attack the second Russian position with such troops as he had at hand. By this time the whole of the reserves of the 6th Section of the blockade were ready to meet the Turkish attack, which, being delivered across the open against a strongly entrenched position, failed, the Turks losing heavily, and Osman himself being wounded. Still the 2nd Turkish Division did not appear, and the situation of the 1st Division had become desperate.

About 2 a.m. on the 10th Lieutenant-Colonel Kuropatkin, Chief Staff Officer to General Skobelov, commander of the 4th Section, had discovered that the redoubts about Krischin had been evacuated by the Turks, and these were soon afterwards occupied by the Russians. By 8 a.m. the evacuation of the Omar, Ibrahim, and Grivitsa Redoubts was discovered by the 2nd and 3rd Sections. The troops of these sections pressed forward and engaged the 2nd Division, which was thus entirely occupied with its own affairs, and unable to render any assistance to the 1st Division. About mid-day the 2nd Grenadier and the 4th Roumanian Divisions began a counter-attack upon the 1st Turkish Division, which was gradually pushed back over the Vid. By 1 p.m. the greater part of the Turkish army was hemmed in in hopeless confusion between the Grivitsa and the Vid. Osman, finding further resistance useless, surrendered unconditionally with his whole army.

The fatal decision of the Sultan not to permit the evacuation of Plevna at the beginning of October had made this result inevitable. In face of the gradual accumulation of Russian troops Osman was unable to keep open his lines of communication, and once these had been cut the surrender of his force was merely a question of time. Osman had however completed his task before the month of October. He had brought the whole Russian plan of campaign to a standstill, and his force had become the chief objective of the Russian armies. Had Turkey, in the month of August, possessed a general capable of taking advantage of the situation that Osman had created, the defeat of the Russian armies would have been assured. The chief lesson of Plevna is not the importance of redoubts and field defences, but the extraordinary power exercised by a comparatively small force striking at the flank or communications of an army greatly superior in numbers. Just as Moore, by his bold advance to Sahagun with his handful of men, shattered Napoleon's elaborate plans for the conquest of Spain, and changed the course of European history, so Osman by his march from Widin brought the mighty power of the Czar to the verge of ruin. There is a lesson in this which it is important for us Englishmen to mark and learn. It is commonly said that in these days, when the armies of the Continent number their conscript soldiers by the million, that any idea of intervention in a European campaign by our little army is ridiculous. To admit this is at once to diminish the influence of England among the nations of the Continent. Fortunately the idea is far from ridiculous. In our unrivalled Fleet and Mercantile Marine we possess the power to transfer our land forces to almost any point washed by the sea. We have therefore in our hands the power of creating Plevnas of our own, and of exercising a decisive influence upon the fortunes of a campaign. It will not be disputed that it would, even with our present military organization, be possible for us to transport to and maintain upon the Continent an army of 40,000 men. At Plevna we have seen such an army neutralizing a force of nearly three times its number, and the chief lesson of Plevna for us appears to me to be that, given that we possess the command of the sea, the power that the British Army can wield beyond the seas cannot be measured in terms of the number of men upon its rolls.

The fate of Osman's army exemplifies the limitations of fortification. Final victory can only be obtained by superiority in the field. Fortifications are only of value when they are used to assist in attaining such superiority. If from some cause or other superiority in the field has not been attained, or has been lost, fortifications, whether temporary or permanent, may legitimately be used to contain a superior force with an inferior force, and to gain time to develop fresh resources, with the ultimate object of resuming active operations in the field. But if this goal is not kept in view, and the retention of a fortress for its own sake becomes the objective of military operations, fortifications not only cease to be of value, but become positively harmful.

Before finally leaving the subject of Plevna, it will be of interest to give here certain tactical lessons from the battles round that place which were deduced by General Kuropatkin, and were issued by him, in his capacity as Commander-in-chief of the armies in Manchuria, to the officers under his orders. Kuropatkin served throughout the campaign as Staff-officer to Skobelov II, and free use of his account of the operations in which he took part has been made in this volume. He says—
" It is unnecessary for us to make any special modifications in our tactics, but we must not repeat the mistakes

which caused us such serious failures in the war of '77-'78 against the Turks. Our campaign was successful, and covered the Russian army with glory, but we finally defeated the brave Turks only at the cost of heavy sacrifices, and of temporary repulses of large bodies of our troops. The failure at Plevna was particularly important, not only because of our heavy losses in killed and wounded, but because it delayed the course of the entire campaign. I consider it advisable to remind you of the causes of our failures and of our heavy losses at Plevna.

" After the capture of Nikopoli our troops marched on Plevna in ignorance of the enemy's dispositions and strength. Our cavalry was not properly used for reconnoitring, we advanced on Plevna in insufficient force, and directed our troops to attack positions, which the Turks had fortified, in unsuitable formations. Our men fought bravely and suffered severely, but were forced to retire. We collected larger forces and again attacked Plevna and were again unsuccessful, because we repeated the same mistakes to an even greater extent. Once more we were in ignorance of the enemy's strength and dispositions. We made two disconnected attacks, and there was no general control. Again the troops fought bravely as separate units, and gained important successes at some points, but in the end we were compelled to retire with heavy loss.

" For the third attack we assembled a very large force and were joined by the Roumanian troops. We studied the position for a long time, and although we exaggerated the enemy's strength, we were generally acquainted with his dispositions. After five days' fighting we remained in possession only of the Grivitsa Redoubt, which was of no particular importance. Our attacks on the centre and left were unsuccessful. We suffered severely, and having decided against a fourth assault, we resorted to a blockade, which ended in Osman Pasha's sortie and the surrender of the Turkish Army.

"The causes of the failure of the third attack on Plevna are particularly instructive, because it was due not merely to our own faulty dispositions but to want of proper preparation. For example, in the centre; although sufficient troops were available for the task allotted them, we frittered them away. A premature attack was made. The regiments were sent piecemeal against the Omar Redoubt, and were unsuccessful. Some of them not only reached the redoubt but entered it and were subsequently driven out by the Turks, and retired to the position from which they had begun the attack. Fresh regiments sent in did not reinforce those already engaged, but had to repeat the attack from the beginning. Formations were too dense, and the attack was insufficiently prepared by artillery and rifle fire. The troops in the centre did not carry entrenching tools and had no engineers with them.

"The cavalry did not assist in the attack. Speaking generally, the part played by our strong force of cavalry and by the Roumanian cavalry was insignificant. Our numerically superior artillery was also unsuccessful. The attack was prepared by four days' bombardment, but on the day of the assault our artillery did little, owing to the fog and rain. Our 4-pounder guns were particularly feeble. On the next day we were severely engaged on our left, which was unsupported, owing to the inaction of the troops of the centre and right. Osman Pasha was able to bring superior force against our left, and notwithstanding the heroic defence made by our troops, after having repulsed four attacks they were finally turned out of the redoubts they had captured under the very town of Plevna, and were compelled to retreat with a loss of half their number. The twenty-two battalions on the left flank had only one engineer detachment of thirty men attached to them, and in the absence of entrenching tools the men fortified the positions they had won with their bayonets, the lids of their canteens, and their hands. Some of the Infantry regiments on the left flank did not make use of the ground in the attack, and advanced in too close order. Insufficient use was made of rifle and artillery fire in the preparation of the attack.

"The work of the staff was not always good in this war. The troops often received their orders too late. Troops were kept waiting for orders when drawn up at their rendezvous, troops arriving at their destinations did not always find officers waiting to show them their places."

Kuropatkin, vol. ii, parts vi, vii. *Défense de Plevna*, chapters vi, vii. *Guerre d'Orient*, part ii, chapters xxvii, xxxii, and xxxiii.

Final Phase of the Campaign in Europe — The fall of Plevna had a decisive effect upon the course of the campaign. By the capture of Osman's army the whole of Bulgaria, north of the Balkans and west of the Kara Lom, with the exception of the fortress of Widin, was cleared of the Turks. The Russians were in undisputed possession of the Hainkioj[1] and Travna Passes, and of the Shipka and Arab Konak[2] Passes, except their southern ends. 100,000 Russians were free to reinforce the armies in the Balkans and to invade Roumelia. It was decided at Russian Headquarters to take the risk of a winter campaign in the Balkans, and to strike while the moral effect of the success at Plevna was still fresh. Gourko's army at the Arab Konak Pass was therefore raised to 80,000 men, and Radetzky's command in and about the Shipka Pass was reinforced so as to bring it up to 70,000 men. The Czarevitch was directed to cover the communications and to prosecute the siege of Rustchuk. Suleyman, at the time of the surrender of Plevna, had the bulk of the force with which he had captured Elena in the neighbourhood of Osman Bazar. He received orders from the Sultan to provide garrisons for the fortresses of the Quadrilateral, and to hurry south with the remainder of his army to defend the line of the Balkans. 30,000 men were at once sent to reinforce the army at Shipka, 10,000 were sent to form an entrenched camp at Adrianople, and with a force of 20,000 men Suleyman marched by way of Slivno on Sofia whither such further reinforcements as could be collected were dispatched.

On December 24 Gourko began a wide turning movement round the Turkish positions at Arab Konak. After great difficulties his columns debouched into the plain of Sofia on December 30 to find that the Turks were occupying a strong position at Tashkessen. On the 31st this position was attacked. The Turkish force

[1] *See* Map II.   [2] *See* Map I.

consisted merely of a rear-guard under Baker Pasha, some 3,000 strong. It was brilliantly handled, and delayed the whole of Gourko's army until Chakir Pasha had withdrawn his force, when it was retired under cover of darkness. On January 4th Sofia was occupied by the Russians without opposition.

On January 5th Radetzky began his advance. He moved in three columns, the right column under Skobelov, moving through Zelene Dveimvo[1] and debouching into the Tundja Valley near Sejnovo; the left column under Prince Sviatapolk Mirski moved through the Travna Pass by Selci and Jenina, while the centre column advanced direct on Shipka. The attack was timed for January 8th; Skobelov's column was, however, delayed, and he was unable to co-operate until the 9th. The movement was, however, completely successful; the Turks were surrounded, and the whole force of 36,000 men surrendered.

Suleyman had meantime gained touch with Chakir's army, which had retired from Arab Konak[2] and had been joined by the troops which had fallen back from Sofia. He was preparing to oppose Gourko's advance about half way between Philippopolis and Sofia when he heard of the surrender of the army at Shipka. He at once ordered a retirement upon Adrianople, but he was overtaken in the neighbourhood of Philippopolis, and finding that he could not reach Adrianople before Radetzky he retired through the Rhodope mountains, leaving a strong rearguard under Fuad Pasha to cover his retreat. Fuad succeeded in holding Gourko at bay for three days near Philippopolis, but he was finally

[1] *See* Map II. [2] *See* Map I.

overwhelmed by numbers and his force driven into the mountains in confusion. The remnants of Suleyman's army were collected on the coast and transferred to Constantinople by sea. The Russian armies occupied Adrianople on the 22nd without opposition, and on the 31st an armistice was signed which led eventually to the Treaty of San Stephano, and ended the war.

FINIS

APPENDICES

APPEN

ORDER OF BATTLE OF THE RUSSIAN ARMY IN
Commander-in-Chief—GRAND DUKE NICHOLAS.

IVth ARMY CORPS.
LT.-GENERAL SOTOV.

- **16th Infantry Division.** Lt.-Genl. Pomeranzew.
  - 1st Bgde. 61st Regt. 62nd Regt.
  - 2nd Bgde. 63rd Regt. 64th Regt.
- **30th Infantry Division.** Lt.-Genl. Schnitnikov.
  - 1st Bgde. 117th Regt. 118th Regt.
  - 2nd Bgde. 119th Regt. 120th Regt.
- **4th Cavalry Division.** Lt.-Genl. Krylov.
  - 1st Bgde. 4th Dragoons. 4th Lancers.
  - 2nd Bgde. 4th Hussars. 4th Don Cossacks.

Corps Troops.
16th and 30th Artillery Bgdes.
7th and 8th Horse Batteries.
21st* and 26th* Cossacks and 15th* Cossack Battery.

IXth ARMY CORPS.
LT.-GENERAL BARON KRUDENER.

- **5th Infantry Division.** Lt.-Genl. Schilder Schuldner.
  - 1st Bgde. 17th Regt. 18th Regt.
  - 2nd Bgde. 19th Regt. 20th Regt.
- **31st Infantry Division.** Lt.-Genl. Veliaminov.
  - 1st Bgde. 121st Regt. 122nd Regt.
  - 2nd Bgde. 123rd Regt. 124th Regt.
- **9th Cavalry Division.** Major-Genl. Lockarev.
  - 1st Bgde. 9th Dragoons. 9th Lancers.
  - 2nd Bgde. 9th Hussars. 9th Don Cossacks.

Corps Troops.
5th and 31st Artillery Bgdes.
16th Horse and 2nd Cossack Batteries.
34th Don Cossacks.

XIIth ARMY CORPS.
LT.-GENERAL WANNOVSKI.

- **12th Infantry Division.** Lt.-Genl. Baron de Firks.
  - 1st Bgde. 45th Regt. 46th Regt.
  - 2nd Bgde. 47th Regt. 48th Regt.
- **33rd Infantry Division.** Lt.-Genl. Timosiev.
  - 1st Bgde. 129th Regt. 130th Regt.
  - 2nd Bgde. 131st Regt. 132nd Regt.
- **12th Cavalry Division.** Major-Genl. Baron Driesen.
  - 1st Bgde. 12th Dragoons. 12th Lancers.
  - 2nd Bgde. 12th Hussars. 12th Don Cossacks.

Corps Troops.
12th and 33rd Artillery Bgdes.
10th Horse and 5th Cossack Batteries.
37th Don Cossacks.

SPECIAL FOR-

- **Caucasian Cossack Division.** Lt.-Genl. Skobelov.
  - 1st Bgde. 30th Don Cossacks. 2nd Kuban Cossacks.
  - 2nd Bgde. Vladicaucas Regt. Terek Regt.
  - 1st, 8th, 10th and 15th Cossack Batteries.
- **4th Rifle Brigade.**
  - 13th, 14th, 15th and 16th Rifles.
  - 1st and 2nd Mountain Batteries.
  - 2 Sotnias Plasstuns.

DETACHED

- **Xth Army Corps.**
  - 13th Inf. Div.
  - 34th Inf. Div.
  - 10th Cav. Div.
- **VIIth ARMY Corps.**
  - 15th Inf. Div.
  - 36th Inf. Div.

* These units were only attached to the IVth Corps in name. Until the arrival of the IVth

DIX I.

EUROPE UP TO THE SECOND BATTLE OF PLEVNA.

Chief of Staff—GENERAL NEPOKOITSHITSKI.

VIIIth ARMY CORPS.
LT.-GENERAL RADETZKY.

- **9th Infantry Division.** Lt.-Genl. Prince Sviatopolkmirski.
  - 1st Bgde. 33rd Regt. 34th Regt.
  - 2nd Bgde. 35th Regt. 36th Regt.
- **14th Infantry Division.** Lt.-Genl. Dragomirov.
  - 1st Bgde. 53rd Regt. 54th Regt.
  - 2nd Bgde. 55th Regt. 56th Regt.
- **8th Cavalry Division.** Lt.-Genl. Manvielov.
  - 1st Bgde. 8th Dragoons. 8th Lancers.
  - 2nd Bgde. 8th Hussars. 8th Don Cossacks.

Corps Troops.

9th and 14th Artillery Bgdes.
15th Horse Battery.
No. 9 Cossack Battery.

23rd Don Cossacks.

XIth ARMY CORPS.
LT.-GENERAL PRINCE SHAKOFSKOI.

- **11th Infantry Division.** Maj.-Genl. Krapovitski.
  - 1st Bgde. 41st Regt. 42nd Regt.
  - 2nd Bgde. 43rd Regt. 44th Regt.
- **32nd Infantry Division.** Maj.-Genl. Allev.
  - 1st Bgde. 125th Regt. 126th Regt.
  - 2nd Bgde. 127th Regt. 128th Regt.
- **11th Cavalry Division.** Maj.-Genl. Tatishtshev.
  - 1st Bgde. 11th Dragoons. 11th Lancers
  - 2nd Bgde. 11th Hussars. 11th Don Cossacks.

Corps Troops.

11th and 22nd Artillery Bgdes.
18th Horse and 4th Cossack Batteries.

29th and 35th and 40th Don Cossacks.

XIIIth ARMY CORPS.
LT.-GENERAL HAHN.

- **1st Infantry Division.** Lt.-General Prosharov.
  - 1st Bgde. 1st Regt. 2nd Regt.
  - 2nd Bgde. 3rd Regt. 4th Regt.
- **35th Infantry Division.** Maj.-Genl. Baranov.
  - 1st Bgde. 137th Regt. 138 Regt.
  - 2nd Bgde. 139th Regt. 140th Regt.
- **3rd Cavalry Division.** Maj.-Genl. de Raden.
  - 1st Bgde. 13th Dragoons. 13th Lancers.
  - 2nd Bgde. 13th Hussars. 13th Don Cossacks.

Corps Troops.

1st and 35th Artillery Bgdes.
20th Horse and 6th Cossack Batteries.

31st Don Cossacks.

MATIONS.

- Black Sea Naval Bgde.
- 3rd Engineer Bgde.
- Siege Park.
- 2 Squadrons Imperial Escort. 1 Sotnia Ural Cossacks.

CORPS.

- XIVth Army Corps.
  - 7th Cav. Div.
  - 17th Inf. Div.
  - 18th Inf. Div.
  - 1st Don Cossack Div.

Corps they acted with the 8th Cavalry Division, and subsequently joined General Gourko.

APPENDIX II

ORDER OF BATTLE OF THE ARMY OF THE QUADRILATERAL, JULY 1, 1877.

Commander-in-Chief: ABDUL KERIM PASHA.

SHUMLA CORPS.
AHMED EYOUB PASHA.

1st Infantry Division.
Nedjib Pasha.
8 Battalions, 3 Batteries.

2nd Infantry Division.
Assaf Pasha.
16 Battalions, 3 Batteries.

Cavalry Division.
Fuad Pasha.
18 Squadrons Regular Cavalry.
6 Squadrons Irregular Cavalry.
3 Horse Batteries.

Rustchuk Brigade.
Mustafa Zefi Pasha.
8 Battalions, 5 Squadrons, 2 Batteries.

ESKI DJUMA CORPS.
SALIK PASHA.

22 Battalions, 9 Squadrons, 6 Batteries.

(3 Squadrons, 5 Battalions detached to Tirnova; 9 Battalions, 4 Squadrons and 2 Batteries to Osman Bazar.)

DOBRUDJA CORPS.
ALI PASHA.

20 Battalions, 4 Squadrons, 6 Batteries.

GARRISONS OF FORTRESSES.

Garrison of Rustchuk.
12 Battalions.

Garrison of Shumla.
10 Battalions.

Garrison of Silistria (including Turtukai).
12 Battalions.

Garrison of Varna.
12 Battalions.

APPENDIX III.

ORDER OF BATTLE OF OSMAN PASHA'S ARMY, JULY 13, 1877.

Commander: OSMAN PASHA.

Chief of Staff: TAHIR PASHA.

1st Division.
Adil Pasha.

2nd Division.
Hassan-Sabri Pasha.

1st Brigade.	2nd Brigade.	1st Brigade.	2nd Brigade.*
Ahmed Hifzi Pasha.	Ali Pasha.	Said Bey.	Sadyk Pasha.
6 Battalions, 1 Battery, 1 Squadron.	6 Battalions, 1 Battery, 1 Squadron.	6 Battalions, 1 Battery, 1 Squadron.	6 Battalions.

Corps Artillery.
6 Batteries.

Corps Cavalry.
3 Squadrons.

Garrison of Widin.
Izzet Pasha.
13 Battalions, 1 Squadron, 1 Battery.

Other Garrisons.
6 Battalions.

* This Brigade was not made up until the detachments from Rahova and Nikopoli joined.

APPENDIX IV.

ORDER OF BATTLE OF THE ARMY OF THE QUADRILATERAL, AUGUST 20, 1877.

Commander-in-Chief: MEHEMET ALI PASHA.

1st CORPS.
AHMED EYOUB PASHA.

1st Division.
Nedjib Pasha.

- 1st Bgde. — 6 Battalions.
- 2nd Bgde. — 6 Battalions.
- Reserve. — 4 Battalions. 3 Batteries.

2nd Division.
Fuad Pasha.

- 1st Bgde. — 7 Battalions.
- 2nd Bgde. — 8 Battalions.
- Reserve. — 3 Batteries. 4 Squadrons.

3rd Division.
Assaf Pasha.

- 1st Bgde. — 7 Battalions.
- 2nd Bgde. — 7 Battalions.
- Reserve. — 2 Battalions. 7 Squadrons. 4 Batteries.

Cavalry Division.
Kerim Pasha.

- 18 Squadrons Regular Cavalry.
- 5 Squadrons Irregular Cavalry.

Rustchuk Brigade.
Mustafa Zefi Pasha.
8 Battalions, 5 Squadrons, 2 Batteries.

General Reserve.
1 Battalion, 3 Batteries.

IInd CORPS.
Prince HASSAN.

1st Division.
Salik Pasha.

- 1st Bgde. — 6 Battalions. 1 Battery.
- 2nd Bgde. — 7 Battalions. 1 Battery.

2nd Division.
Ismail Pasha.

- 1st Bgde. — 7 Battalions. 1 Battery.
- 2nd Bgde. — 8 Battalions. 1 Battery.

Cavalry Brigade.
9 Squadrons. 1 Battery.

Independent Brigade.
Salim Pasha.
10 Battalions, 5 Squadrons, 3 Batteries.

www.ingramcontent.com/pod-product-compliance
Lightning Source LLC
Chambersburg PA
CBHW081519160426
43193CB00015B/2729